D1563467

Branch Rickey

For Louise, Beth, Alex, *and* Robert

*Here it is Spring, eternally new, eternally hopeful,*
  *And here we are, participating in a season*
*Which year after year, gives the lie to all philosophies*
  *of chaos and futility.*

HAL BORLAND

# Branch Rickey
## *A Biography*

### Revised Edition

MURRAY POLNER

*foreword by* Branch B. Rickey

McFarland & Company, Inc., Publishers
*Jefferson, North Carolina, and London*

LIBRARY OF CONGRESS CATALOGUING-IN-PUBLICATION DATA

Polner, Murray.
    Branch Rickey : a biography / Murray Polner ; foreword by
Branch B. Rickey.—Rev. ed.
        p.    cm.
    Includes bibliographical references and index.

    **ISBN-13: 978-0-7864-2643-0**
    (softcover : 50# alkaline paper) ∞

    1. Rickey, Branch, 1881–1965.   2. Executives—United
States—Biography.   3. Baseball—United States—History.
I. Title.
GV865.R45P64   2007
796.357092—dc22                                         2007007619
[B]

British Library cataloguing data are available

Cover photograph: Branch Rickey on Pittsburgh's WQED
(Courtesy Branch B. Rickey)

Manufactured in the United States of America

*McFarland & Company, Inc., Publishers*
    *Box 611, Jefferson, North Carolina 28640*
        *www.mcfarlandpub.com*

# Contents

*"He that will not reason is a bigot.*
*He that cannot reason is a fool.*
*He that dares not reason is a slave."*

FRAMED AND HUNG IN BRANCH RICKEY'S OFFICES<br>IN ST. LOUIS, BROOKLYN, AND PITTSBURGH

"As a matter of fact I do not deserve any recognition from anybody on the Robinson thing. It is a terrible commentary on any of us that a part of us should not concede equal rights to everybody to earn a living."

BRANCH RICKEY TO FRANK STANTON,<br>JANUARY 18, 1949

"The most important single qualification a man should have to marry one of my daughters is infinite kindness. Infinite kindness will sustain a marriage through all its problems, its uncertainties, its illnesses, its disappointments, its storms, its tensions, its fear, its separations, its sorrows. Out of infinite kindness grow real love and understanding and tolerance and warmth. Nothing can take the place of such an enduring asset."

BRANCH RICKEY

"Luck is the residue of design."

BRANCH RICKEY

"Intuition is our subconscious reaction in time of stress."

BRANCH RICKEY

# Foreword to the Revised Edition

## by Branch B. Rickey

WHAT COURAGE IT MUST TAKE to be a biographer. To begin with a blank sheet of paper and sentence-by-sentence build the history of an individual, to endeavor to capture and communicate the related achievements, the relationships, the very essence of a person—how can you but admire someone willing to face that daunting task.

Murray Polner's biography of my grandfather, Branch Rickey, does just that. He honors me in asking that I furnish a foreword, one that is naturally shaped by the perspective of a grandson reflecting on his grandfather. *The New York Times* asked me to write about him almost a decade ago and now I want to share some of my recollections in this revised edition of Polner's book, originally published by Atheneum in 1982.

So many images linger with me, even 40 years since my grandfather's passing. They are mainly first hand recollections, but also impressions when I've encountered his former colleagues in and outside of baseball. Inevitably, on meeting me and hearing my name, they would burst forth with a vivid recounting of events that invariably concluded in portraying him as the most extraordinary person they had ever known.

How does anyone capture a person like that in words?

It always seemed to me that his energy would cause him to go on forever. He once said, memorably, "I want to tell you a story about courage..."—the last line I am told he spoke before collapsing at the podium, the final speech of his life. It was less significant to him, I earnestly believe, that he was being inducted into the Missouri Sports Hall of Fame, than that this was an opportunity to convey his faith in heroism, determination, enthusiasm, and spirit—what makes anyone and everyone special. For decades he fought to change the rules delaying Baseball Hall of Fame inductions, explaining, "no one should ever be inducted posthumously." Ironically, baseball inducted him posthumously.

"Baseball people, as a rule, are generally allergic to new ideas." This is a phrase I heard my grandfather utter on a number of occasions when I knew him in his 70s and 80s. Even at that advanced age, he had an enormous capacity for fresh ideas—which made him, naturally, a danger to the defenders of the status quo.

He was Victorian in manner, rumpled Churchillian in appearance. He was the kind of person who always had something creative and exciting going on around him. Whatever he did, he did with zeal—and it constantly surprised even those who knew him well. He blended philosophy, politics, economics, decades of baseball lore and always, with a dose of religion.

Having known him from my earliest years and having listened to him at so many family meals expounding on issues of social conscience, it seems natural to me as I look back that he would be the one to orchestrate the elimination of baseball's shameful gentleman's agreement to keep the game lilywhite.

I grew up listening to his stories and his memories of his childhood. There was a moral to every story he told. He remembered so much of the rural influence of his childhood, having grown up on a farm in Duck Run, in southern Ohio, not far outside of Portsmouth. His education there was in a one-room schoolhouse, but he was so adept academically that he overcame the limitations and went on to Ohio Wesleyan University and the University of Michigan Law School. He played pro baseball in the summers and excelled in Latin and Greek in the winters. Academic excellence was his conviction, but baseball was his passion, as Polner's biography recounts.

Baseball consumed him, and he infected everyone around him with the same sense of dedication. There was no small element of the game that escaped his scrutiny. Veteran baseball coaches, young and older players were drawn to him for his insights. He was always teaching, inspiring, lecturing, tutoring and motivating. He saw what others missed. "I would not mind," I remember him saying only half facetiously, "if my epitaph read: *He had something to do with converting Stan Musial to an outfielder.*" Stan Musial had originally been a pitcher...

My memories of him are personal and deep. But since his death in 1965, I have also grown to appreciate him for his role in signing Robinson and thereby allowing other black players to enter major league baseball. It proved to be an electrifying move that reverberated throughout our nation and far beyond, powerfully affecting people and groups working for racial equality.

The genesis for the signing of Jackie Robinson actually dates to 1903, when my grandfather was a coach at Ohio Wesleyan University and went on a trip with his team to Indiana, where the lone black player on his team was refused a room at a local hotel. After a brief argument between my grandfather and the desk clerk, the young student player, Charles Thomas, was allowed to use a cot in my grandfather's room. When he arrived he found Thomas there sitting at the foot of the cot, pulling at the skin on his hands as if he could rub away the color. With tears coming down his face, he said, "Mr. Rickey, if I could just get this color off I'd be just as good as anybody else." It was a traumatic moment that always remained with grandfather, and it led to his resolve to one day make a difference.

And he did. Many have characterized Robinson's signing as "The Great Experiment" or "The Noble Experiment"; even my grandfather used such words. But it seems to me that the historic signing of Robinson was hardly an experiment and had much more in common with, and more closely parallels, other events when pioneers set out to climb a mountain that has never been scaled. These courageous men and women were willing to risk everything. No, signing Robinson was not an experiment; rather, it was the carrying out of a powerful personal commitment, meticulously planned by two strong-willed, well-prepared men.

Both men signed that first Brooklyn contract knowing there were enormous risks. As general manager of the Brooklyn Dodgers in the '40s, my grandfather was well aware that every other team in major league baseball would oppose him, as they had when they voted 15–1 against permitting any team to sign a black player. He knew that his reputation, which had taken him a lifetime to build, was clearly at stake. All the same, he was unwilling to be cowed or bullied by the majority.

As it was, the thought and planning that went into scouting the Negro Leagues and signing Robinson to a Dodger contract had begun years before. As early as 1943, my grandfather quietly recruited allies and allocated sufficient resources to carry out the search. A few scouts were enlisted and discreetly prepared. Fictitious articles were planted about a Brooklyn Brown Dodgers team that was never really in the plans. Details were refined; coalitions developed and broadened—all to forestall the expected firestorm of opposition.

# Foreword (Branch B. Rickey)

While a member of the Dodgers, the notion that Robinson was kept "on a leash" has often been used to characterize Robinson's first three years in baseball because my grandfather supposedly did not want him to retaliate when taunted and mocked.

However, I see a much more complex facet to this relationship. After a grueling first meeting with my grandfather, before signing his Dodger contract, the two men struggled through an exhaustive and painful series of hypothetical encounters of what might happen on and off the field by bigots who would not accept him. But given Robinson's keen intelligence and perhaps uncanny insight, he immediately understood the importance of not responding to certain provocations. But there was a fire burning within Jackie Robinson. On a leash, ... hogwash, as my grandfather would say. Branch Rickey could never have shackled his competitive intensity. There was only one way to even channel it, and that was through Jackie's own overpowering determination not to fail, either on the field or to his obligation to a larger world than baseball.

Another misunderstanding is the simplistic view that credits Robinson with breaking the color barrier. What dim-witted, faint praise. This man did not simply cross a line but rather crossed over from being an excluded American forbidden to play major league baseball to setting new standards of excellence. He not only played, he triumphed, and in doing so, captured the respect of every rational person in the country. He not only broke the Jim Crow rule but also proved that those who had previously been barred were capable of extraordinary achievements. And, so, he was strong enough to turn the other cheek for those first few years.

Though Branch Rickey and Robinson were the architects of a new era in baseball, I never knew my grandfather to seek credit for his role. As Roger Angell said of him in his introduction to *A Baseball Century*: "His ultimate alteration of the game, the destruction of baseball's color bar, was an act of national significance.... He refused to accept awards or plaudits for the deed since it had only reversed an ancient and odious injustice. It would shame a man, he said, to take credit for that."

Such was the grandfather that I knew.

So it was with Jackie Robinson. Jackie had the courage to do what he did, but it was with Branch Rickey that he found direction and further resolve. What a partnership they made. Professionally, it lasted from 1945 until 1950, when my grandfather's unanticipated departure from the Brooklyn Dodgers and relocation to the Pittsburgh Pirates forced them into a somewhat different relationship, but one that remained steadfast.

In November 1950, Jackie wrote my grandfather. "Finding the right words come hard," Robinson said. "Your exit from the Dodgers has been tough on everyone in Brooklyn, but much worse for me. It has been the finest experience I have had being associated with you. And I want to thank you very much for all you have meant not only to me and my family but to the entire country and particularly to the members of our race. I hope to end my playing days in Brooklyn as it means so very much, but if I have to go any place I hope it can be with you."

Indeed, they are now both enshrined in Baseball's Hall of Fame, one's plaque not far from the other. Bonded by adversity, confident in their trust in each other, these two men fought a battle that went far beyond baseball. It seems to me that their struggle and their victory was personified by the framed quotation by Sir William Drummond, a 19th century scholar, which hung on the wall behind grandfather's desk and which read: "He that will not reason is a bigot; he that cannot reason is a fool; he that dares not reason is a slave."

In Branch Rickey and Jackie Robinson, America experienced two fearless men of conscience, two men who refused to accept the cruelty of bigotry, two men who dared to break out of the slavery of injustice.

For me, Jackie was and ever will be my childhood hero. The other man was simply my grandfather who showed his special love for a grandson every time he and I were together.

Branch B. Rickey
*President, Pacific Coast League*

# Preface to the
# First Edition

SEVERAL YEARS AGO, having left our daughter at college in Albany, New York, we drove to Cooperstown, the home of baseball's Hall of Fame and Museum. I explained to my wife that the experience would prove stimulating for our youngest son, but we all knew it was I who wanted desperately to go. For, like so many boys reared in Brooklyn in the 1940s and 1950s, baseball—really, the Brooklyn Dodgers—held a special place in the memories of my growing up years.

We reached the museum at dusk and immediately entered, wandering about until we reached the bust of Branch Rickey. "There, Robert," I said to my son, "there's the man I want to write about." Naturally, he had never heard of him and even if he had, it would be in association with the coming of Jackie Robinson. No mean achievement. All the same he was far more than the one who broke baseball's color bar. As I started exploring Rickey's roots and life, he came to be, in my eyes, a genuine American hero and not the instant celebrity we encounter so often now. He was, too, the son of poor, rural southern Ohio farmers, who taught their three sons—and by extension all who came after them in succeeding generations—the worth of an ethical and moral way of life grounded in religious faith.

I am indebted most of all to the Rickey family, primarily his five daughters and the wife of his late son, Branch Jr., and their respective families. They granted me exclusive permission to examine the Rickey papers held by the Library of Congress prior to those papers being made available to the general public.

I am also obligated to many other people, but I want to thank especially Catherine Barber of the Missouri Historical Society, Kenneth Blackburn, Roy Campanella, Hobert Clements, Bill De Witt, Bob Howsam, Mickey McConnell, the Charles Pfizer Chemical Corporation for information concerning John L. Smith, Branch B. Rickey of the Pittsburgh Pirates, Pherbia and Pinky Thornberg, Keene Landis (who told me where I could find his grandfather's papers), and William G. Turner.

Stephen Berkowitz was an unerring guide at the start, providing me with a detailed outline of the life and times of Rickey, plus an initial bibliography. Hanna Desser kindly read the manuscript. My daughter, Beth, helped me sort out various legal decisions. My sons, Alex and Robert, and I talked about the project frequently, and I derived much from their insights and suggestions. Thomas Stewart, my editor, was consistently helpful. My agent, Julian Bach, was a source of strength when I seemed to lose faith in the manuscript. And finally, I owe far more than I can express to my wife, Louise, critic and editor, occasional researcher and much-needed prop. "A woman of valor who can find, for her price is far above rubies."

Needless to say, I am solely responsible for any and all errors.

# Preface to the Revised Edition

HAS ANY SPORT EXECUTIVE EVER HAD as many words written about him than Wesley Branch Rickey, a former catcher and manager turned executive who ran the St. Louis Cardinals, Brooklyn Dodgers and Pittsburgh Pirates and possessed the most creative mind in the game's long history? Long after his death in 1965, his name and achievements have not been forgotten.

Rickey created baseball's farm system, was a prime mover in expanding baseball to more American cities, but most famously and significantly, was responsible for desegregating baseball when he hired Jackie Robinson. It was an act of extraordinary courage before President Harry Truman desegregated the U.S. armed forces and long before the Civil Rights movement of the sixties.

For a number of years there had been pressure by some groups and individuals to allow black players into major league baseball. Outspoken black sportwriters such as Sam Lacey, Wendell Smith and A.S. "Doc" Young, among others, carried on unremitting campaigns. But somehow, someone in baseball had to make the first move.

That someone was Branch Rickey.

"It was Rickey alone who broke the color line," wrote Red Barber.*

When I originally began writing the story of his life one of the larger questions I wanted to know was why a conservative evangelical Christian could become so obsessed in fostering racial equality. But we humans are motivated and moved by many forces, some contradictory and unex-

*Red Barber, "Game Today Would Make Rickey Ill," Miami Herald, February 15, 1970.

# Preface to the Revised Edition

pected. My partial answer for his dedication to achieving social justice, often dismissed or disputed by some, was that his religious faith was as decisive a factor as his well-known business acumen. Certainly Rickey foresaw the economic gains ahead by adding black players to his roster. He was, too, wrote Steve Sailor in his interpretation of the Rickey-Robinson revolution, "as renowned as [Judge Kenesaw] Landis for his righteousness." But, he added, "No one should look down upon Rickey, however; pursue his self-interest he certainly did, but with infinitely more intelligence and courage than his rival owners.... Rickey chose Robinson because they had so much in common: both were Methodists who didn't smoke, drink or chase women, and both were smart enough to know the historic importance of their undertaking. Most importantly, both were too competitive to back down."*

To Rickey, baseball was, yes, a business, but it was also a civil religion and "my game and my sport," as he once said years after while promoting the Continental League. His forced departure from Brooklyn, however financially profitable it was personally, was for him a great disappointment. "My eight years in Brooklyn gave me a new vision of America, or rather America gave me a new vision of a part of itself, Brooklyn. They were wonderful years ... a baseball club in any city in America is a quasi-public institution, and in Brooklyn the Dodgers were public without the quasi."

Hired by the Pittsburgh Pirates, he never again achieved the success he had experienced with the Gas House Gang of St. Louis or the "Boys of Summer" of Brooklyn, in Roger Kahn's memorable phrase.

All the same, his legacy to baseball and the nation remains secure. In 1957, at age 76, he and Rutgers University philosophy professor Houston Peterson visited a black church in Pittsburgh one Sunday morning. Peterson told me that when Rickey entered, cane in hand, the congregants began shouting out, "God bless you, Mr. Rickey," while the minister intoned "Amen."

When Jackie Robinson died in 1972 of diabetes and hypertension, some wrote that his coming required no special courage on Rickey's part and would have eventually happened. Others, more cynical, deemed Rickey's driving force as greed. But the truth is that before Branch Rickey no one had done it. And that is his legacy to baseball and the nation.

*Steve Sailor, "How Jackie Robinson Desegregated America: Perhaps the Least-learned Lesson of the Saga of Jackie Robinson Is That Competition Can Transform Self-interest into an Engine for Racial Fairness," National Review, April 8, 1996.

## Preface to the Revised Edition

*Branch Rickey: A Biography* was originally published in 1982 by Atheneum and later issued in a paperback edition by New American Library (Signet). This new McFarland edition contains textual changes, different photographs, a new Foreword and new Preface as well as an updated bibliography.

# Chapter One

Accompanied by his secretary, Kenneth Blackburn, a former World War II army captain, he was chauffeured to a maximum security penitentiary. His years of glory were ended and his name seemed to have faded from the headlines, but still a group of prisoners had asked him to visit with them. It was 1958 and Branch Rickey was seventy-seven years old.

He planned to speak of Jackie Robinson and inject, as he so often did, his favorite references to Jesus and his redeeming and forgiving spirit. On the long drive he jotted notes on the back of a Pittsburgh Pirates letterhead until they passed through the prison gates. There, the visible restraints seemed to astonish him. A warden described the many restrictions demanded of visitors, particularly involving times and schedules. At precise moments, he was warned, lunch began and ended, lights were turned on and off, and recreation permitted and forbidden. Branch Rickey listened in silence, his eyes darting about at the unfamiliar scenes before him. The warden was still talking. At a fixed time, he said, the bell would ring and Mr. Rickey would begin speaking. When it rang again, he would stop. Rickey nodded, as if in agreement, smiled politely, and turned to Blackburn, murmuring, "This man's got my rabbit up."

The bell pealed and he rose to talk. Soon the bell sounded again. The prisoners shifted uneasily as Rickey paused, all eyes turned to the rear where the warden sat. The warden was still for a few seconds and then raised his hand. "Oh, go on, Mr. Rickey. These men aren't a-goin' anywhere, anyway. Take all the time you need." The men stood and cheered, and he spoke for almost an hour longer, and then they stood and cheered again. After, he wandered among them, shaking hands, grinning, signing autographs. On the long drive home he scratched a line on an envelope, "We are all men of God."

Daniel Brown spent the night hiding in nearby woods as his parents and two brothers and two sisters were being murdered by invading Indians. Neither they nor anyone else in the tiny Massachusetts settlement lived through that frigid winter night and Daniel waited, hidden, shivering until the next morning, when he walked fifteen miles through deep snows and empty forests to the closest houses to sound the alarm.

Branch Rickey was a Brown on his mother's side and he heard the story of young Daniel many times and how the Browns had come to North America with seven other intrepid Scottish families in April 1646. He also heard with pride from his mother how future Browns included George, Daniel's grandson, one of the principal founders of the Methodist Church in America.

David Brown and his wife, Sallie Hubbard, Rickey's great-grandparents, were the first of the family to migrate westward. Sallie Hubbard's family were wealthy eastern landowners and they included seventeenth-century colonial clergy, the author of a once well-regarded history of New England, and a member of President Millard Fillmore's cabinet. When she introduced David Brown to her family as the man she loved they were aghast at her selection. David drank heavily, which their Methodist sensitivities found unforgivable. He was also unsettled, restless, outspoken, brash, and sparkled with ideas and notions, all of which the more conventional Hubbards found boorish and unbecoming. When Sallie refused to abandon him they disowned her, and she and David were married without their blessing.

David Brown was as adventurous as he was crude. Not long after the War of 1812 ended, and when the "West" still meant Kentucky, Indiana, Illinois, Missouri, Tennessee, and Ohio, he and his pregnant wife, with twenty-five cents in their possession, traveled overland from Buffalo to the Allegheny River, then to Pittsburgh and the Ohio River. There they rented space on rafts, drifting southward until they alit on a small site known locally as Sciotoville, not far from Portsmouth, in the free state of Ohio in 1816.

When he and Sallie had four children, David decided to strike out for more advantageous land, wandering with his family farther into the wilderness on a cart drawn by two oxen for which he had traded some clothing. His wife handled the reins, a baby was lashed to the side of the wagon, and David walked up ahead, hacking the way clear with an ax through the dense underbrush.

He built a farm and planted corn, turnips, and potatoes near the Scioto River. Soon a settlement grew up about them, and his produce helped feed his neighbors until their own crops were harvested. For nearly a decade they lived in this harsh manner, hardly unique in the annals of frontier families, while Sallie bore seven more babies. And then one day, David decided the family should move again, this time to another site in Ohio, called Little California, "where he turned his boys loose in the Briars and swamps to root hog or die. But they had rugged constitutions, endured the hardships and the ground seemed to stick to them."

These successive transplantations into the unknown rarely troubled Rickey's great-grandfather. Taming a wilderness, suffering the inevitable diseases in the midst of medical and dietary ignorance, working until exhausted, the Browns nonetheless survived in the hope of independence and future comfort.

As David worked hard so he played hard too, drinking heavily, womanizing, talking endlessly on any and all subjects including his beloved Democratic Party—"When General Jackson was a candidate for the presidency [in 1828] he made a barter at a gathering that he could throw down anyone who voted against General Jackson and he received a broken leg in trying to make good his boast"—while Sallie held the family together, prepared their young for adulthood, and passed on to each of them her unquestioned and passionate faith in Jesus as savior.

If David was a displaced Yankee trader who "loved a slick horse-trade," as the unofficial family historian put it, "Grandmother was a kind-hearted woman [who] cherished an ardent love for the Christian religion and the Methodist church and instilled the principles of religion into the minds and lives of the children, always taking an interest in establishing schools and churches in the county in which they lived. Not a saloon keeper nor a backslider can be found among them."

It was one of their granddaughters, Emily, born in 1856, who undoubtedly passed these stories on to her second son, Wesley Branch, in his growing up years. In 1873 she married a local farmer's son, Jacob Franklin Rickey, whose family had settled originally in Connecticut and Vermont in the seventeenth century and then gradually moved west, at first to Elmira in the southern tier country of New York State and then to southern Ohio. Jacob Franklin, Branch's father, whom everyone called Frank, was born in Tioga, New York, in 1856. Like the Browns, he and his family went west on the Ohio River, landing from a raft at a point just above the village of Portsmouth.

The Rickeys were Baptists. Frank's father and grandfather had been lay preachers during the years of evangelistic piety and revivalism that swept through the "Burnt-Over Districts" in New England and New York during the 1820S and 1830s. It was an intense and emotional time when

God was portrayed as demanding that the "saved" perform "good deeds," broaden the boundaries of Christ's Kingdom, and accept personal responsibility for bettering society. Armageddon was fast approaching and the Second Coming could not therefore be far behind. Rickey once observed that as a boy he felt drawn to his paternal grandfather, Ephraim Wanser Rickey. The two of them—grandfather and grandson—often sat together for hours, the older man speaking softly about the imperatives of absolute faith and uncritical suspension of judgment before God's mysteries, and the boy listening and absorbing every word.

Following their marriage, Frank and Emily Rickey gravitated toward the Wesleyite Methodists, a tolerant church in which no heretic had ever been tried and where John Wesley's words "Think and let think" were their guiding inspiration.

Someone once described Branch's father as "the most pious, devout, religious man I ever knew, a genuine New Testament Christian, always the main man in the church." Years after, Rickey remembered that when his father wasn't farming he was wandering about the region, provoking religious disputations, organizing competing churches based upon shades of barely discernible doctrinal differences, forming and reforming them whenever he felt the congregation or the pastor had gone too far or done too little. Often, Branch mused later in life, his father appeared uneasy, dissatisfied, a man about whom controversy seemed to swirl continuously, anxious lest a day pass without something of significance having happened.

When the Rickeys first moved to Duck Run they attended the Free-Will Baptist Church and after, in 1892, when they moved to Lucasville, another southern Ohio hamlet, the Flat Woods Methodist Protestant Church, four miles from their home. For the remainder of his life Rickey recalled the joyful days they hitched Clay and Nell to their surrey and loudly sang in four-part disharmony their beloved hymns, "Jesus, Lover of My Soul" and "When the Roll Is Called Up Yonder," his mother in her soprano voice, his father the tenor, and he and his older brother, Orla, shrieking at the top of their lungs.

When Wesley Branch Rickey was born in 1881 in Little California—soon renamed Stockdale—his birth certificate cited November 20 rather than December 20 as his day of birth. "It will be corrected," he told inquirers time and again, although it never was. The doctor "who sent in the registry or whatever it may be called and much later than my birth" inadvertently made it November, he explained fifty years later. "My mother told me the true facts. I was born on December 20, 1881, in a little town two miles north of the Cosuda County line and I was born, therefore, really in Pike County, Ohio, forty miles north of the Ohio River."

Little California was a barren and hilly country. When his younger son was two years old, Frank bought 102.8 acres in Duck Run, for $320, money he borrowed from his father. On a late morning in November 1883 the family packed their belongings onto their wagon and set out for their new home. The four Rickeys moved slowly along the Scioto River path, crossing over near Rushtown, and passed through Lucasville, a village of 350 persons, six miles from Duck Run, on past the towering elms that shaded its main street in the summer, past Chandler Moulton's General Store, across two covered bridges, up a road into a hollow, and there young Branch set eyes on a scene he was able to describe in detail all his life—the two-story house, the barn across the dirt road, the creek where he, his brothers and cousins swam on warm days after work and school, the sycamores and raspberry bushes, the land he revered.

Life on the farm was unchanging. They planted corn and sorghum and raised a few cows. Everyone rose early, fed the hogs, and milked the cows. Branch, who was awkward with his hands and almost entirely unmechanical, filled a sack of hay each morning for the horses, adding several ears of corn for nourishment. He worked alongside Orla and his father, churning butter, slaughtering chickens, husking corn, and as he grew older, hunting game in the foothills of the Appalachians.

In 1886, when he was five, he was enrolled in school, and each morning after chores he and Orla walked four miles down Duck Run Road to the canal and across Little Buck Knob to a one-room schoolhouse to memorize *McGuffey's Reader,* with its emphasis on blind obedience to authority and its simple-minded faith in American moral superiority. It was a comforting world for children, even children as poor as the Rickeys.

Branch's parents, however, must have been less than overwhelmed with *McGuffey's,* and for all Frank's sense of righteousness, he wanted more for his boys than a life of plowing. Thus when Reilly's Bookstore in Portsmouth burned and its water-logged and singed volumes were placed on fire sale, Frank hitched the wagon and drove to the county seat ten miles away—a round trip consuming almost six hours—and bought eleven books for $2.25: an illustrated version of Dante's *Inferno;* a four-volume collection of Washington Irving's stories; a book on natural history; Gustave Doré's drawings; one book titled *The Devil and Tom Walker,* and another describing hunting in Africa, *Mr. Godkin in Africa;* Charles Foster's *Story of the Bible;* and a New Testament, in which the father wrote an inscription to his young son. For the remainder of his life Branch lovingly remembered each of the books he received that evening in their quiet, kerosene-lit farmhouse and how much he loved the special odor and the texture of their charred cloth and paper and how much they contributed to his lifelong love of literature. He was still unable to read them but he devoured their pictures. When at last he learned to read, he said, he read and reread every book and committed many of their passages to memory.

Frank also allowed newspapers into their home, which many local religious literalists took to be the voice of the devil. The Lucasville *Transcript* arrived weekly, and when an occasional visitor brought the far more worldly Cincinnati *Enquirer,* the boys were permitted to read it. "We didn't have a newspaper in the house every day because there weren't any available. But if someone brought the *Enquirer* nothing was said about it. The so-called violation of the Sabbath was frowned upon very much, but I don't recall father ever finding fault with my older brother or with me, if the Sunday paper came into the home at Duck Run," said Rickey.

If Frank Rickey was his son's primary teacher, then Emily Rickey was the sustainer, the strong-minded nurturing mother who offered her sons religious fervor, constant love, attention, friendship. It was she who helped build Branch's strong ego and stimulate his ambitions. She had a sense of making her husband and sons believe she was unique in their lives. "At the age of fourteen, March 12, 1871, I first met her, and after becoming acquainted I found that her great principles and character were far beyond any that I had ever met—and too, I discovered I was not worthy of her—this I never got over," said her husband.

Neither overbearing nor smothering, Emily proceeded to give Branch the strength to sustain himself in later life, the ability to draw endlessly on his inner reserves, a lifelong love for his community, the land, religious faith. She gave him as well a growing sense of self-worth and confidence that he could lead his own life in any way he chose.

By the testimony of those who knew her in Branch's earliest years, she was an exceptionally outspoken and assured woman, vigorous, concerned with the state of the moral and religious education of her youngsters, yet offended by the growing secularism and areligiosity that seemed to be affecting nearby towns and cities. Her friends considered her "proud and candid" in her views and unafraid to enter into disputes where she thought her principles were at stake.

All his life Rickey paid homage to his mother. He vaguely remembered being four years old, listening intently as she read to him nightly. He recalled all his life her inexhaustible wealth of stories designed to illustrate a conversational point or a moral, a technique he adopted naturally and which became the hallmark of his public personality. "She had a vast supply of folksy stories and could always find one from the Bible to illuminate any point she wanted to make." He sensed that he had inherited her "character, industry, frugality, and sobriety."

Nor did she punish him corporally. Once—following some act of misbehavior—he remembered his mother asking him into her bedroom and bidding him to kneel with her to ask that God forgive her for having failed to instruct him properly. The sight of his adored mother castigating herself for his antics was, he said on many occasions, "a solemn and unforgettable moment," forever etched in his memory. "I felt as though I had hit her, and I was thoroughly chastised."

Then too, as he grew, she never seemed to pull him back possessively, always seeking to embolden him, daring him to take risks and reap the rewards, soothing his many doubts while upholding his moral rectitude. It was this upbringing and this relationship with his mother that instilled in him a zest for living, and which gave him the idea, a sportswriter once suggested, that it was good to be a Rickey, it was good to be a Duck Run farm boy, it was good to be alive.

Four years later, in the fall of 1892, the family moved again, this time into Lucasville. Emily gave birth to a third son, Frank Wanzer. Part of the reason for their move was their belief that Branch was especially bright and the one-room schoolhouse had given him all it could; Lucasville had a better school, with more than one overworked teacher and with a more complex curriculum. His father was to work the farm through Saturday and come into Lucasville Sunday for church.

The 1890s were a difficult time for a farmer. The emergence of the transcontinental railroad and the rise of large cities had compelled him to produce for distant markets while he bought goods in shops or by mail order. The old way of growing and marketing corn and sorghum was now unprofitable. To manage financially, Frank knew he would have to mortgage his future crops and borrow heavily for seed and provisions, for harvesters and machinery. He was not, however, prepared to make that jump and decided instead to draw in his belt, sacrifice, and trust to the precepts he had learned from his father. "Frugality, industry, and sobriety are simple virtues any man can cultivate. The opportunities for success, like the opportunities for salvation, are limitless and heaven can receive as many as are worthy," he preached, later adding: *Make first things first, seek the Kingdom of God and make yourselves an example.*"

When Lucasville was founded, the Scioto Valley Railroad, a short spur to Portsmouth (then a city of 11,000 people), was built. It raised false hopes in Lucasville that the village might boom economically; corn, lumber, and cross ties were the hoped-for basis for prosperity. A grain elevator and a steam flour mill were constructed, and after that, four general stores and two livery stables opened.

By the time the Rickeys arrived, the optimism had been thoroughly dashed. Still, the village represented a rise in status for them. When they moved into Squire Crain's house on Valley Pike across from Chandler Moulton's store, the village had a hotel ("Just a big house," said Rickey), a handful of fairly well-off families with some political influence—the Moultons most prominent among them—and a superficial egalitarianism that hid the drudgery and heavy drinking from sight and emphasized an easy social mixing inherited from Ohio's frontier years.

They rented three rooms on each of two floors with separate entries at the front and rear. Rickey swiftly decided that the landlord "was a numbskull, a quick-witted, ignorant man." The landlord in turn disliked the boys' exuberance and noise, their friends, and would not allow a day's delay in payment of the rent.

All the same, they were reasonably content with their lot. Orla received his teaching certificate from Scioto County and moved away to take up a teaching job, leaving Branch to attend school and the fifth grade alone. The Lucasville school offered instruction in twelve grades but no diploma. Yet its two-story wooden building, bustling halls, and three large classrooms were a dramatic change from Duck Run. And whatever its physical and scholastic limitations, the school was blessed successively with two spirited and resourceful young superintendents, both still students at Ohio Wesleyan University, who chose teaching, as did many rural young men, as a stepping-stone to professional careers elsewhere. The first was twenty-three-year-old Frank Appel; his successor was James H. Finney, a vigorous, talented, and athletic farm boy. Finney quickly developed a reputation as a pedagogic innovator and a firm proponent of a humane liberal arts education with stress upon classical literature; as Rickey recognized later in life, he was a born psychologist too. "He was a pace setter," he said in admiration, "a man who understood boys, who could win their confidence and merit it. He was a big man."

Finney's technique was relatively simple. He sought to build self-esteem among the small town and farm boys and girls he educated and open their eyes and minds to the great ideas of the past by introducing religious aphorisms and teaching morality to guide them into more Christian lives. Like most Methodist children in Lucasville, Rickey must surely have been familiar with Finney's efforts to explain life as derived from John Wesley's "The Use of Money," a celebration of individualism, enterprise, and charity. "Gain all you can, without hurting yourself or your neighbor," read Finney aloud on any number of occasions to his youngsters. "Save all you can, waste nothing, living or dying, on sin or folly. And then give all you can, or in other words, all you have to God."

At first his classmates made fun of Branch. He came from a farm and they from a village, however small it was. He started stuttering and only in retrospect understood that his peers' taunts forced him either to retreat into fearfulness or else to develop strong defenses. Slowly, by a force of will and self-discipline he was barely conscious of, he began to rid himself of the impediment, aided immeasurably by Finney. Together the pupil and teacher sat each afternoon, the elder man patiently correcting the boy's defect. Before long, Branch's words began pouring out as a torrent, a cascade of sentences and phrases that overwhelmed many of his classmates and teachers. By the end of his first school year, the other students were increasingly respectful of the small, good-looking boy.

"From as early as I knew him," said a former classmate, "he was able to make up his mind, take responsibility on himself, dedicate himself to whatever he wanted to do, unlike the other kids."

He even changed his name. Two cousins living in Harrisonville were both named Wesley, so he dropped it. By the age of twelve, he was Branch Rickey.

In the next year, in 1895, he decided he had had sufficient schooling. In an era of early departures from school when relatively few children of the working and farming classes completed elementary school's eight grades, classroom work seemed unimportant to the young Rickey. The world outside, his father's harsh workaday labors, the give and take of daily affairs seemed more manly and appropriate. He must also have fretted about the ceaseless efforts of his parents and their bitter struggle to see him through school as they tried to cope with the sharply plummeting prices in com and sorghum. He decided to return to the farm "where I belonged."

In April school closed for a week for the planting season. Branch approached his father with his idea.

"I'd like to help you, work alongside of you," he told his father. "Dad, I want to quit school and go to work."

His father was silent. They were standing in the corn field on Saturday afternoon, and Frank picked at a plant. Orla had finished high school and gone on to teaching. What was Branch's future without some kind of schooling, he must have thought. Uneasy, he nevertheless replied evenly, "Certainly, son. You have reached the age where you have to make up your mind about your life. You can go to work for me tomorrow."

For four days he was sent into the hills by his father to work near Duck Creek.

"It was spring and they were planting corn. Father said: 'Now, son, take this hoe and follow the corn planter. It will miss covering up grain corn once in a while. I want you to cover up the grains if necessary.' I followed that corn planter all day long and at the end of the day was never so tired in my life."

His father returned home, leaving his son at the farm.

"I hung in there the next day and for the next two days, too, but at the end of that time I felt like I imagine a runner feels when he is finishing a marathon.

"Well, the next day Gus Massey, the tenant, said he had to go to Lucasville to see my father, and would I like to go along? Would I? No one knows the boyish struggle I went through to save face! How could I get back and let my father and mother know that I really wanted to go back to school? I would have to take back everything I had said.

"Father made it very easy for me. He repeated all the arguments with greater strength and force and put the matter up in such form that I would simply have to give up to parental authority. That was a great 'out' for me. Thus I, with apparent regret and, of course, with a show of contrite hesitation, consented to do as he said and go back to school. This is what Dad had planned all the time. He was a wonderful father."

The next month Orla returned from his teaching job. He and Branch discussed their education and work, and Orla, said Rickey, displayed little interest in returning to teaching. He was nineteen and a passionate follower of baseball, and the Red Stockings in Cincinnati in particular. Orla always seemed to be carrying a ball with him, and he started to initiate his younger brother into the ways of the game. Their mother made baseballs by hand for them to play with and weekdays, following Branch's return from school, the two would form a regular tandem, the left-handed, sidearm fastballer Orla throwing and Branch catching. Often townspeople stopped to watch the two boys, among them Finney, who announced not long after that he wanted to form a town team to play on Saturday afternoons.

By the summer's end Orla was Lucasville's best pitcher, while Branch shared catching duties with someone else. Yet he was beginning to draw the attention of the Ohio farmers and villagers who watched the games from their buggies or along the baselines. Squatting behind the plate, his boyish muscles bulging through his rolled shirt sleeves, learning to see all positions from his vantage point behind home plate and possessed—as Finney said in admiration—"with an instinctive grasp of tactics," he began to assert a growing degree of confidence. "I was a natural left-handed hitter with fair power," he said in a self-description of those early days. "I had an excellent throwing arm but I threw a heavy ball. My speed was a shade better than average."

In one game, coach Finney put him into the lineup in the fifth inning. "Right away, he took over as though he owned the whole game," recalled one of his teammates. "He barked orders to everybody, held a meeting with the pitcher, raced back to the plate, punched his glove, shouted more orders, and put new life into the game. He was the catcher after that."

The Rickeys lived down the street from Chandler Moulton's general store. The Moultons were the town's most prominent family and their large house and huge porch with its swings for their children and willow rocking chairs impressed Rickey. While still a boy, Rickey was attracted to Moulton and tended to see him as an important man—the keen small-town businessman and landowner with a substantial interest in the world outside Lucasville.

Chandler Moulton—who would one day become Rickey's father-in-law—was born in Vermont in 1839, the grandson of a Revolutionary War veteran. In 1848 the Moultons settled in Scioto County. In time, Moulton became a Republican member of the Ohio legislature, "a man of commanding influence in business and politics. He takes everything easy and does not worry about anything. Job could have taken lessons of him and improved his book," said an admirer.

Following his marriage to another prominent Ohioan's daughter, Moulton moved to Lucasville where the fourth of his six children, a daughter named Jennie (later called Jane), was born on February 16, 1882. Rickey knew her from the time of his arrival in town, but at some point—he always claimed it was "love at first sight"—in their adolescence he saw her as a young woman and fell in love. This feeling was unshakable and in 1898, when he was seventeen and she sixteen, they began to correspond after Jane and her sister Mabel were sent to the Western College for Women, in Oxford, Ohio, where she studied French and drawing, read Caesar, sang in the chorus, played piano, joined the school's athletic club, and participated in golf, tennis, basketball, cricket, and battle ball. From there she wrote a steady stream of "My dear Branch" and "My dear Friend" letters to Branch back home.

> My dear Branch—[began one such letter] It is almost time for the last bell to ring to close this beautiful yet windy Sabbath day, and I suppose you must have your letter [they had agreed to correspond once weekly].... As to "Dearest Jen" I don't see that I am any dearer than last time to you.

A week later, though, she confessed that she could not concentrate on her studies and told him she had failed a French recitation because of him.

His most immediate problem after finishing school was finding a job. He briefly considered a military career and took the West Point exam receiving the fourth highest grade in the area, but only the top two were sent to the academy. He considered farming, but with Orla at home and prices and profits declining, he took a job as a door-to-door salesman peddling self-help medical books and cookbooks. He quickly discovered his potential customers could barely afford the expense.

It was James Finney who came to his rescue. If Branch would agree to take the upcoming summer exam for Scioto County primary-school teachers, Finney would tutor him without charge.

Rickey responded with uncertainty. His family's farm was more precarious than ever and he felt a great obligation to stay home and help as best he could. Still, Finney was persistent, arguing that the $30 monthly wage he would be paid as a teacher would benefit his family. Besides, Finney told Branch's parents, the months away would help the boy mature. If Branch really wanted to help his family and himself the first step was teaching. "I ought to be with Mama and Papa and Frank," he told Finney, who refused to hear his objections. So it was that very early on a July morning Rickey left home for the 8 A.M. test at the Portsmouth courthouse. Two weeks later he received a two-year teaching certificate, enabling him to teach "Orthography, Reading, Writing, Arithmetic, Geography, English Grammar, U.S. History, Physiology and Hygiene." And two weeks after that, he was instructed to report to a one-room school in Turkey Creek in the Friendship, Ohio, postal district. At Finney's urging, the local Republican Party had put in a good word for him with the school superintendent.

Turkey Creek, seventeen miles from Lucasville, was as nondescript as Duck Run. The name Friendship belied the local population of combative, battling, brawling, and drunken loggers and moonshiners who comprised most of the townspeople. Some of the biggest stills in the county were there. Fighting and knifings were commonplace, and severe injuries and death accepted as ordinary.

Rickey learned this only after he arrived in September. He also learned, to his horror, that one of his predecessors had been beaten by a schoolboy and hospitalized in Portsmouth. "Just before the Christmas holidays one of the boys hit the teacher in the scalp," said the shocked Rickey, "and after they had taken him to the hospital down in Portsmouth they had the teacher arrested besides." He added: "He never came back to school."

His most immediate predecessor—"a tremendous big man," Rickey described him—arrived as a replacement and lasted for only two weeks. The students spat tobacco juice on his shoes and he fled, cowed.

Alarmed, Rickey nevertheless chose to confront the worst of his students directly.

On his first day, he promptly sized up his enemies: tough male adolescents, virtually his own age, scions of the lumber camps and stills. (The quiet ones in class included Joseph and Mary Preston Myers, a black brother and sister.) One of the boys he put down as "criminally inclined, strong talking, vile talking, a roughneck," who entered his classroom with the smell of corn liquor on his breath. Instantly, Rickey challenged the boy. Out they went, and to the amazement of his students, Rickey beat him in a bloody fist fight. After that, there were more fights when he had to take on the dares and taunts of his students. In one brawl, on a hot night under the moonlight, using cheap gloves and surrounded by students and the men of the area, he took a savage beating. "The fellow nearly killed me a couple of times, but I was not whipped," he said. In another, he faced a student who spat into the coal bucket and dared Rickey to run him off.

> He brought the book *Black Beauty* with him. That was the only book he had. He was just about my age, maybe a few months older than I, and about my size. Slovenly in dress, one leg left outside the boot and the other inside, his hair uncut apparently for months, hung clear down to his shoulders, and he was a pile loader up at the railroad station at Turkey Creek. Said he made $1.10 a day ... and I told him that was a little more than I was making.

The boy waited for Rickey after Friday's class. "Do you want to run me out of my job?" Rickey asked sharply, squeezing his shoulder hard, and adding: "Well, you just can't do it, do you understand?" The boy pulled away and grabbed the coal bucket and emptied its contents on the floor while Rickey shoved him out of the room, "banged the door shut and went up and rang the bell with great dexterity," to warn others of his trouble. Even so, the boy—Rickey remembered his name, Gordon Tatman, for the rest of his life—was impressed by some facet of his teacher's personality and became his major defender among the other hoodlums in class and eventually, in Rickey's words, became "a real student."

When the school year ended a measure of discipline had been established, but he was happy to be relieved of the burden and done with Turkey Creek. It had gone fairly well, he thought, despite the aggravating moments. In fact, Turkey Creek asked him to return at $40 a month. Word had spread of the young teacher who had contained their local toughs, and every male adult in the hamlet signed a petition calling for his rehiring. But when Pike County offered him a teaching job for the following year at $65 a month he was thrilled.

Back home again in Lucasville he confessed his love to Jane and "when I told him I love him" he left the Moulton porch with "eyes full of tears of joy."

Yet there remained the problem of where to teach the next year. As far as Rickey was concerned, it was Pike County, and he was surprised to hear his father question his judgment. Frank was so disturbed he called on the Scioto County superintendent to talk about Branch's plans. "They really made the decision for me," he said. "I would have tried to get the job up in Pike County or have done something else. My father was the one who said that under all circumstances I must return for a second year. He felt that it was a job that had not been finished."

Rickey accepted without much objection. "At the time I was not disposed to dispute with my father about his very set opinions," he told Arthur Mann years later. Young and extremely dutiful, he returned to Turkey Creek. Yet he wasn't quite the same boy who had left home for the first time the year before. His imagination had been stirred by the news that two Lucasville boys were attending Ohio Wesleyan University in Delaware, not far from the state capital at Columbus. He knew too that Chandler Moulton's children all attended college. And his idols, Finney and Frank Appel, had both graduated from OWU.

He had indeed started to change, yet he often retreated into diffidence and self-consciousness. He was aware that he lacked social graces, and he still wore Orla's hand-me-down clothing, his large hands protruding past the cuffs of his shirts. He had no formal diploma, very little money, and only one year of schoolteaching. He also felt guilty about even daring to think of the luxury of a college education while his family remained sorely pressed merely to keep their farm operating. One day he spoke to his older brother about his doubts. Orla told him straight out that if it was college he wanted, then to go ahead. But Rickey wasn't satisfied: Wasn't it his obligation to stay and help the family? Orla shook his head. "You go ahead, Branch, Frank and I—we'll stay and work the farm."

Still, he hesitated, and did not bring up the subject with his father. While Branch pondered, he received a letter from Frank Appel, then school superintendent in Wheelerburg. He and Finney had been talking about him, Appel wrote. They agreed that something had to be done to help him go on to college, especially—it was meant to be a joke—as the OWU team needed a reliable catcher. Would, therefore, Branch be willing to spend the summer in Wheelerburg with Appel cramming for the entrance exam for OWU's prep school, a pre-college academy which shared the OWU campus and faculty in Delaware? If he passed the exam, and afterwards the prep school courses, he would be admitted into the college, Appel explained.

Rickey jumped at the chance but also thought again about a military career and decided to take the United States Naval Academy examination, which Jane had been urging him to do.

"I think it is just fine," she wrote him on April 9, 1899, "and the best chance you could have.... I think you stand the best chance of anyone at Lucasville. You know all the studies well and you have a strong constitution. Mark Crawford [another local applicant] has a weak heart, so Father said, and you stand as high as any of them. Why don't you try? I know I would if I were in your place. You know the last two years you would get to be on the ocean all the time. Then what an opportunity to see the world. To be sure you would have to go to war if there was one but there won't be one so you are safe for a long time anyway. I believe I would try at least."

When the results were in, he learned he had placed third, losing to Jane's cousin. Branch was crushed; "a very bitter disappointment" was the way he described his feelings. "I was sick about it," but in writing Jane he confessed his growing love for her was greater than his sadness: "I am true as steel to my trust," he wrote.

Appel's tutoring offer was a clear alternative. In late June he rented a room in a boardinghouse across the road from Frank Appel's house. For the next eight weeks, six days weekly, they spent much of the day studying geometry and reading Caesar, Cicero, and the school's basic text, *Grove's Latin Grammar.* But for Sundays, when he visited church, each day was an academic grind and each evening was spent ingesting and memorizing the required materials.

By the end of August, exhausted by the intense heat and endless round of study, looking thin, drawn, and ashen, he returned home intent on talking with his father about his dream of college. One evening he felt his father was ready to listen, and he poured out his hopes and fears. Frank listened without interrupting until, at last, Branch had finished. He then scotched the idea of college, saying that he was "really opposed" to the very idea. Frank Rickey firmly believed that, unlike West Point or Annapolis, an ordinary college might corrupt his son as he thought it corrupted other men's sons. He had heard tales of dancing and drinking and gambling on campuses. But even more, there was another reason he was against his going. Years after, when Rickey talked about the evening's conversation, he was still amazed that his father thought him unprepared for further studies in spite of his summer in Wheelerburg.

Young Rickey had no high school diploma, argued Frank; besides, college was for the sons and daughters of the well-to-do city people and Chandler Moulton's kids, people with money.

Finney and Appel went to see Frank Rickey, probably at Rickey's request. What sort of life had Frank in mind for his son? they asked. Dirt farming? Storekeeping? Schoolteaching? The boy, they argued, had a first-rate mind, and Frank ought to be encouraging him.

Frank sat back and considered the arguments. Very reluctantly he agreed that if Branch truly wanted, he could go. But then he raised another objection: why OWU and not Ohio State University? Patiently the two educators explained once more about OWU's unique prep school. But Frank was trying to defer a final decision. At last, a decision was made. Branch could—if he still wished—enter college after his second year at Turkey Creek.

The school year went well for him and having received permission to leave earlier than usual, he prepared for his new life.

At 5 A.M. on March 7, 1901, Branch awoke to prepare for his long day's trip north to Delaware, Ohio, home of the OWU campus. As he began dressing he heard his father speak from the bedroom. "Branch," he began, "I think you should go to Ohio State and not Ohio Wesleyan. I know Mr. Rightmore"—actually, he had a nodding acquaintance with George Rightmore, an OSU alumnus and local school administrator—"and he will take care of you." Branch did not reply. His father's voice rose, filled with anxiety over his son's leaving. "In fact, Branch, I don't believe you should go." Branch continued dressing, saying nothing, his first rebellious act. Then, in an even more exasperated and fretful voice, his father shouted, "I think you ought not go to college at this time."

His mother was preparing breakfast and brewing a pot of coffee. She helped her son pack and included *Grove's Latin Grammar* and a catcher's mitt in his satchel. He would wear his only suit on the train. She also gave Branch a torch made up of rolled copies of the *Transcript* bound with a string, and some matches, to flag down the Norfolk and Western train for Columbus at the Lucasville depot. Packed, dressed, fed, he embraced his mother, shouted good-by to his unhappy father, and left for the station with $62 in his pocket. At 6 A.M., the Columbus-bound train stopped, and four hours later, in the state capital, he changed to the Hocking Valley Railroad and reached Delaware a little past noon.

"I wanted to go to college more than anything else in the world, and I didn't care how I got there," he said. "I just wanted to go."

# Chapter Two

OHIO WESLEYAN UNIVERSITY was founded in 1844 in the hope it would become the great American Methodist university. By the time Rickey arrived on a blustery and raw March mid-afternoon, the school was approaching the peak of its intellectual flirtation with laissez-faire liberalism—its acceptance of the principles of evolution, its tempered dislike of too much government, its firmly held faith in the marketplace as a political and moral arena for the self-made man.

By 1901, the school had twelve hundred students, most of them the sons and daughters of midwestern smalltowners and farmers, and ministers serving in the church's foreign missions. The era of world wars and mass slaughters was far off and the searing depressions of the 1890s but a dim memory for most. Student life, the college's memoirist rejoiced, "was a happier, more buoyant experience" than in earlier decades.

Rickey's tuition was $10 a year plus an added $12 for general fees. His most costly expenditure was room and board, and he read in the 1901 catalog he carried that first day: "Some students who are boarding themselves bring their actual expenses at the college down to $45.00 a term. Others who are living better and spending more for books, entertainments, expenses of $75.00 to $100.00 a term."

When his train pulled into the small railroad depot on West William Street, two Lucasville friends, Clay Brant and Ed Appel (Frank's younger brother), were on hand to greet him.

"No boy could have had fewer clothes than I had my first year in school, and no boy could have had less money," said Rickey, pigeon-toed, bowlegged, lean, angular, his only suit so old that it was shiny.

"What's in the bag?" asked Appel, peering down at his shabby suitcase.

"Oh, that," Rickey answered, beaming. "My other suit." He stooped down, unfastened the straps, opened the bag, and proudly held up his Lucasville baseball uniform.

Laughing aloud, happy to be together again in their new setting of independence, the three boys started down the street to 4 Michael Avenue, where Appel had found a tiny flat for him for 50¢ weekly, a room so small, Rickey said, that he had "no place to sit down—more or less a closet with a single bed in it."

Ed Appel was especially pleased to have Rickey at school with him, not only because of his elder brother's attention but because they had been close friends at home. Ed, who had written glowing letters about OWU to Rickey, was now a sophomore, with a veneer of sophistication and worldliness, ready to guide the untried Rickey, steer him into the Delta Tau Delta fraternity, and teach him the ways of the campus. Walking to the rooming house, Ed decided to concentrate first on his friend's seedy appearance.

"Branch," he whispered, suddenly stopping and putting the bag down on the walk. "Branch, turn your toes out when you walk." Clay nodded in agreement, adding that Rickey looked too much as if he was straight off the farm. "Aw, turn your own damned toes out," Rickey snapped back. "It's the way I walk."

The next morning Rickey headed for the campus prep school. "On the first day I took all my books and went to Cray Chapel for the morning service, and it was after chapel that I roamed about the corridor in front of the big billboard and that was when Shorty Gutshawl came into the picture—a big 6' 6½" fellow, he was the only one there. I was hanging around with my arms full of books and I went up to him. I said, 'Where do you go now?' and he looked me over and he shocked me with his reply. 'Wherever you damn please.' So I went back to 4 Michael Avenue."

The incident filled him with self-pity and homesickness, but when he repeated the story to an upper classman in the boardinghouse he laughed and told Branch to return to school. In fact, the young man went on, Rickey could even use his larger room in the front part of the house for study when he was away. And another student invited Rickey to eat at his mother's table for $2.50 weekly, far less than he was paying.

Loaded with the required texts, Branch went back to the campus and registered for classes. Along with everyone else, he had to appear daily at compulsory chapel, which became the centerpiece of his daily schedule. Conducted each morning, prefaced by a hymn, followed by a scriptural reading, a short prayer, and then a final hymn accompanied by student choristers and an organ, chapel thrilled Rickey though others stayed away when they could. From the first day he believed that the spirit of chapel moved him immensely, reassuring him in his anxiety that certain principles were immutable, bedrocks he could always lean on in times of stress: "Duty, conscience, loyalty, devotion and reverence for Christ and for Methodism and for Democracy," was the university motto, and the young man believed it was the lodestar he would follow.

On his third day at college, he walked into Professor John Grove's Latin class. Grove, who also served as prep school principal and taught elementary law, immediately announced that the required text would be Virgil, which he distributed to the class. Then he called on Rickey.

"Will you take up the text at this point?" he asked, pointing to the opening chapter.

Terrified, Rickey rose and his recitation went badly, his long-forgotten stutter returning, his mastery of Latin weak. "I would give an English word for a Latin word," he said. Grove then asked him several textual questions, none of which he could answer. The professor said nothing, removed his glasses as if in thought, pushed his chair back, and crossed his legs.

"Mr. Rickey, sir, what Latin grammar did you study?"

"Scared to death and trembling, and ready to flop, I answered quick as a flash, but not meaning to be a smarty, 'Yours, Professor' because his Latin grammar was the one Frank Appel had given me at Turkey Creek."

The other students started howling and one boy fell out of his seat, laughing and holding his ribs. Even Grove shrieked with laughter.

Rickey sat down, "the tears ran down my cheeks ... I knew I was going to go home right then." There was a train leaving at 2:10, and he told himself he planned to be on it.

When the class mercifully ended, Grove called him to his desk. "I'm going home, Professor, I'm not ready for college," he blurted out. Grove would not be diverted, and he asked Rickey questions in fundamental grammar. Satisfied, he asked the boy to visit with him at 7:20 each morning for tutoring, saying he was confident he could pass the work.

In time he mastered the course and his other subjects. But he had to wait on tables and tend furnaces to relieve his financial pressures. His mother mailed him occasional dollar bills, although clearly the gifts strained her budget. All the same, her letters, and the reconciliation between father and son she negotiated, bolstered Rickey. "There was a closeness between us that I just have never known," he said about his mother. "I had no secrets from her, intimate as they might be. And as for my father, nothing could really ever separate us."

Study and work consumed him in his early months, relieved only by long and solitary walks into the neighboring countryside, and thinking about Jane still in Oxford. "I never thought of myself as lonely. There was so much to do," he admitted. "I was lovesick, though. I didn't have dates with anybody. I had no interest at that time with girls, only just this one girl who was off somewhere else."

One afternoon the university's athletic director called on him in his tiny room. As both sat on the bed Rickey was asked to join the football team. The athletic director had heard of Rickey's athletic agility from the other Lucasville boys, and the team, he confessed, was desperate for new blood. Rickey jumped at the invitation and two days later appeared on the playing field, wearing a worn long-sleeved shirt with sewn patches on the elbows. Within a matter of days he was the starting halfback, and his touchdown run later in the season against arch rival Ohio State enabled OWU to win 10–6. In spite of his demanding work-study schedule, Rickey managed to play in every game.

The next semester he enrolled for twenty-one credits, the maximum permitted by school rules. He also awaited Jane's arrival on campus as a new student; she and her sister Mabel were to live in Monnet Hall, the women's residence. Even so, he barely found time to visit with her, caught up in his heavy schedule and still shy because of his one shoddy suit, hard-pressed for cash, and wary of the prim atmosphere concerning dating. For him and Jane to date he had to send her a note: "Mr. Rickey requests the pleasure of..." They were not allowed to walk the streets, nor be seen alone in local restaurants. For a while, then, they were content to stare at one another from afar, only occasionally stopping to talk, walking together only on Sunday afternoons.

In March, baseball coach Dan Daub, who had once pitched for six seasons in the National League—five with the Brooklyn Dodgers and one with Rickey's beloved Redlegs—asked him to join the baseball squad. Daub had an almost all–Lucasville infield: cousin Eph Rickey at first base, Ed Appel at shortstop, and Clay Brant at third. From behind home plate Rickey barked orders, moved players about with a wave of his hand, took charge of pitchers and outfielders. He batted lead-off and hit well as the team won eleven and lost but two games in the spring of 1902. Once Daub sent him in to relieve and he barely survived the inning, giving up a double, triple, three walks, hitting two batsmen, and throwing a wild pitch. After that, he remained a catcher.

When the school year ended he was eager to explain to his father what he had passed through during the year. Ed Appel had preceded him by several days and he visited Frank Rickey to extol Branch's first year. James Finney had also dropped by the farm and told Frank that his son had been chosen for the mythical all–Ohio football team.

Frank's pride grew with each visitor, and when his son finally arrived home he blurted out cryptically, "Son, I'm going to make some moves so that I can help you." He didn't explain and Branch did not ask, but there was a bond of trust between the two that the strains of going away to college had never ruptured.

Rickey soon cast about for ways to earn money. A friend told him that the semiprofessional Portsmouth Navvies (the town was a river port, hence the nickname) were looking for a catcher at $25 a game. Hired immediately, he traveled that summer with the team through a number of southern states, playing games in Knoxville, Louisville, Memphis, and Birmingham, cities he had never before seen.

In the autumn he returned to Delaware, where once more he threw himself into a heavy academic program, registering again for twenty-one credits, working round-the-clock at an assortment of part-time jobs, and looking forward to the football and baseball seasons. One morning, the librarian stared uneasily at him as he sat reading in the large study hall. Rickey innocently disregarded the stares until another student approached him and asked him how he felt about becoming a celebrity. The boy carried with him a copy of the Columbus *Dispatch,* and told him that the Cleveland *Plain Dealer* and Cincinnati *Enquirer* had also carried items about him, none favorable. Rickey was appalled and stunned. Other than the college newspaper and the Lucasville and Delaware week-lies his name had never appeared in print. The *Dispatch* article, he read swiftly, reported he had been disqualified from all OWU athletic programs because he had violated his amateur status in accepting payment from "Maj." Andrews, owner of the Portsmouth Navvies. Unknown to him, the "Ohio Conference," a bloc of the state's colleges, had been organized during the summer months but was not ratified by all the cooperating schools (including OWU) until the autumn, after he had left the Navvies.

Not only was he overwhelmed by the spectacle of newspaper coverage, but he was frightened by its implications. Quite innocently he had chosen to play summer baseball for fun and for money. From elation at being back at school his spirits fell precipitously. When he received word that Dr. Bashford, the college president, wanted to see him he panicked. "When Dr. Bashford sent for me, I was scared to death—I didn't know what in the name of common sense I could have done that the president of the university would send for me. Anyhow, I was professional and could not play anymore. But when I got into his office, he greeted me pleasantly and told me he had a letter he wanted me to see, and with that he handed me a letter signed by Maj. Andrews, written in lead pencil, ungrammatical, and very vulgar." Andrews wanted to protect the young man who had played so well for him in July and August.

"Dear President," it began. "Whoever said I had paid Branch Rickey any money was a Goddamned liar. I never paid him a damn cent."

Rickey read the letter silently and shook his head, handing it back to Bashford.

"It isn't true," he said firmly.

Bashford said nothing and turned his chair around to stare at the campus through his large window. Then he turned back, put the letter into his desk's center drawer, and simply said: "I understand." And with that he indicated with a nod that Rickey was to leave his office.

Once outside, Rickey was vastly relieved, and he tried to rationalize what had happened. He hadn't been dismissed from college; he hadn't been penalized academically in any way; he had however been barred from interscholastic sports but "the football team was secondary to me and making $25.00 a week at that time meant my getting back to schoolwork." The money he had received from the Navvies, he reflected proudly, had been enormously helpful to his parents and younger brother. "I think I would have played even if I had known about the rule or if it had been in existence at the time."

It didn't take long for Rickey to realize that, his amateur status lost, he could still play for pay. He joined the semipro Shelby Steel Tube Company football team not far away, practicing in the early evenings and playing Saturdays for $50 a game. Shelby Tube was one of the precursors of Ohio professional football, and as many as 2,500 people watched its games from the sidelines and behind each goal post. The team had never before had a college player. Rickey started out by playing end, but before long was asked to help in the coaching as well. But it was all over after the third game when he broke his ankle against Ohio Northern University in Ada, refused to leave the game, continued to play for several plays, and then had to be carried off the field by his teammates when the pain became too severe.

For the next few months he hobbled about on crutches; he managed to tend furnaces, although waiting on tables proved too much for him. Far more troubling to him, though, was the jealousy he felt when he heard that Jane was being courted by another student, the editor of the Ohio State University newspaper, who, complained Rickey bitterly, "proposed repeatedly" to her. Rickey saw him as a serious rival and obviously told her how upset he was. When she had to leave school in the middle of the year because of her sister's illness, he was greatly relieved. Columbus was far from Lucasville, and before going home, Jane and he discussed their relationship and she reassured him of her love.

After her departure, he devoted even more of his waking hours to his studies. He wrote Jane that economics, Latin, Greek, and German were challenging ("Mrs. Davies talks nothing but German and sometimes I get disgusted," he complained to her) but history, English, and grammar were a pleasure. With pride he wrote her: "I'll give you my grades so that when you get the *Lucasville Transcript* you can compare them with those who received honor grades." He then listed his grades:

Virgil—91%
Physics—94%
English—93%
Sophomore History—93%
Greek—96%
Livy—85%
German—89%
Grammar—93%

"My term average [was] 91¾%." He had discarded his crutches, he wrote, and had a new part-time job digging ditches on roads just outside Delaware.

"I long to see you and be near you. I must not let myself long for you so much for it makes me despondent and careless but honestly, my own true sweetheart, I think the happiest boy in the world will be I when starting home to see you. I want to see my parents and all but really—I don't know why—I don't think of coming home but to see you. Can you love me just the same then? Will my absence alienate your affection in the least? Darling, always know that I love you just as much as anyone can and that someday you are to be my wife." He signed the letter, "Your own true lover, Branch."

Once again, President Bashford called for him, a rather unusual request since the president customarily dealt directly with faculty and not students. This time, the interview was entirely unexpected. Dan Daub, the coach of the baseball team, had quit, Bashford told the young man. Would Rickey be interested in the job? Bashford said he had been impressed with Rickey's honesty in refusing to lie in his sophomore year when confronted by the Navvies' owner's letter; he had also spoken with faculty and all were taken with the prodigious schedule Rickey was able to maintain without damaging his scholastic record. To a man and woman, they praised his sense of responsibility and integrity, especially, said one professor, for someone only twenty-one years old.

Assured by Bashford that he would be paid for coaching he accepted, though he continued at occasional part-time jobs, juggling exhausting academic programs, reading all the books assigned, and writing all the papers required. But now he was even more: a part-time quasi–college instructor who on occasions was even allowed to sit in—without speaking or voting—on faculty meetings. Delta Tau Delta now boasted of his membership when they sought to recruit new pledges, and professors sought him out with offers of stipends and grants.

In the midst of this good fortune he received a letter from his father asking if he remembered his father's pledge to do something for him. The time had come, Frank Rickey continued: he had decided to mortgage the farm so that Branch could concentrate on his work and interests rather than on exhausting part-time jobs. The young Rickey was astonished at his parents' generosity but, even more, deeply moved by their sacrifice. "I don't know how in the dickens he ever got hold of that amount of money," said the dazzled Rickey when he received $15 for Delta Tau Delta's initiation dues. Now, at least, he could turn seriously to coaching and drop the other paid jobs.

Rickey's first baseman was Charles Thomas, one of OWU's few black students. They had first met two years earlier on the football squad and liked one another. Thomas, whom Rickey called "Tommy" and others "Cha," had grown up in Zanesville, Ohio, where his parents had moved after his birth in Weston, West Virginia, in 1884. Three years younger than Rickey, he was on first base in the season's 1903 opening game against Kentucky.

When they saw Thomas, the southern college players objected vehemently and, said a student seated behind first base, they insisted the umpire "Get that Negro off the field or we don't play."

Rickey was twenty-one years old, a novice coach. Seated on the bench, he heard the catcalls. "Get the nigger boy off the field," one of the opposing players shouted. "We aren't going to play with him," screamed another.

Rickey rose and ran toward the Kentucky bench. Pointing his finger at their coach and waving it again and again, he shouted angrily, "You will play Tommy Thomas or you don't play OWU."

He then strode back to his bench and ordered his team to throw the ball around and stay loose. The Kentucky coach approached Rickey and spoke with him. Rickey started shaking his head furiously, and the crowd began to cheer him on. "We want Thomas, we want Thomas," they started chanting, as the Kentucky squad huddled and rehuddled. At last, after one hour they relented and took the field. "Rickey stood his ground," said a spectator. "He was only a kid."

At the close of his third year at college, Rickey joined the Terre Haute club of the Central League, played a few games—no record is available—and decided to move to a higher-paying job as a catcher with Le Mars of the Iowa–South Dakota League. Playing in 41 games in July and August, he batted .265, stole 12 bases, committed 13 errors, and had a fielding average of .956. In one game he had three hits—a single, double, and triple. After the game the manager complimented him, saying he had "caught a good game." Rickey, though, was unimpressed. The manager, he wrote Jane, rarely engaged in flattery or even more rarely complimented his players. "So I must not knock myself all the time, I need confidence."

Rickey, a village boy now in a larger small town, found Le Mars exciting and vibrant. The town had a biweekly paper, had "everything doing" he wrote Jane: carnivals—which he loved to visit—races, and above all, prizefights. "My Dear Little Sweetheart. There was a prizefight at Dalton two miles from here last night—bloody and fierce—a go-round draw. I'm seriously thinking of entering the ring."

"I want you to be my wife so badly," he blurted out in a non sequitur, "and I'm just crazy to know I have you for all time. I love you more and more but please write me good letters."

Back at school in 1903, he rejoined the Shelby Tube Company football team. Football was, however, his nemesis: again in the third game he broke a bone, this time in his leg. He received a pair of crutches from the local dispensary. He was still hobbling when spring came and his baseball team reported for practice.

In April, the baseball team traveled to South Bend, Indiana, to play Notre Dame. Advance registrations had been made at the Oliver Hotel. But when the players entered the hotel lobby the desk clerk was stunned to see the black among them. The desk clerk told Rickey that only whites were welcome at the Oliver; Rickey immediately turned to his student manager, Barney Russell, and told him to run to the nearby YMCA and ask about lodging for Thomas and the entire squad. Thomas, though, was stunned by the clerk's attitude. Perhaps it would be better for the team and himself if he returned to Delaware, he told Rickey timidly. "'I'd like to go back."

Rickey waved him off. "No, no," he answered, "we'll be all right."

Rickey asked to see the manager of the Oliver. After thirty minutes behind closed doors he emerged, smiling. Management would allow

Thomas to wait in Rickey's room while a room in a black neighborhood could be found for him. On the way up to his room, Rickey whispered to Russell: "Forget about the YMCA, Tommy stays with us."

From his room he ordered a cot. When the hotel manager protested Rickey had violated his trust, Rickey announced in stentorian tones, "Under no circumstances will I leave or allow Thomas to be put out."

"We went upstairs," said Rickey. "I summoned the captain to discuss plans for the game, Tommy stood in the corner, tense and brooding and in silence. I asked him to sit in a chair and relax. Instead, he sat on the end of the cot, his huge shoulders hunched and his large hands clasped between his knees. I tried to talk to our captain, but I couldn't take my gaze from Tommy. Tears welled in the large, staring eyes. They spilled down his black face and splashed to the floor. Then his shoulders heaved convulsively, and he rubbed one great hand over the other with all the power of his body, muttering, 'Black skin ... black skin. If I could only make 'em white.' He kept rubbing and rubbing as though he would remove the blackness by sheer friction.

"'Come, come, Tommy!' I barked. 'If you can't lick it, how can you expect us to help? Buck up.'"

Charles Thomas was again his first baseman. Thomas remembered those days vividly in 1958, years after he had become a dentist in Albuquerque, New Mexico.

"From the very first day I entered OWU, Rickey took a special interest in my welfare. I think I was the first Negro player on its teams and some of the fellows didn't welcome me any too kindly, but there was no open opposition.

"I have always felt that Branch set them straight. During the three years that I was at OWU no man could have treated me better. When we went on our trips, Rickey was the first one to see if I was welcome in the hotel where we were to stop. On several occasions, he talked management into allowing me to occupy a double room with him and his roommate, Barney Russell."

For the rest of his life Rickey tried to explain the effect of that scene on his life.

"Whatever mark that incident left on the black boy, it was no more indelible than the impressions made on me," he said. "For forty years I've had recurrent visions of him wiping off his skin."

It was 1904 and the farm boy from Duck Run was struggling, often unconsciously, toward a concept of an evolutionary and willing acceptance of blacks by the white majority. His experiences with black people were extremely limited: he had had two black students, a brother and sister in the school at Turkey Creek; his father—he noted with pride for years after—had reared him "without snobbery or racial bias." By instinct and by inheritance he believed in fair play, hard work, exhortation to reason, all of them in his mind's eye basic precepts of a harmonious world. Watching Charles Thomas' humiliation was, however, the first time he may have wondered whether the moral code he lived by was denied to black people.

The team did well his first two years at the helm. In the spring of 1904 he was asked to coach football as well. Bishop Herbert Welch, the college's new president, said, "Rickey applied some of his well-known brains in devising new methods of attack and defense; he was the first to use line-shifts and other new strategies." For the yearly big game against Ohio State, his parents and young Frank traveled to Delaware for their first visit and heard the marvelously silly cheer that swept the stands that afternoon:

> Speak to me, State, only speaky-spiky-spoky;
> Why are those tears on your cheeky-chiky-choky?
> You can't make first down against Rickey-Riky-Roky.
> Amen.

He graduated in June. Three and one-third years after he left home with one suit and $62, he finished prep school and the university and earned a B. Litt., a course of study that normally took five years.

# Chapter Three

He returned to Lucasville with a degree but with no sure notion of what he wished to do. A friend from his Navvies team told him the Dallas club of the Texas League was desperate for a catcher, and he wrote a letter outlining his experience and asking for a tryout. Back came a telegram offering him $175 a month if he reported within three days. For a brief while he hesitated: Texas was farther away than he had ever been. Yet he wanted badly to repay his parents, to marry, and to go on to law school. A law degree, he thought, would help impress Chandler Moulton, who considered baseball beneath the dignity of a college graduate.

Above all he needed money, and $350 for the summer was a dazzling figure.

That summer he played in 41 games and hit a respectable .261. A few days after Labor Day he was promoted to the Cincinnati Reds. The team was fighting for second place against the Cubs and Pirates and needed backup help in catching. The Reds had always been his boyhood favorites and he was elated at the possibility of playing in Cincinnati, the largest city by far he would ever have lived in.

Not Jane, though.

"What are you going to do about baseball a year from now?" she wrote angrily when she heard the news. "This is my plan, only under necessity will you play, and the necessity to be decided by both agreeing that such is the case. If you would save your money, kid, there is no necessity.... By managing properly there is no necessity. I say $400 will furnish a house as cozy as one could possibly want. It is all up to you, kid, you have got to think about it."

Arriving at the Red ballpark on a Tuesday morning, he sat on the bench and watched his new club perform. These were the first major league games he had ever seen, and seated alongside him—it must have seemed unbelievable to him at the time—was his boyhood idol, second-string catcher Heinie Peitz. "I was as green as grass and happy as a kid with his first fish on the line, being out there with the players I'd dreamed about. Heinie was swell, even loaned me his chest protector and mitt since I didn't have any equipment of my own," he said happily.

After Saturday's game—which the Reds won from Brooklyn 6–1—Rickey entered the clubhouse "whistling and grinning," he remembered, shut his locker, and packed his bags to return to Lucasville for the weekend. Heinie was seated on a stool next to his locker.

"Hey, kid, where are you going?" he asked.

"Not far, Mr. Peitz—I'll be back bright and early Monday morning."

"*Wh-a-a-a-t?*" screamed player-manager Joe Kelley, who overheard the rookie catcher. Kelley had been in the big leagues since 1891 and had spent six years with John McGraw's fire-eating Baltimore Orioles. He was livid with rage at Rickey's remark. "Listen, busher, beat it over to the owner's office and get your release!"

The president, Gary Herrmann, was a powerful local politician and ally of the Taft machine, who genuinely liked ballplayers and baseball. Rickey knew nothing of the man as he sat across from him in a leather armchair—the first one, he thought, he had ever been in—listening to Herrmann express surprise that a rookie would refuse to play on Sundays. Patiently Herrmann explained that Cincinnati, together with the Cubs, Cardinals, and Browns, had broken the ban on Sunday ball that year, a ban until then so powerful and pervasive that an evangelist had declared that several players had been hurt precisely because they performed on the Sabbath. Even so, Herrmann predicted, before long most ball clubs would follow the Reds' lead and play every day of the week.

Rickey nodded. He was impressed with the Red president's calm and comforting manner, so unlike Kelley's open contempt. But he had made up his mind not to play or even appear at the ballpark on Sundays. He knew his mother would not approve. He told this to Herrmann, adding that he considered his abstinence a moral act in consonance with his family's faith.

Herrmann was intrigued with the explanation and sought to understand him. Coming to the Reds was the chance of a lifetime, he told Rickey. Why, young men throughout America would leap at the opportunity. And besides, he went on, the Dallas club had failed to tell him of this idiosyncrasy when the trade was negotiated.

Nervous and upset, Rickey would not budge, telling Herrmann that while he never doubted what playing for the Reds might mean to

In 1903 and 1904 Rickey (second row, left), coached baseball and football at Allegheny College, a liberal arts school in Meadville, Pennsylvania. He taught a wide variety of courses, such as freshman English, Shakespeare, German and Greek drama. He also lectured publicly at the YMCA. His pet topic was—reported the local newspaper—"Evidences of True Manliness on the Athletic Field." (Allegheny College Archives, Wayne and Sally Merrick Historical Archival Center, Pelletier Library, Allegheny College)

others, for him it was only a way of accumulating enough money to marry and go on to law school.

"Mr. Herrmann then asked me to remain seated and he asked me again why, exactly, I refused to play. I repeated my feelings. He listened and smiled and then he said, 'Son, you go home and come back Monday. Then tell Kelley I sent you. Report every day but Sundays.'"

But Kelley wouldn't give way and he refused to play the young catcher. Soon Rickey was summoned to Herrmann's office again. The president informed him that he had to go. But first, he said, what, if anything, did he think the Reds owed him?

"I knew I hadn't been much help to the Reds. I just asked for board and expenses. Herrmann fiddled with his pencil and paper and then he said, 'Between expenses and salary for one month, it comes to $306.50— that all right with you?'"

Rickey was amazed. Herrmann had chosen to defy his manager who wanted him fired for insubordination and instead offered him his pay plus additional money for having caught seven innings in one practice game.

"That was more money than I had ever seen in the world, so right quick I said to him, 'Mr. Herrmann, I don't deserve any part of that.' But I didn't argue too hard."

The Reds returned his contract to Dallas, who then sold him to the Chicago White Sox. But by then it all seemed academic since he was back in his usual routine in Lucasville and Duck Run, working the farm, spending evenings and Sundays with Jane on the Moulton porch, playing pickup ball with his friends at home. Baseball, he always claimed, was secondary to earning money, and by now he bad decided to return to OWU to earn the far more coveted B.A. degree.

Before returning to Delaware, though, he received word that a few OWU faculty members had nominated him as football coach at Allegheny College, a small liberal arts school in Meadville, Pennsylvania. He was hired and Jane was overjoyed, for the position held out possibilities of permanent employment plus the chance to teach academic subjects, too.

For two years he coached baseball and football at Allegheny and taught a wide variety of courses, such as freshman English, Shakespeare, German, Greek drama. He lectured publicly at the YMCA, his pet topic— reported the local newspaper—"Evidences of True Manliness on the Athletic Field."

Allegheny was a typical Rickey performance: fevered, frenetic, overcommitted, exhausting, as he rushed here and there consumed by his many jobs and yearnings. Still, there was an air of insecurity about him at the time, often revolving around Jane's criticism of sports as a career. She and her father "felt that professional baseball was not a cultural undertaking. They didn't go with the idea of a college graduate going four years to some university in order to prepare himself to play professional sport."

He remained on professional baseball's roster of active players and during the winter was traded by the White Sox to the St. Louis Browns for the more experienced catcher Frank Roth. When he was told of the transfer he wrote Jane a long letter telling her that the Browns wanted him to report in the following spring (1905). "Unless I join them, I fear my chances for a berth on the team will be small—consequently you quickly see that my plans for the future will be altered."

He was trying to do the right thing by himself and Jane, he told her, but did not know what the right thing was. Should he return to OWU for the B.A.? Study law? Go into business? And, the crux of the matter, "Will you marry me while I am a ballplayer...? I think this thing of going along single is getting monotonous. I'm tired of living alone and I intend to marry—and that before I stop playing ball.

"If you think it impossible to consider marriage so long as I play baseball, then the culmination of a happy past must be indefinitely removed.

"I want you to give up this old prejudice of yours against baseball. On the other hand, I must sacrifice. Seriously too, my sacrifice is much greater than yours. Your prejudice is one existing only in your fantasy— a mere mental state & to change it results only in injury to your feelings. My sacrifice is material.... For me to marry you may impede my progress both financially and intellectually.... My future might be narrowed."

In another letter he suggested that since their separation was too aggravating to him, they marry secretly.

"I am opposed to a clandestine marriage," Jane wrote back.

"Such a course as we are now considering means, dear heart, a life of deceit. It seems to me a big black cloud is just waiting to envelop us. How happy, dear, will you be with the knowledge that I am your wife, yours to protect, help, love, and whose life you expect to fill with gladness? How happy, even to overflowing, will I be to know you are my husband, and that my life's work is to make you happy.... How can we hide it, dear, how much will it detract from it to know no other must know it, to hide it as if ashamed of it?"

Life seemed more complicated when he notified Robert L. Hedges, the Browns' owner and president, that not only would he not play Sundays but would only be available between June 15 and September 15, due to his college commitments.

Hedges agreed, since he needed a catcher badly. Thus Rickey traveled to Philadelphia to meet his new teammates at the Continental Hotel, as they prepared for a four-game series against the Athletics. He always recollected his first vision of that city and what baseball meant to its fans.

"I remember, as we alighted from the old horse-drawn omnibus at our hotel entrance downtown, looking around at the milling fans in front of a large newspaper office where they were gazing at a huge scoreboard with red and green lights, flashing the detailed progress of the game. I saw the name of the St. Louis players on the left and of

Philadelphia's on the right, and then in a summary certain significant letters such as AB (at bat), H (hits), etc."

In the opening game he came to bat three times without reaching base safely. Afterward, still troubled by Jane's letters, he returned to the Continental to find a telegram from his brother Orla. The words were ominous; their parents were ill and he wanted his younger brother to return home immediately. Their mother was even sicker than their father, and Orla, who recognized Branch was her favorite, wanted him to tend to her. Rickey bought a return railroad ticket that evening, and his baseball contract was returned to Dallas.

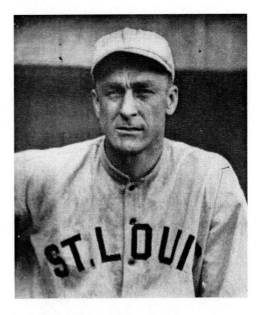

Rickey played for the St. Louis Browns in one game in 1905 and in 64 games the following year when he caught and batted .284 in 64 games. (National Baseball Hall of Fame Library, Cooperstown, NY)

What next, he must have asked himself as he rode westward toward Ohio. Baseball was still secondary to him, and he badly needed to find and settle into a more stable and worthier profession. Jane's cautionary words rang in his ears: "A man without enthusiasm would never interest me."

By August his parents were well again, and he decided to concentrate on law. Following his return to Allegheny College in September, he wrote his parents asking them to ship him "M.L.D. Barr's law books and papers immediately," particularly those concerned with criminal law. He set his mind on reading for the law in his free time. He still owed Frank and Emily $875, the money they had received for mortgaging the farm. Law, he believed, would enable him to repay the debt sooner.

In the spring of 1906 the Browns asked him to report again, offering $450 a month. He and Jane visited Chandler Moulton, who agreed they could announce their forthcoming wedding on June 1 with the "understanding that I would read for the law during the winter and the following summer would be my last in baseball."

As it turned out, 1906 was his finest year as a player. Proudly, he wrote his parents he played "in more games than either of the other catchers," batted .284, the third highest on the team. One Sunday he wrote his mother: "I attended three services, once in the A.M. & twice in the evening."

The *Sporting News* described him as "a high strung youngster with ability and enthusiasm" but his refusal to play on Sundays still aroused curiosity. A skeptical Cleveland *Press* reporter cornered him to ask, "How do religion and professional baseball mix?" The next day he wrote "Catcher Rickey looked bored" on hearing the question.

"Why shouldn't they mix well?" asked Rickey. "I try to be both a consistent ballplayer and a consistent Christian. If I fail it isn't the fault of the game or the religion, is it?

"It isn't a thing a fellow likes to talk about. My hometown is Portsmouth, Ohio, and my people are all Methodists. Sunday to me has always been a day apart. I can't help it. It was bred in me. You might almost call it a prejudice.

"So I won't play Sunday ball. I made them put it in my contract that I wouldn't have to. Instead, I go to church. I'm a member of the St. Louis YMCA, and whatever city I'm in, I generally find the time to visit the local association.

"You see I'm doing the things I was brought up to believe in. It doesn't necessarily follow that the other fellows have to believe as I do.... I'm not a missionary and the boys on the team would have a right to resent it if I should have the nerve to try to convert them.

"The boys don't need conversion. They're good fellows, they have made me one of them, and I know no reason why, in such company, a man can't play professional ball week days and be a consistent Christian all week 'round."

After an eastern road trip he temporarily left the team on May 29 for his wedding in Lucasville. When he arrived, hot, exhausted, and looking rumpled after the long coach trip, Jane said, "He looked as if he had been through a three-day operation." They were buoyed by their impending marriage and the news that Bishop Herbert Welch, OWU's new president, had just offered him the job of coach plus the chance to study for a B.A. degree.

On a sunny and warm June 1 morning they were married in the Moulton home, filled with family and friends and decked everywhere with red roses. Rickey told his younger brother that he was still tired and Jane was miffed because a prankster had taken her "bridal night dress" and locked it away in the railway depot baggage room.

Their honeymoon trip was another baseball road trip, working their way with the Browns through New York, Boston, Washington, Chicago, and then returning to their new, if temporary, apartment in St. Louis.

For the first time, direct contact with the game allowed Jane to sense the meaning it had to her husband. It was, of course, a means of earning money for other ends, as he had always insisted. But she realized now for the first time that it meant far more to him as she observed his feeling for the sport and for the men who played it. She saw how much baseball's power and speed defined the gesture of heroism in the American male consciousness. There was no *why* in the game; one either loved it or not. "I saw through his eyes with all the eagerness and his basic knowledge his keen mind had stored away." With a good teacher's instinct and patience for explaining, illustrating, and clarifying, Rickey opened her mind and heart to baseball.

But 1906 was a long season. It stretched past the September date he had set with Hedges for leaving; by the twenty-fourth he wrote his parents that he hoped to leave within the week. Fatigued by the searing heat of the St. Louis summer, his stomach troubling him, he confessed to his parents he was no longer able to attend church services. "In all my life I never had such a summer as this & let us hope I may never have another like it."

He was also peeved at manager Jimmy McAleer, who insisted he stay on beyond the fifteenth or else have his pay reduced. He was forced to accede to McAleer's demands and Bishop Welch moved the reporting date at OWU to October 7, but Rickey seethed at his manager's behavior. He appealed to Hedges, who allowed him to leave on the fifth, but before leaving an angry Rickey vowed he would never again play for the Browns, if he ever played for anyone else at all.

He and Jane rented a six-room frame house on Franklin Street near the campus for $40 a month. It was also close to Edwards Gymnasium, where he would spend much of his time. He was assigned the baseball, football, and basketball teams and paid $1,100 for the year.

They slipped easily into their new life; people and places were familiar and Delaware was a second home to them. As a new wife, Jane hadn't any real ideas about cooking, and Branch presented her with *Dr. Chase's Cook Book and First Aid,* the volume he had once tried unsuccessfully to sell door-to-door in Lucasville. He also quickly established a lifelong pattern of filling his home on a whim with people he wanted about him. "He brought home his fraternity brothers unexpectedly without a moment's notice, a trait he never got over," explained Jane, "confident that I would somehow manage and welcome them." She understood his deep-seated disquiet with idleness and his desperate need for continuous activity and hubbub. They were well-suited for one another, she confided in a friend at the beginning of their married life, she stronger and more secure and he requiring reassurance and emotional support. "I understand Branch very well," she told a friend in Delaware.

Jane chose blue as the predominant color in the house. Jacobean furniture was installed in the dining and living rooms and Grand Rapids early American in their bedroom. They made lifelong friends with Wesley Page, the director of athletics, and his wife, Ethel, both of whom thought the Rickeys in 1906 "the most loyal friends in the world." Together, the four took long walks into the countryside, picnicked and ran foot races, attended church services and sought out lectures offered at the Delaware YMCA. Weekday evenings Rickey reserved for himself to study his textbooks, write his papers, and work with a student-tutor as he sought to prepare for his B.A. qualifying exams.

He wrote his mother for "any quilts and pillows that you have ever planned to give me ... I want my house to show just as much of my mother's handiwork as it can." He also asked for her photograph so he might have it placed "in my watch." Later he added: "You know I'm hoping before this year is over to make Papa and Mama fall in love with Delaware & just decide to live there. I believe Papa could do something to make a living."

He was awarded the B.A. degree shortly before they returned to Lucasville for the Christmas holidays. At home their days and evenings were filled with family and friends. It was a hectic homecoming and Jane, now pregnant, found little time for rest. On their way back to Delaware, she became ill, and when the train arrived at 11 P.M. at the West William Street station he ran for a doctor, who promptly ordered her into the Jane Case Hospital. Three hours later, at 2 A.M., he learned that Jane, in her sixth month of pregnancy, had miscarried their first baby, a girl.

The following afternoon Jane's mother arrived to comfort her in her grief. Letters of sympathy flooded their home and visitors, especially Ethel Page, stopped in daily to see her. Sorrowing, they drew closer and they extracted those elements of their faith that allowed them the strength to grieve without despairing. "Branch's devotion and love for me overshadowed the loss of the child," she wrote. It enabled them to look ahead.

In the spring of 1907, his basketball and football squads won their conference championships. Yet still smarting at McAleer's treatment, he told Hedges that he could never play for the Browns. The Browns owner complied with his wish and traded him to the New York Highlanders— the predecessors of the Yankees—for infielder Joe Yeager. When the news reached him he said he didn't know whether to cheer or moan, for in December he had hurt his arm throwing a baseball in the gym. "I couldn't throw accurately and at a time when my arm would be cold, I couldn't throw the ball hard and it was painful up under the shoulder."

He felt obliged to tell Clark Griffith, the Highlander manager, about his condition and his private doubts about joining the club with his handicap. Griffith, though, felt otherwise and instead suggested Rickey spend two weeks in a Hot Springs, Arkansas, spa, basking his arm in the mineral waters and heated pools and having it massaged. Two weeks later, feeling no improvement, he took the train to New York City and then a subway to the Highlanders' park in northern Manhattan in time for the opening game. He learned that the first-string catcher, Red Kleinow, was hurt. "Grif came to me and asked me if I would catch—and I said I'll try, of course, but you know—well, he said, go in and catch—and [Deacon] McGuire, a very old catcher, was the other man [McGuire was forty-four years old, a veteran of twenty-three years in baseball and had just come from the Red Sox] and he was doing very little catching, almost none. I tried to catch—and the first three or four men that tried to steal I tried to throw them out." His arm was gone and despite a leaping save in right field by the Highlanders' Wee Willie Keeler on a wild Rickey throw, thirteen opponents stole bases that day, the last "six or eight" uncontested.

He had established a major league record for stolen bases allowed in one game. He was embarrassed, less because of the dismal showing he had presented than because his throwing ability had been the one athletic asset he took pride in above all else. By the time the 1907 season was finished, he knew that his playing days were over. He had been in 52 games, hit .182, and fielded a poor .862.

In Delaware for another year, he and Jane threw themselves into the active life of the college community. Bishop Welch knew and liked the couple, and since it was obvious they could use more income, he helped Rickey find a job as administrative secretary of the Delaware YMCA. As always, Rickey needed a multiplicity of outlets and he simultaneously enrolled as an evening law student at Ohio State University in Columbus, about twenty-five miles away. And when Professor John Grove, his onetime Latin teacher and guide, fell critically ill, he taught his elementary law course, refusing to accept any fee so that Grove's family could continue to receive his full salary.

He found the YMCA position challenging and intriguing, as he admired and respected Dr. Welch. Certainly he regarded his religious faith as exemplary. But what fascinated Rickey most of all about Welch was the way he applied religion to contemporary issues. Welch, as everyone on campus well knew, was prominently associated with the rising Social Gospel movement, just then beginning to supplant traditional laissez-faire liberalism. The more Rickey associated with Welch, the more he became aware of Welch's deep passion for social reform and profound interest in the lamentable condition of black people in America.

Herbert Welch was the New York City–born son of a banker and merchant, the first in his family to enter the ministry. Early on, he came under the influence of the doctrine of "Christian social responsibility," which arose from and had its intellectual and moral underpinnings shaped by British Methodism. Welch spoke with evangelistic fervor on the lecture circuit, rarely shrinking from controversy. "The Hope of the Negro," "The American Lynchings," and other denunciations of the mistreatment of black Americans were among his favorite subjects. In one of his YMCA orations, witnessed no doubt by Rickey, Welch expressed his concern for "the neglected and the oppressed, crying aloud for social justice, for equality of opportunity." And speaking as OWU's president, he said: "I was stirred to a new vision of what the Church might be and do in following the Christ who was not only a preacher, but a teacher and healer and transformer." In 1907, Welch was one of twenty-five bishops of the Methodist Federation for Social Service who called for a living wage for working people, the abolition of child labor, and the equitable distribution of corporate profits.

As YMCA secretary, Rickey helped bring to Delaware a glittering array of speakers reflecting Welch's views—Jane Addams ("The Conscience of Women and Social Amelioration"); Graham Taylor ("Industry and Religion," a call for the improvement of laboring conditions); United States Commissioner of Labor Charles P. Neill; the Danish-American journalist-documentary photographer of New York's Lower East Side slums, Jacob Riis; the two prophets of the Social Gospel, Washington Gladden and Walter Rauschenbusch (the latter telling his listeners to "let the [ex-]slave realize that he is Christ's freeman and can hold his head erect as any").

In the autumn of 1907, Rickey and Welch played host at the YMCA to Booker T. Washington, who delivered the first analysis of black Americans Rickey or probably anyone else in the audience had ever heard delivered by a black man.

It was during these years too that Rickey developed a passion of his own. Early one May evening in 1908 as he and half his football squad were strolling they approached a crowd gathered in front of the railroad depot to listen to a speaker standing on a baggage truck.

"What's that fellow doing?" Rickey asked his reserve end, Herman

"Rusty" Shipps. Someone else called out a reply: "Coach, he's making a 'wet' speech." Rickey raised his thick eyebrows and answered in his booming voice, "If you get me a box over on this corner I'll make a 'dry' speech." He then began speaking at the top of his lungs on the menace of liquor, drawing some of the crowd across the way to his side as his players cheered him on. Drawn to controversy as a fish to water, he was thrilled with the response he received. A few days later he heard from the Anti-Saloon League in nearby Westerville. The League, which had been proselytizing in Ohio among evangelical Protestants and Wesleyans, had developed close ties nationally with the American Anti-Saloon League, following its formation in 1893. They asked him to join their cause as a speaker in smalltown Ohio for $10 a talk plus expenses. The current issue was local option—whether a community should be permitted to forbid the sale of liquor.

He bought a used Maxwell automobile and set off for Chillicothe, arriving in the early evening. Looking for a place to sleep, he visited a hotel but was rudely told there were no vacancies. The hotel earned much of its income from its saloon, they told him, and wanted no part of dry agitators. He tried the town's second hotel and got the same response.

Confused and uncertain, he wandered aimlessly down the main street when someone called out his name. "Branch Rickey, what are you doing in Chillicothe?" It was—Rickey later told Rusty Shipps—a boyhood chum from Duck Run.

"And what are you doing here?" asked Rickey, just as surprised. "I'm tending bar, what are you doing?"

"Well, I came to make a dry speech and I can't find any place to stay. The hotels won't let me in."

His Duck Run friend smiled. "That's all right, Branch. Come down and stay with me."

The next day he started delivering his polemical talks and then he moved on to nearby towns. By all local newspaper accounts a fiery speaker, he began to develop a more dramatic delivery at each successive performance. His ability to snap back at hecklers grew more polished, his shouted warnings of the evils of alcohol more ominous, his orations peppered with his mother's stories and anecdotes.

Jane soon joined him and they roamed the state until it was time for the school year to begin. His reputation as a speaker spread and reached the ears of the powerful Ohio Republican Party in Columbus. By October 1908 he was working for the William Howard Taft for President Committee, crisscrossing central Ohio again in his battered

Maxwell, speaking until he was hoarse, yet miraculously finding time to attend night classes at Ohio State, teach Grove's class, and run OWU's athletic program.

A month after the presidential election and into the first months of 1909 Jane grew alarmed at his physical appearance. His round-the-clock activity had taken its toll, and he developed a chronic cough and was often racked with spasms. He was fatigued all the time, so unlike the animated man she knew so well. He had also started losing weight. One night, after an especially strenuous session with his football team, he arrived home drenched with sweat. "I had night sweats and I didn't know that I had a running temperature at all. I had no appetite and lost approximately thirty pounds," he said.

Jane kept after him to see Dr. Seaman, the local doctor, but he resisted until he began coughing up blood. The medical examination soon revealed he had contracted tuberculosis.

Tuberculosis! It was the dread disease of the day, the foremost killer of the time. The news terrified him and Jane and their families, for there was no known cure. "I was distraught and discouraged and all that," he wrote to a friend. "My plans, everything, had suddenly 'gone to pot.'"

He notified Bishop Welch, who, as always, went out of his way to help him. Earlier, Welch's secretary had contracted the disease and with Welch's assistance gone for treatment to the Trudeau Sanitorium in Saranac Lake, New York, in the Adirondack Mountains. Welch told Rickey of her experiences and progress and how well the famed sanitorium dealt with its patients. Welch offered to speak with his influential friends in New York City and ask them to reserve a bed for him.

They spent several days settling their affairs and learning what they could about the course of the disease. From Dr. Seaman and a handful of articles in the library, they learned that the main curative treatment at Trudeau was somehow to prevent the disease from spreading beyond the lung. Too often, though, that was a matter of luck. If the bacilli spread into Branch's bloodstream or lymphatic system and reached his central nervous system, death was inevitable. All medicine could do then was comfort the patient and offer solace to the family.

Equally frightening to the Rickeys was the sure knowledge that the customary course of the disease was slow, and it took a very long time to recover, or die. Given the state of medical awareness in 1909, the only "cure" was absolute rest, constant exposure to clean, dry air, and control of the deadly bacillus.

Branch and Jane traveled by railroad through Buffalo and Rochester and then boarded a small branch line to the tiny hamlet of Saranac Lake in the Adirondacks. They were probably filled with premonitions of death, but at least Rickey had his wife with him; families of more seriously ill patients were barred and the sick often abandoned and stigmatized.

Arriving late in the evening, they spent the night at Saranac Inn, telling no one he had TB since the Inn, along with the nearby Lake Placid Inn, excluded all tuberculars. The next morning they rode out to the sanitorium five miles away.

Their first stop was at the cottage of Bishop Welch's secretary, who shared her sanitorium experiences with them. Later, an alarmed Jane described her as looking deathly ill, despite Welch's optimistic prognosis. They then went to another cottage, where, again thanks to Welch's intercession, a room was rented for Jane in the home of a Trudeau physician who had herself recovered from the disease.

Satisfied that Jane was comfortable and safe, Rickey finally checked into the Administration Building. Following an extensive physical examination, he was ordered to bed for ten days of total rest and advised to eat as many high-calorie foods as possible. He was given a series of tuberculin tests.

"They would give these tests starting with a small dosage," he explained to Arthur Mann in 1956, "testing your reaction to these injections, and it was supposed to indicate the extent of the disease and thereby regulate your exercise. I reacted to the third tuberculin test. If you didn't react to the fifth one, you were not supposed to have tuberculosis."

He felt no pain but was experiencing a lassitude he had never known. After his enforced bed rest he could limit himself to two hours of mild exercise daily, which meant slow walking each morning and after lunch and never permitting himself to break into a sweat, which sanitorium officials believed to be a sign of a relapse and fever.

When, at last, he was allowed to leave his bed he was assigned to the Jacob Schiff cottage, the first one at the entrance to the grounds and, he said with relief, "a three minute slow walk" from Jane's room.

Trudeau's director and Rickey's personal doctor was Dr. Lawrason Brown, who had contracted TB as a third-year medical student at Johns Hopkins University. Brown, described by Elizabeth Mooney, whose mother was a patient at the sanitorium, as the most sensitive and sympathetic of the medical staff, "a gentle and nervous man," founded *The Journal of Outdoor Life* for the patients. Its pages emphasized the sanitorium's central healing principle—ingestion of the clean, crisp air of the mountainous region. Like everyone else, Rickey slept in an unheated room all year round.

He read *How to Get Well,* a booklet written by a patient counseling other patients to eat heartily, fumigate their quarters, scrub down everything they handled with disinfectant, and above all, beware of their more seriously ill fellow patients.

Gradually, he began to feel stronger and soon found work in the sanitorium's picture-framing workshop, for which he received a modest honorarium. Always hovering above him was the fear that the fever could return unexpectedly. His room was filled with the paraphernalia of the very sick—the sputum cups to see if his lungs were free of blood, the stone hot-water bottles which he called "pigs," and the blankets in which he wrapped himself during the frigid nights he slept outdoors.

It was a stroke of fortune that Jane was nearby, for otherwise his confidence would surely have eroded and his hopes been dashed. They dined incognito at the Saranac Inn, where he drank beer on doctor's orders regularly if very reluctantly. He simply had to gain weight, they told him. He and Jane read prodigiously, played bridge, chess, and checkers, rode sleighs in the winter, went bird-watching with the coming of spring, picnicked, walked the lovely trails near Tupper Lake, and spent time with some of the other recovering patients. Jane especially benefited from having Dr. Wynne, in whose home she lived, explain each of the medical stages Branch was passing through. It was their time of troubles and testing. But to Jane the year at Saranac Lake, however threatening, became a time of long and unhurried days together, leisurely wandering over the quiet mountain roads, hiring carts pulled by ponies, exploring the countryside, and observing the changing seasons. "Our love for each other was consuming," she said. "Simple pleasures helped our love of each other and being together meant much to us."

As the summer of 1909 drew to an end his fever abated and the medical staff determined that he could leave, reasonably healthy, but with a warning that he would always have to concern himself with the possibility of a relapse.

# Chapter Four

THEY WENT HOME TO LUCASVILLE in September and took stock of his condition. He was twenty-seven years old, three years married, a recovered consumptive with only $200 savings and no job or career. Nevertheless, they thanked God and believed his recovery was a heartening sign, so much so that Jane and his mother agreed he could enroll at the University of Michigan Law School. In the end, they thought, the practice of law would be a calming, dignified, and stable profession for him.

He moved alone to Ann Arbor, Michigan, while Jane remained with her parents. He had just enough money to eke out a marginal student's existence. Even the $92 required for matriculation, the $42 he spent for textbooks, and the $7 weekly he paid for room and board at 643 South Thayer Street strained his budget. (After Christmas he moved to cheaper lodgings.) He and Jane agreed she would join him early in the second semester, and their surviving correspondence reveals the pain of separation. Meantime, both Jane and his mother repeatedly cautioned him about overtaxing himself and taking on too much too early. Yet in spite of being apart from his wife, he wrote that while the first weeks in Ann Arbor were in sharp contrast to their closeness at Saranac, he still thought school was invigorating and a welcome change from the deliberate pace he had been forced to follow at Trudeau.

"I am taking pretty heavy work and I expect to *do* the work I'm taking, too," he wrote his parents early in September. "I believe my health will continue to improve this year. I feel first rate and I think the work will not hurt me in any way."

Part of this was sheer bravado and a way of reassuring his anxious family, for he well knew how delicate his condition was and the shattering effect a recurrence would bring.

"A relapse would end it all," he wrote Jane in a fit of depression. He had just come from a Case-Michigan football game and was feeling poorly. "From my standpoint, the game was disastrous. I'm not used to excitement and it nearly laid me out, gave me a high pulse and a fever, and I've been uneasy all evening. I shall not go to all the games, I've decided."

He continued consuming large and high-caloried meals but gave up drinking beer. He tried to avoid dwelling on the Trudeau experience but found it difficult to erase from his memory. What, he thought moodily, would have been the fate of his parents had he died? Taking pen in hand, he wrote a lengthy and rambling letter to his father, whose business acumen Rickey doubted.

"Deal straight with a good tenant," he advised his father in a letter that must have astonished the elder Rickey, "and get every cent that's due you. A landlord makes more enemies by loose, easy dealing with his tenants than he does friends." Writing regularly to his parents, he continually offered them gratuitous, and often sophomoric, advice on how to manage their lives. "Your work is to develop the farm, get more property, get out of debt, make a nice home and a living income for future days. Your work is now to shape up the property you have, and make it no burden to you when the declining years do begin to come. God doesn't mean for us to worry. He wants us to remove the cause. And I've given you the recipe: keep Mother quiet and get interested in your work. The more money you make the more you can give to charity and to the church. The more peaceful, hopeful and cheerful the life, the more joy and help and comfort you will be able to spread about you and the more you will render unto Him that which is His due. Power to make others happy is the greatest asset in the world, I think. We must believe in the doctrine of 'Loving God and one's brothers.' Jesus Christ made people happy just by loving them—He loved God and his brothers. But he had substance too. Didn't he heal the blind and the sick? And didn't he supply food and drink? Don't you see? You are to make as much as you can."

In this period he discovered that the law was easy to master and his first-semester grades were outstanding. At the start of his second semester he received permission to take an advanced placement test for Elementary Law—based upon the course he had taught for Professor Grove at OWU—and for Criminal Law and Personal Property, which he had studied on his own while at Allegheny College. Once he passed all three exams, he registered for twenty credits, an unheard-of academic load, hoping to complete the three-year course in two. To a friend he boasted, "I know how to study."

At the close of his second year he learned that Lew McAllister, a crusty, tobacco-chewing, acerbic former minor league catcher, had quit his post as coach of the Michigan baseball team. McAllister's style was well-known at Ann Arbor. Once, Rickey told Arthur Mann, he called for a pinch hitter and to the nervous youngster's question "What'll I do, Coach?" answered, "Strike out, you sonofabitch, you never done anything else."

Phil Bartelme, Michigan's athletic director, was happy with McAllister's departure and began to hunt for a more sensitive replacement. He had almost decided on another ex-ballplayer when he received a call from Keene Fitzpatrick, the school's track coach and director of physical education. Did Bartelme know that a former major leaguer and college coach was a student in the law school?

Rickey, meanwhile, sat down and planned a systematic campaign to get the job. Writing to all the OWU, Ohio State, and Michigan alumni he had ever met, he asked them to write Bartelme on his behalf.

"Day after day those letters came in," complained Bartelme, until at last he surrendered, calling in Rickey and telling him he would hire him if only to "put a stop to those damn letters that come in every day." And provided, too, he added, that Rickey could persuade the dean of the Law School that he could study and coach baseball at the same time.

The dean objected to the idea and told Bartelme "it was absolutely impossible for Rickey to successfully coach the team and maintain passing averages especially in view of the fact that Rickey was carrying more than the average number of hours required by an outstanding law school." Rickey responded that he had done very well thus far and would continue to do so, and quite easily, if only given the chance. Following a two-hour meeting between the three men, the dean reluctantly ruled Rickey could coach if he was called on every day in every class to test his ability to maintain the academic pace.

Once installed as coach, Rickey acted much as he had in Delaware, driving about Ann Arbor and its environs in a newly bought Chalmers touring car, his players piled one on the other in the front and rear seats and standing on the running board, listening as he delivered nonstop comments on life, baseball, and academia. After weekend games he invited them to his apartment, where Jane prepared mugs of hot soup and coffee.

His players considered him "patient and tolerant," so unlike "the roughhouse manners of McAllister." "He treated me more as a son than as a player," said another of his players. Rickey was twenty-nine years old, and his solicitude for his players was already widely recognized on campus.

"If I had a sore arm, he would personally rub it in the evening, or just before a game," one player recalled. When Michigan's team toured the South playing Kentucky, Georgia, Vanderbilt, and other universities during the spring vacation in 1912, he spent an afternoon with a sick player, "watching over me like a patient."

From all accounts, his players adored him, especially when he talked continuously on any and all subjects "from astronomy to Sanskrit," dispensed advice on personal and public matters, and shouted "Balzac" and "Judas Priest" when incensed or disappointed. Clearly his marriage, his recovery from tuberculosis and his success in college and law school had made him more relaxed, more content and willing to give vent to his sense of humor.

It was during that southern trek that he watched a University of Georgia baserunner try to score from second base on a single to center when a strong throw home seemed to beat the runner. When the umpire yelled "safe," Michigan catcher Goodloe Rogers spun about and hit the umpire while players swarmed onto the field.

"Rogers was always getting into fights," said Rickey later, in barely concealed glee. "I never could find out whether or not he started them, but he was always involved. We were playing down at Georgia. I was on crutches as a result of a broken leg [a batted ball in practice had fractured a small bone in his foot]. Well, as usual, a fight started around home plate, and I hobbled off the bench and must have prodded several players with my crutches."

Rogers, the team's colorful, zany, and angry man—the sort of personality Rickey always loved to have on his ball clubs—watched his coach in action.

"When the brawl was over, there lay B.R. flat on his back near home plate, his leg in a cast sticking straight up in the air. One of his crutches was found in the Georgia dugout. The other was up in the stands."

When the rhubarb was over, the teams returned to their benches where Rickey told his players to be good sports. "Even if we don't win this game, let's let this crowd know that we are good enough sports to take a break against us." The game was resumed and Rickey, who had inadvertently rushed to the plate without his crutches, decided they were unnecessary and never used them again.

The dean's misgivings about Rickey's schedule were unjustified. As he had promised and planned, Rickey completed three years of law school in two, graduating in 1911 as a member of the prestigious law school *Review* with an A average and receiving his Doctor of Jurisprudence.

Armed with his degree, he and two fraternity brothers from OWU, Frank B. Ebbert, an ardent dry, and Howard "Jim" Crow, decided to form a law firm. They elected to settle in Boise, Idaho, because Rickey's still delicate health required he live in a mountainous and dry climate. Boise seemed eminently suitable to the three young men; they thought it on the verge of an economic boom since a major railroad line was rumored to be building a spur through the town. Then, too, Idaho's most famous personality of the day, the politician and lawyer Senator William E. Borah, was so preoccupied with Washington political life that they hoped to pick up some of the business he hadn't the time for.

Visiting Boise, Branch and Jane bought "a little place upon a mountainside and I slept practically outdoors trying to get well." During the summer he passed his Idaho bar exam, and the firm leased office space in the town's most prestigious building, hung out its shingles, and waited for clients.

Unfortunately the railroad never came through Boise, Borah's superfluous clients failed to materialize, and Rickey's only case was a minor civil dispute. It was apparent that their fortunes were at a dead end. Rickey, the poorest of the trio, felt the absence of income most severely, and he and Jane soon returned to Ann Arbor, where he took up coaching again. He told his partners that if things improved he would be back the following June.

Subtly, baseball began to supplant the law in his mind. He was developing a certain stature as a college coach and becoming known in midwestern and southern college circles. Aside from his constant need of money, the job—and especially the teaching associated with it—fascinated him, and he began experimenting with a variety of techniques and tactics.

He taught catchers how to run down men caught between bases; he never hit balls straight at the outfielder but usually placed them at such long range that the fielders could catch the balls only after a long run—his method of learning which outfielder could judge and catch fly balls and how much ground they covered in doing so. Players assiduously practiced their bunting and fall-away sliding. He showed his Michigan players how to take one-way leads from first base. He taught them that the runner was always balanced to return to first base and had a longer lead than he could otherwise employ; when the pitcher tired of throwing to first base unsuccessfully, the runner could reduce his lead but be positioned to break for second base the moment the pitcher ignored him, as was so often the case. He encouraged catchers to call for pitchouts. If the tactic failed, he would shrug his shoulders and rationalize the play as daring and therefore excusable.

# Branch Rickey

One of his pet devices for correcting batting flaws was to rig a rope and pulley to the batter's leg so that a batter with a tendency to "put his foot in the bucket" could not step back from the plate as the ball approached him. If he did, he found himself flat on his back.

"He's a dynamo," said one of his players, "a perfectionist." Said another: "Rick drilled us for hours on cutoff plays, the squeeze—we beat Notre Dame in eighteen innings on a squeeze play."

His players had to have "one foot on the bag when catching the ball," and use two hands when possible. They had to practice bunting, he said, for a sacrifice missed was an opportunity lost. He spent three weeks that spring teaching a diminutive former high school mascot to bat left-handed, to bunt, to wait out pitchers. He timed the boy as he raced down the path to first base. And when the season was over the tiny onetime mascot had hit over .300, broken the school's records for walks and bunt singles, "fielded splendidly," said his proud coach, "and become a first-class third baseman whom I turned loose to hit whenever the pitcher wearied of pitching to him too carefully."

Above all, Rickey demanded of his college players a sense of—and it became one of his pet bromides—"adventure," of derring-do on the bases, of constantly attacking their opponents' weaknesses. Playing against Cornell in Ithaca that spring, he signaled his slow-footed catcher Russ Baer to steal second simply to underscore his point. "Branch gave me the signal to steal," said Baer, "and thereupon all the players on our bench arose in unison and cheered me on my lumbering way to second base, where I was tagged out by ten feet." When he picked himself up and dusted off the dirt, Baer returned to the Wolverine bench, his teammates still applauding and his coach sporting a huge grin. "Adventure, Russell, adventure," he shouted.

This engrossment in the game's minutiae began transforming him into a keen judge of athletic ability. Among the Michigan players he nurtured into the major leagues were Clarence Lehr, Johnny "Doc" Lavan, Goodloe Rogers, Jack Enzenroth, and a painfully shy adolescent from Nimisila, Ohio, George Sisler.

If coaching brought him emotional satisfaction, he nevertheless thought of quitting it for a better paying position as a lawyer. Yet the news from Boise was not good. The small law firm was failing rapidly. More and more he began to see his future life on a college campus as a coach and ultimately as a director of athletics. Until, that is, Hobert Lee Hedges, the owner and president of the St. Louis Browns, unexpectedly reappeared in his life. In April 1912, Hedges visited him in Ann Arbor.

When Rickey first met him in 1905—the season he appeared in

one game before returning home to attend to his ailing mother—he impressed the Browns owner less with his ballplaying talent than with his refusal to play on Sundays, which Hedges took for a principled act. When Rickey returned to the club the following year as his first-string catcher, Hedges observed him closely, attracted by his performance, of course, but probably more so by his abstinence from liquor (Hedges, too, was a teetotaler), his youthful poverty (Hedges' father had died early and penniless), his rural roots (Hedges grew up in Hickman Mills in Missouri), and his generally courtly and erudite manner, so unlike the coarseness and ignorance of so many of his players. Early on, Hedges confided to an assistant in the front office that the college boy from Ohio bore watching. A few years later Hedges wrote Rickey, then in law school, and asked him to scout a few players in the Central League.

Hedges was a self-made Horatio Alger character and bold entrepreneur who had made his millions as a carriage manufacturer. He had been persuaded by Byron Bancroft "Ban" Johnson, with his vision of establishing a rival league to the Nationals, to enter baseball by buying the bankrupt Milwaukee Brewers. So it was that in 1901, for the sum of $35,000, Hedges became an owner and immediately transferred the Brewers to St. Louis—in part because the German workingmen there wanted Sunday ball and in part, as he boasted, because it was "the city that's just a little better than any city on earth."

Before long, Hedges had revolutionized St. Louis baseball, "stealing" the Cardinals' Jesse Burkett, their leading slugger, by offering him more money, and signing their brilliant shortstop Bobby Wallace and veteran catcher Joe Sugden, who had befriended Rickey in 1905. He built the first concrete and double-decked stands in either league, renamed the Browns' ramshackle ball park Sportsman's Park, planted grass in its outfield, hired burly security guards to police the stands and eject the bums and layabouts, and founded Ladies' Day. Each Wednesday that the team was home he stood at the entryway behind home plate, distributing a fistful of free tickets to any woman accompanied by a male. By 1908, he had earned a net profit of $168,000 on his invested capital of $80,000 as the Browns drew a spectacular 618,947 customers.

One goal eluded Hedges: He wanted nothing more than to win a pennant. Yet in 1908, their finest season financially and otherwise, the club had only reached fourth place and thereafter in a series of terribly disappointing seasons fallen to seventh and last place finishes. In the two years before his sudden arrival at the Rickey apartment, the Browns had been hopelessly last.

"I went into baseball purely as a matter of business," Hedges told a reporter a few months earlier. "Before I began to organize the St. Louis team in 1901, I had not seen a dozen games of professional baseball in my life. But although I went into the thing for the purpose of making money, I have an entirely different feeling today. I am full of the spirit of baseball. Let me have a winning team four or five years and I'll be satisfied, regardless of the money earned."

Hedges finally came to the point of his visit: He was thinking of buying Kansas City, a minor league club. Would Rickey agree to run it for him? Both Branch and Jane were staggered by the offer and its potential impact on their lives. Still, his response was a quick "no" since he had a moral obligation to return to Boise at the close of the summer.

"Tell you what, then," said Hedges, reluctant to return to St. Louis without an understanding with the younger man. "You take the summer off with your wife, do some scouting for me in the Pacific Coast League, then return to Boise. You can even continue coaching Michigan next spring. I'll pay for the West Coast and the trip to Boise. All I want in return are scouting reports."

In August, as they were readying for a return from the coast, Hedges called from Salt Lake City and asked them to meet him there. It was important, he said, and worth delaying the trip north to Boise. When they arrived, Hedges announced that he wanted him now, and for the Browns, not Kansas City. He wanted a number-two man to administer his policies, select and trade players, choose prospects in the forthcoming draft, negotiate contracts, develop a winning team, all the details Hedges despised. For this he offered Rickey $7,500, plus one more year of coaching at Michigan, where he was receiving $1,500.

Above all, Hedges wanted a brainy man who might implement an idea he had been tinkering with for years—what he called "multiple ownership" and others referred to as syndicate baseball. Most likely the idea had originated with the Cincinnati Red Stockings in 1895, when their owner John T. Brush (who also owned the Indianapolis Hoosiers of the Western League) initiated the technique of "loaning" a sufficient number of ballplayers to the Hoosiers to insure successful Western League seasons. The *Sporting News,* in late 1895, described the practice as "farming out"; by the end of the century, many other ball clubs were emulating Bush. "The advantage of this system is that whenever a player develops," continued the *Sporting News,* "or whenever he is needed, whether it be in mid-season, he can be called in." By 1910, such clubs as Brooklyn in the National League and Cleveland in the American League, for example, controlled sixty players each.

When Hedges took up the idea, he emphasized "gentlemen's agreements." By this he meant that his Browns could help fill a minor league team's roster, with the oral understanding that at some future time they would have first choice of that team's players.

Rickey was eager to accept his offer and therefore, upon reaching Boise, was rather pleased to learn that the firm was still without clients and ready to disintegrate. They also were split over the 1912 presidential election, one partner favoring Woodrow Wilson's candidacy while Rickey and the other backed Theodore Roosevelt's Bull Moose Party.

The firm was dissolved and Rickey wired his acceptance to Hedges, then threw himself on the bed, laughing. "Jane, $9,000—it's more than we ever dreamed."

For the next several months he traveled extensively for his new employer, attending baseball's draft meeting in Cincinnati, claiming thirty players (ten of whom eventually played in the majors), discovered Jane was pregnant again, appeared briefly in St. Louis in January for preliminary meetings, returned to Lucasville for the birth of their daughter Mary, moved Jane and the child back to Ann Arbor, and at last, in June 1913, walked into the Browns' offices at Sportsman's Park and sat down at a chipped and worn desk across the room from part-time scout Charlie Barrett and a fifteen-year-old office boy named Roscoe Hillenkoetter.

# Chapter Five

Sᴛ. Lᴏᴜɪs was the country's fourth largest city and a local booster's pamphlet described it as "a large, Progressive, Busy City, entirely Surrounded by the U.S." A cosmopolitan city of 750,000 swelled by 300,000 more in neighboring areas, St. Louis was also racist and segregated.

In 1913, the year Rickey arrived, baseball seemed the same as it had been when he'd last played there six years earlier. It was still a rural game, slow-paced and quiet, a sporting event without any serious commercial competitors.

All the same, in spite of its superficial stability, the nation and baseball were changing. By 1913 the rush to industrialize and urbanize had already transformed an insular republic into a world power. The coming of technology, the railroad, the telephone, telegraph, typewriter, camera, and linotype machine revolutionized the game and the way it was reported to the public by a growing number of newsmen. Clearly, baseball's sun had risen; in 1910 and again in 1913, the president of the United States had thrown out the first ball in opening day ceremonies in Washington. Superstars such as Ty Cobb, Honus Wagner, and Christy Mathewson dominated the sport pages. Pitcher Rube Marquard was dubbed "the $11,000 beauty" because of his high wages, and John McGraw was the best-paid manager, with an $18,000 salary. And when Barney Dreyfuss of the Pirates paid an unprecedented $22,000 for the untried pitcher Marty O'Toole, fans and writers were shocked.

Big money was entering the game, and baseball began assuming a new emotional significance—in historian Harold Seymour's keen phrase: "Baseball was a cohesive factor for a diverse, polyglot population.... With the loss of the traditional ties known in a rural society, baseball gave to many the feeling of belonging."

"Baseball is still in its infancy," a sportswriter of the day predicted.

"The owners are staking their own cash in monster stadiums of iron and stone, and laying out their business plans to care for profits that must be counted in millions."

As Hedges' protégé, Rickey was at first odd man out in the tiny Brown organization. Some resented him for his college background and others because he seemed too theoretical, despite his major league credentials. And, of course, others were annoyed because he was young and had caught the boss's eye. He tried to shrug off their pique. "I got a salary. That pleased Jane and me. Salaries helped me grow up. They tend to make men of boys."

He had no specific duties other than the owner's wish for him to remove the daily burdens from his shoulders. Yet Hedges regularly bombarded his young assistant with calls, letters, and visits directing him how to act and what to say concerning the most minute details of the operation. Player sales, railroad expenses paid to Brown employees, lineups, no matter was too insignificant for Hedges.

The overriding problem, however, was how the Browns could compete with the wealthier ball clubs for players.

"I was not accustomed to daily defeats," Rickey said after his first weeks as an executive. "Michigan had been a winner. In St. Louis, though, there had been a continuous series of defeats. The Pittsburgh Pirates, the New York Giants, and the Chicago Cubs were one, two, three all the time. What could you do about it? The Browns had no money, no money even for scouts. So through my acquaintance with college coaches plus agreements to put out players for minor league experience (although we couldn't always get those players back) we sought to improve and overtake the rich teams at first."

In Rickey's first month in office Hedges loaned four Montgomery, Alabama, businessmen $12,000 to buy their local baseball club. For the money spent the Browns were to have the right to all Montgomery players at $10,000 each at the close of the season. The agreement collapsed when the local owners fell out among themselves. The next year syndicate baseball was banned by baseball's ruling National Commission. Now all major league clubs were forced to seek alternative sources of players.

To find the right men and build a winning and profitable team Rickey started in the only way he knew—by systematically compiling the names of all the promising college players he had seen or heard about who might be able to make the big leagues. He kept the list in a small notebook he always carried with him, which people quickly dubbed "Rickey's Bible." He also began to correspond with college coaches and athletic directors and, deciding the Browns needed a full-time scout, hired Charlie Barrett whom he had first met in the Texas League.

Roscoe Hillenkoetter, the fifteen-year-old office boy and Hedges' distant cousin, soon developed a bad case of hero worship. Rickey, he said decades later, was different from all the other baseball people he had met, "never rough, never swore, never got mad at you, he was jovial and pleasant. We all adored him." So much so that he confided in another teenage office boy named William De Witt that he was going to decline an appointment to the United States Naval Academy so that he could stay with Rickey and the Browns. Thinking Rickey would be pleased, he confessed his plans but the older man turned beet red at "your incredibly stupid and shortsighted decision." Rickey shook his finger at the boy. "Roscoe, if you don't go, I'll fire you and you'll never get another job." He dealt with De Witt in the same manner, telling the boy he had no future without an education. He could have his job with the Browns only so long as he went on with his schooling. (Hillenkoetter did accept the appointment and eventually became an admiral.)

These personal interludes were overshadowed by daily crises, the most serious of which concerned Brown manager George Stovall. Stovall was a hardworking, fiery-tempered first baseman who had spent a decade with the Indians and the Browns and was called Firebrand by his teammates for good reason.

One steamy afternoon he roared out of the dugout protesting a call by Umpire Charlie Ferguson and was soon ejected from the game. Stovall fumed and raged. Third baseman Jimmy Austin was standing alongside the two men and watched as his manager challenged the umpire by strolling leisurely toward first base to retrieve his glove and then, "maybe even slower" (said Austin), past the livid Ferguson, who told him to move more rapidly. At which point Stovall spun about and spat at him with his forty-cent tobacco plug, getting juice all over Ferguson's white linen jacket and face.

Hedges and Rickey were disgusted with his behavior. Hedges wanted to clean up baseball and improve its rough-house reputation. Rickey echoed his employer's feelings but went beyond him, expressing his view to his small staff that baseball players ought to serve as role models for young boys. When Ban Johnson, the American League president, fined Stovall the Browns refused to appeal. And when Johnson also urged that umpires "be treated with respect," Rickey publicly agreed, telling a reporter that otherwise there would be anarchy on the field.

Then Hedges, too, reached the end of his patience. After seven straight Brown losses under the broiling sun in August, he phoned Austin.

# Chapter Five

"Jim, will you come out to my apartment tonight?" he asked. "Sure," answered Austin, wondering where the owner lived, "but why?"

"I want you to meet Mr. Rickey. Mr. Rickey is going to be the manager next year, but we'd like you to finish out as manager for the rest of the season."

"Pepper" Austin was a Welsh-born infielder two years Rickey's senior. He had been in the majors for five years and his .266 average was the highest in his career. Very reluctantly he agreed to take charge as a bitter and sullen Stovall was kept on as a player and returned to first base. Austin managed for eight games, losing six, until Hedges exploded again. Storming into the Browns' office on a September afternoon, Hedges spied Rickey dictating a memorandum to Roscoe Hillenkoetter. "Branch," he sputtered angrily, "I want you on the damn field this afternoon. I want you running the team."

For Rickey's first spring training he took the ballclub south to Florida, the first club ever to train in St. Petersburg.

"I shall have three batting cages, three handball courts, one sliding pit, and a place for running dashes at the training camp in St. Petersburg, whether anyone approves of it or not. If this is theory, it is blamed good practical theory.

"Hitting alone will not win ball games," he declared. "I want speed on my team and I also want every man on the squad to know how to slide. I intend to have my players taught how to run. Few players know the slightest thing about sprinting. I will teach my players how to make hook slides to both sides. Handball will help get my players in condition, brighten their eyes, and make them alert. I don't say that we will win any pennants—no, far be it from me to mention anything of that kind—but I do think that my systematic training will be laying the foundation of a pennant winner."

In St. Petersburg Rickey threw himself into the role of manager. "He's a bear for work," marveled an astonished reporter. Every morning Rickey walked from his office to the jerry-built ball park put up by a local businessman, Al Lang. To Rickey, St. Petersburg seemed a splendid choice with its white sandy beaches, small-town atmosphere, rainless days, and wondrous sun. The Cubs were across Tampa Bay, and by journeying across the bay in small boats they could play practice games.

Each day began with a lecture. At 9 A.M. he stood alongside a blackboard, the cigar he had taken to smoking locked in one hand and chalk in the other, the white dust already covering his dark outer jacket. No subject was too esoteric or irrelevant and he talked as he had to his college players, covering every aspect of the game, their moral development, their families. Many of the players thought him boring and patronizing and the *Sporting News* early on caught up to his quirkiness:

> Branch Rickey is a funny cuss,
> Though cussin he forbids;
> His rules have started quite a fuss
> Among his Brownie kids.
> When Sunday comes he leaves his team
> Completely in the lurch
> And Jimmy Austin rules supreme
> While Branch hikes off to church.
>
> He's got a time clock on the field;
> Don't let his Brownies smoke
> Those nasty cigarettes, or yield to
> Poker and go "broke,"
> And when he wants to bawl them out
> for some queer bone-head play
> He doesn't stage a swearin' bout
> He does it highbrow way.

He was, he believed, making progress. As always, he was everywhere possible: praising and appraising players, looking for gimmicks to stimulate attendance, trading and dealing constantly with other teams. Even so, peripheral issues tended to dog him, especially his refusal to attend Sunday games. Those who knew of this practice disregarded it, but others, new to the team as players or reporters, continued to accuse him of hypocrisy. "He may not be at the game," went a familiar charge, "but he's always at the cash box on Monday to count the gate receipts."

"Just for the sake of argument," asked a reporter in 1914, "suppose every man on the team would decline to play Sunday baseball. What would be your policy if this was the case?" And for the umpteenth time Rickey answered: "Beyond a doubt both parties would observe their contract."

He also had supporters, and a few of them composed some doggerel and passed it on to him at the start of the season:

> We're for you, Branch Rickey, and that is no joke,
> We like your ideas of the game;
> We'll sit and we'll root while watching your smoke,
> And see the Browns rise up to fame.
> You may be the Moses who'll pilot them out,
> You may be the dark horse, who knows?
> An any rate, Branch, we will boost, never doubt,
> So buckle right to it, friend Mose.

Managing, though, was quite different from administering an organization from an office. It tended to make Rickey tense and anxious. In one exhibition game, he seemed to lose control of himself and the confidence of his team as he used nineteen players—four pitchers, five pinch hitters, two catchers, and a pinch runner. He warmed up pinch hitters in the bullpen with instructions to keep their eyes on balls thrown by bullpen pitchers. Pinch runners were sent to every corner of the field to limber their muscles and legs. Later, during the season, he pinch-hit twice without success. To some, he was, as a writer put it, "almost panicky." Yet the Browns rose three notches to fifth place, the first time they had improved in years.

He was also becoming known in influential circles. The Public Question Club, organized by Wiley Rutledge, dean of the Washington University Law School (and later a justice of the United States Supreme Court), invited him to join and comment on private talks given by powerful people. He also began speaking wherever and whenever he was invited, at Y's, churches, and as an after-dinner speaker. By the end of March 1914 the *Post-Dispatch* estimated he had already spoken on sixteen separate occasions that year.

Ominous events were taking place elsewhere, threatening the idyllic and isolated world of Americans, yet when the European war erupted in August it seemed to him terribly remote. His job, his family, his religious and social activities consumed his attention. But then the assassination of the Austrian archduke and his wife in faraway Sarajevo seemed distant to most Americans, whose real last war had ended in 1865 at Appomattox Court House.

St. Louis's large German population cared, but opposed any American intervention on behalf of the English and French. Rickey was never sympathetic to their pro–German approach, but at least at the beginning of the war his attention remained riveted on baseball.

In 1915, for example, George Sisler reported to the Browns, setting off a harsh and acrimonious legal and personal battle that led eventually to the destruction of the governing three-man National Commission and smoothed the way for a one-man ruling czar.

The facts of the matter were never in dispute, only who had the right to Sisler's services. Since he had once signed a contract with Akron, which was eventually transferred to the Pirates, he was considered Pirate property while he attended college.

By 1915 he was the preeminent college player in the country, and a bevy of scouts trailed after him, hoping Pirate owner Barney Dreyfuss would cede his rights to the young man.

For several years the National Commission wrestled with the thorny Sisler case while the young man played for Rickey at Michigan. Unknown to the commission or to Dreyfuss the Sislers had turned to Rickey for unofficial legal advice. Rickey traveled to Manchester, Ohio, to speak with Sisler's father and make certain the young man had signed the contract without parental approval. Once he was sure of his facts he suggested the elder Sisler inform the commission (and especially Rickey's former Cincinnati boss, Gary Herrmann, a member) and dare them to defy his paternal authority in the courts. Sisler's father did exactly that, adding that in his opinion (probably Rickey's as well) his son ought to be declared a free agent. Rickey also spoke with George B. Cobb, Detroit's mayor, and influential University of Michigan alumni, including a number of eminent Detroit attorneys.

Then he wrote the National Commission on Sisler's behalf, urging them not to enforce "this illegal contract," or else run the future risk of offending families, high schools and colleges when gullible young men signed contracts and then had them withdrawn, as was the case of Sisler.

After several years of delaying tactics, the commission ruled Sisler had the right to sign with whomever he chose. When the decision was handed down, Dreyfuss, wild with indignation, swallowed his pride and offered Sisler $5,200 to play for the Pirates. But in June Sisler telegraphed the Pirate owner: "Have decided to join the St. Louis American League team." The Browns offered him $7,400 with a pledge of regular future raises. Besides, he said, he really wanted to play for Rickey.

That was too much for Dreyfuss, a driving and nervous man, and he exploded at Rickey. The Pirate owner accused him of tampering with another club's property, of a serious breach of ethics, of an unparalleled conflict of interest, and of a series of acts detrimental to baseball and simple justice. Dreyfuss, who loved to be called the "Little Gentleman" because of his diminutive size, was widely respected in the game as a penniless immigrant boy from Germany who had arrived in the United States in 1881 and made a fortune in whiskey and baseball. Dreyfuss told Rickey he would never deal with him again, the breach made deeper each passing year by Sisler's spectacular success on the field.

But Sisler was now a Brown. From the very day he set eyes on him at Ann Arbor, Rickey knew he had a talent beyond the reach of most athletes. When the gentle, almost agonizingly shy young man joined his team at Comiskey Park in August, he was greeted by Rickey: "Be aggressive, George. I want you to be nervy on the baselines. It doesn't make much difference whether you are successful in your attempts this year.

Rickey with two of baseball's greatest hitters, George Sisler (left) and Rogers Hornsby (right) before a game between the Pittsburgh Pirates and Hornsby's St. Louis Browns. (*Pittsburgh Post-Gazette*)

It will be good training for you, and give you an idea as to just how much liberty you can take with the different pitchers and different teams."

Sisler nodded, in awe of his tutor, reverent and respectful of him all their adult lives, calling him "Mr. Rickey" when others were present even after a friendship of half a century. Rickey, in turn, idolized Sisler—his manner, his family life—and he often cited him as a model to other athletes.

By the end of the season Rickey stated unequivocally to the press that Sisler would soon be the equal of Ty Cobb as a hitter and fielder. Skeptics smiled. The brash young Brownie skipper with the large vocabulary and never-stop method of talking was at it again, said a writer. "Judas Priest," exploded Rickey to a young minor league executive, Warren Giles, a few years later, "when I read that nonsense I knew even more that my prognosis was correct and my faith in George's abilities would prove valid." Giles remembered smiling at hearing Rickey's words, sure even then he could bet on Rickey's judgment.

In 1915 the team sagged and finished in sixth place. Rickey continued to express confidence in their future, but Hedges was getting tired of his unrequited love affair with the Browns. He decided to sell the team.

Rickey was upset when he heard the news. He genuinely liked Hedges but thought he had panicked in the face of uncertainty. But Hedges argued that war created instability and he didn't intend to lose one cent more on his investment. More than anything else he was afraid of the Federal League's antimonopoly suit against the American and National leagues then being heard in Chicago before federal judge Kenesaw Mountain Landis. For two seasons, 1914 and 1915, eight teams from Brooklyn and Baltimore to Chicago and Indianapolis had competed in a third league aimed at breaking the iron grip baseball owners held on the players. Hedges was worried by the suit because, he told Rickey, Landis was the judge who had fined John D. Rockefeller's Standard Oil Company $29,240,000 in an antitrust case a few years before. "But Landis was overruled by an appellate court," Rickey broke in. "Never mind," added Hedges, "he could rule against baseball. And then where would I be?"

He sold the Browns to Philip DeCatesby Ball, who had made his fortune from ice machines sold to Armour and Swift meat-packing plants and major beer breweries and now owned the Federal League's St. Louis Slufeds. Ball was a screamer, yet another poor-boy-to-millionaire who always had to have his way. People who knew Ball had heard of his experiences as cowboy, railroad laborer, Texas buffalo hunter, and especially as a Shreveport, Louisiana, minor leaguer whose career—or so he always told listeners—was cut short in a savage barroom fight that left his left hand partially paralyzed.

But how he loved baseball!

"How much did that Brown club cost you," the fifty-six-year-old Ball was asked in 1915 by Harry Sinclair, the oil baron, wheeler-dealer, and fellow Federal League owner. "Oh," answered Ball, "fifty thousand a year, maybe a hundred thousand."

"You're out of your mind," Sinclair shot back. "Not for a baseball team, I'm not," replied Ball.

Immediately following the sale, Ball appeared in the Browns' office and asked Roscoe Hillenkoetter for Branch Rickey. "I am Mr. Rickey, sir. Branch Rickey, field manager and general manager of the Browns. And you, sir, who are you?"

Chapter Five

Ball nodded, his lips puckered. "So you're the goddamned prohibitionist," he blurted. "I'm Ball."

If Ball had had his way Rickey would have been dismissed.

But Hedges cared enough for his erstwhile protégé to see to it that he had a contract for the 1916 season which Ball was bound to respect. Ball did not like the idea of keeping him on, and he particularly resented his hawkish challenges to the Slufeds and the Federal League. Moreover Ball liked and admired his Slufed manager, Fielder Jones (whose name really was Fielder Allison Jones, a fifteen-year major leaguer who started with the Dodgers in 1896).

Ball took a chair, sat down, and looked about the shabby quarters. "Rickey," he said abruptly, "you're out as manager and Jones is in. You'll be my business manager."

The office boy sat gaping at the new boss as he went on pumping Rickey for information.

"Now that you're running the club's business, what'll you do with the club, Rickey? *What are your plans?*"

Rickey found himself stuttering (which Hillenkoetter had never before heard him do). "Mr. Ball, we-we-we're going to ..."

Rickey started to sweat and Roscoe Hillenkoetter, seated mutely on the other side of the room, watched as Ball coolly crossed his legs and then shouted: "Well, goddamnit, do it. You're the boss." He then rose, grabbed his hat and coat, and strode out the door, leaving Rickey speechless.

It was an inauspicious introduction for both men, and they took an instant dislike to one another. Ball thought Rickey's ideas too radical and Rickey's endless talk and large vocabulary made him uncomfortable. Rickey was, in turn, uncomfortable with Ball's crudeness; he considered Ball uncouth and, in matters of baseball, virtually illiterate. Approaching Ball not long after their first meeting, he asked him to release him from his contract if something better came along. Ball—Rickey asserted for years afterward—agreed and told him he would never stand in the way of an ambitious man eager for advancement.

Until then, however, they had to work together and submerge their differences. Ball loved his new role but his temper and undiplomatic manner led him into a constant series of public battles, the first of which occurred when the Cardinals finished last in 1916 and declared themselves bankrupt. The team then announced a public sale of stock to raise cash and pay existing expenses. Ball rejoiced publicly at their plight and boasted it could never happen to the Browns.

But insofar as he was concerned, what happened was far worse. The

Cardinals' investors had approached seven local sportswriters and editors for their advice: whom should they hire to run the club? It was a secret vote and Rickey was their unanimous choice. He was offered the club's presidency. He was overjoyed, for it was the opening he had been waiting for.

"I went to Mr. Ball and talked to him about it and he felt it was a great opportunity for me and didn't want to stand in my way and again he orally agreed to have me go on with the Cardinals under these arrangements. But Mr. Ban Johnson, who had become, a sort of, I would say, good friend of mine and a benefactor and much interested in me, protested very vigorously, later, to Mr. Ball about my leaving the American League and there wasn't anything in writing at all about it and Mr. Ball frankly changed his mind and said he had decided that he would not let me go to the Cardinals. Well, that brought up quite a dispute, and even got into the courts. It was a very sad experience for me."

They sued one another and Rickey suffered from a stream of invectives by Ball, the kindest including "contract buster" and "traitor." The suits were eventually dropped in court, but it bothered Rickey for years to come.

Now with the Cardinals, Rickey took stock of his assets. Miller Huggins, a graduate of the University of Cincinnati Law School, was the manager. Huggins, though, had a grievance against the Cardinal owners, who, he claimed, had promised him the chance to buy the team. With the millionaire yeast king, Julius Fleischmann of Cincinnati, they had been negotiating the sale when they learned the owners had sold out to a local syndicate for $375,000, throwing in ramshackle Robison Field as well. Huggins stayed one year and led the Cardinals to third place and then departed to manage the Yankees. In 1918, Rickey hired Jack Hendricks, a successful minor league manager, who promptly led the team back into the cellar.

Looking ahead, however, Rickey issued a glowing report to his board of directors, noting that better days lay ahead. He had on his roster, he reported, a young hitter named Rogers Hornsby, "an exemplary hitter, a remarkable batter, indeed." He traded for his old favorite, Brownie shortstop Bobby Wallace, bought Willie Sherdel from Milwaukee, the strong-hitting Austin McHenry from the Reds, and following a tip from a former colleague in the college coaching ranks, purchased Penn State outfielder Cliff Heathcote.

In June the War Department issued a "work or fight" order to baseball players. Despite baseball's efforts to identify as closely as possible with American patriotism—flags hung from ball park flagpoles and the national anthem was played in a growing number of stadiums—players (unlike actors, opera singers, and other entertainers, who remained exempt) had to choose between essential civilian jobs and joining the military. Confronted by the end of baseball, Rickey found it hard to keep the war at arm's length. Still, when he was approached by the YMCA and asked to organize a committee to help off-duty servicemen religiously and socially, he was uninterested. He believed he could do more for his country.

One morning—he told Arthur Mann—he was standing on a corner of downtown St. Louis, staring at a shop window, and noticed a hand-drawn sign: "Closing up after six months in business. I am going to war." It was as if he had received a sign. Nothing, he said, had so great an effect on him. "Perhaps it was foolish but I developed a deep desire to fight, in combat if possible. I imagine many men of my age plagued themselves the same way. If so, we were all frustrated by a growing sense of useless-ness. We kept telling ourselves we are not too old to die."

He was almost thirty-seven years old, the father of four children (Mary was born in 1913, Branch in 1914, Jane in 1916, and Mabel Alice in 1918), and part of an era of uncomplicated appeals to patriotism, obe-dience to authority, and easy acceptance of such emotionally charged news as alleged German atrocities and the sinking of the *Lusitania*.

On a trip to New York City he spoke with Boston Braves president Percy D. Haughton, once Harvard's football coach, who knew many bright and influential young men who had gone to Washington for the duration. If Rickey wanted to go to war Haughton said he had a mar-velous idea. The army was forming a gas warfare branch. Would Rickey care to enlist? His friends in Washington could see to all the arrange-ments.

He was commissioned a major. But how to break the news to Jane? He was an over-age Cardinals president in no danger of being con-scripted; his family life was, as he wrote, "orderly and organized." Why then risk it all, he must have asked himself on the long train ride to the Midwest. Certainly he was no man of violence. Nor had he ever exulted in displays of cruelty. Yet like so many of his countrymen, war was an abstraction and "making the world safe for democracy" a shibboleth in which he firmly believed.

Jane was both hurt and furious when she learned of his decision. "I thought about leaving him," she confessed years after to her granddaugh-ter. She and the children were sent back to Lucasville while he boarded a troopship, developed flu on board (and did not tell her until many years later), and had to be carried onto French territory by stretcher.

In France, Major Rickey, accompanied by captains Ty Cobb and Christy Mathewson and Lieutenant George Sisler, drilled the troops in air-tight chambers on the dangers of mustard gas. A few cryptic notes among Rickey's papers reveal his horror at his first glimpse of war, including the dead and maimed that passed regularly through his sector. "Discolored skin" "shock" were notes found on bits of scrap paper, undated, but clearly a reference to what he had seen.

Surrounded by the screams of suffering young men, eager to return home as the war drew to an end, he was no doubt pleased to receive a letter from the sports editor of the St. Louis *Star* soon after the armistice. Talking baseball instead of war, Clarence Long wrote, "We still insist on you being elected to the position of president of the National League. I picked you for that job many months ago, if you remember, and I'm still plugging away for you."

The war ended in November and five weeks later Rickey disembarked in Manhattan. He had served four months and sixteen days in the 1st Gas Regiment of the Chemical Warfare Service.

He returned to baseball in 1919, on the eve of what historians often describe as the "Golden Age of Sports"—an allegedly euphoric ten years sparked by higher real income and reduced working hours. Together with the development of radio and the mushrooming of automobiles, they spelled prosperity for baseball.

Following a meeting in early January with the Cardinal board Rickey was left with the unsurprising suggestion he control spending carefully but at the same time try to shape a winning and profitable club. So poor were the Cardinals that spring that training was held at local Washington University rather than in Florida. Rickey had the better uniforms stored away while players wore—in his words—"shoddy suits, dry cleaned and mended." His office was downtown in the Railway Exchange Building to save money on rent. He encouraged his parents to mortgage their farm for $5,000 and invest in the club. His only assistant was stenographer Bill DeWitt, his onetime Browns summer employee. And when a potential investor scheduled a meeting with him he borrowed Jane's Oriental rug to impress the man.

The team's reserve list numbered twenty-three players and all but three were quickly released because of the team's financial plight. Recalling those days, he said, "I went without salary to help meet the payroll, as long as I could still meet my personal expenses." He owned two hundred shares, for which he had paid $200, a mere pittance. Yet the Cardinals were so desperate for any additional funds that he laughed delightedly when told that Sam Breadon, a young automobile dealer in St. Louis, had been persuaded to buy a similar number of shares.

To save an additional $10,000 Rickey doubled as field manager, a job he both liked and disliked, depending on the extent of his success. Yet in spite of all their efforts at paring down the expense budget, he told DeWitt the payroll was growing; in 1917, for example, his best players had been earning $7,500, a considerable sum at the time. Now they were up by $1,000. The club paid for expenses away from home, medical care, fines imposed by the league, the laundering and repair of uniforms. In the event of illness or injury, salaries were continued. And against these realities, only 173,604 fans paid their way into Sportsman's Park in 1919.

If little could be done to remedy the desperate fiscal situation, he was determined to develop a first-class team. At the winter meetings in New York City he bought Milt Stock, a third baseman, catcher Pickles Dillhoefer, traded for his old Michigan shortstop Johnny "Doc" Lavan, and got Burt Shotton and Jimmy Austin, his erstwhile Browns Sunday managers. He turned regularly to his "Bible" for a steady influx of newcomers. "Judas Priest," began a bemused sportswriter, satirizing Rickey's apocryphal comments while leafing through his detailed notations: "I initially encountered this fine young man when he was three, performing admirably behind the plate for the Duck Run Tigers. I disliked his tendency to throw sidearm and transformed him into a second baseman. After that, at the age of seven..."

But the lack of money presented insurmountable difficulties and members of the board prevailed on Sam Breadon to loan the club $18,000, for which he was granted 72 percent of the stock, the remaining percentage passing to Rickey. Once the deal was done, Breadon emerged from the shadows suddenly and named himself president and demoted Rickey to the vice-presidency, asking him to stay on as manager. The Cardinals had finished seventh that year, and Rickey was crestfallen at what he took to be a slap in the face by Breadon. "I never wanted to manage," he complained to friends, depressed at his loss of status.

For a while he even considered leaving St. Louis. When an American baseball squad toured Japan he asked a Japanese promoter named Ben Shimada to see if Waseda University needed a coach–athletic director. And when his old friend Phil Bartelme quit at Michigan, he was sorely tempted by an offer to replace him. "I dislike the 'give and take' of professional baseball and I dislike some of its associations," he wrote his sponsor. "I love college work as you know...." But he had second thoughts and wrote again, "I regret indeed, that it is impossible to permit you to recommend me to the Board of Regents ... not on account of salary. That has never been the most important part with me in any job that I have ever undertaken. It is a matter of doing the thing you start to do and I must make a great ball club successful artistically and financially in a town where there is every handicap under the sun.... Until that time, I shall not leave my present work."

He now had to learn to live with Breadon, who was quite different from himself. Breadon had grown up in Manhattan's ninth ward and never completed grade school. Born five and one-half years before Rickey to Scotch-Irish parents, he moved to St. Louis in 1900 because "there seemed more opportunity in the West." Like Ball and Hedges before him, Breadon was the sort of figure Rickey generally tended to find attractive: a rags-to-riches man who had married ingenuity and verve with new marketing techniques and thereby earned a good deal of money. Breadon sold White Steamers automobiles with Marion Lambert of the pharmaceutical family and then bought a Ford agency on the eve of the auto boom in the 1920s. When he and Rickey met for the first time, he was a millionaire several times over.

J. Roy Stockton, a close observer of both men for many years, thought their relationship "always a strange one." Certainly they were temperamentally opposites. "Singing Sam," as he was called in the easy jargon of the sports pages, loved to drink, socialize, and sing at the top of his lungs. Like many self-made men, he distrusted Rickey's extensive formal education and possibly even resented it too. They rarely spent time with one another outside of the office and even more infrequently talked about anything but baseball. Breadon, however, was in awe of Rickey's knowledge of the game, precisely the attribute he so sorely lacked.

At first Rickey objected to Breadon's miserly approach to salaries for players and in fact "frowned on Sam's watchdog scrutiny of the books," but there was little he could do. He also quickly learned that despite his penurious attitude toward athletes, Breadon could be extremely generous: from 1918 until 1922, Rickey received $10,000 a year; for the following five years, he was paid $15,000 annually.

"Rickey was the dreamer, Breadon the hard, sound businessman," wrote Robert L. Burnes of the *Globe-Democrat*. Rickey oversaw everything but the hiring and firing of managers; this Breadon reserved for himself since it gave him the ultimate source of power.

Otherwise, a remarkable relationship developed between the two. Breadon permitted Rickey to flourish as a baseball man. He gave him the freedom to speak his mind in public. More than ever now, Rickey wanted to speak out on public, even non-baseball issues.

"Virtue, fortitude, self-respect, unselfishness, consciousness of right and wrong," he scribbled on a piece of paper before a talk at the YMCA. These were the themes he stressed.

But he was really stressing unquestioning faith, bucolic values, passionate Methodism. His competitive juices were stirred when a promoter asked him to debate the famous agnostic, antiprohibition lawyer Clarence Darrow following Darrow's decimation of William Jennings Bryan in the Scopes "monkey trial." He was offered $7,000, but Jane was strongly opposed. More than anyone, she knew his weaknesses as well as his strengths. The intensely opinionated Darrow—whom they knew personally and whose company they enjoyed—was unlike anyone he had ever confronted, a brilliant opponent who might easily overcome him. Even so, Rickey couldn't resist a joke and proposed playfully to Jane his plan to conquer Darrow. "I would beat him at his own game. I would take that $7,000 and pass out two thousand tickets to the event to two thousand friends with instructions on what to do. Every time I would deal a telling blow I would wave my hands with thumb extended, whereupon all two thousand of my guests would stand up and shout approval. I would win the debate hands down and brother Darrow would be put in his place."

Jane laughed but nevertheless insisted he decline the offer. He did, but then invited Darrow to their home, for a friendly if unobserved argument.

"Talk at the Rickeys' was always brisk and stimulating," recalled a former neighbor who knew them well. "My young boys sensed that. One day my five-year-old son, Jack, wandered over alone to the Rickey house. Mrs. Rickey's sister asked him to do some small errand, but the boy wasn't interested. 'Auntie, I didn't come over here to work—I came to talk.'"

Rickey adored the limelight and the attention accorded him by the press and his peers. He seriously believed that what he said publicly mattered. He wrote his own speeches, drafting and redrafting them on large foolscap paper, hotel or team envelopes, sales receipts, on any scraps of paper. He was the intellectual in an anti-intellectual profession, a reader among men for whom books were suspect, an anomaly in a sport where simply the wearing of glasses earned players the sobriquet of Professor or Specs.

Breadon paid him to administer but also to manage. His clubs were mediocre at best. It was as an executive that he blossomed; his imagination stirred and his dreams proved fruitful. In the early 1920s he adopted the red bird as team symbol after he had seen red cardboard cardinals propped up on white tablecloths in a Presbyterian church in Ferguson,

Missouri. Within days, he asked Edward H. Schmidt, a commercial artist, to design a team logo—a red bird perched on a bat in front of a large ball. On another occasion he aped earlier efforts by the Dodgers and Giants in allowing schoolboys to enter the park free if accompanied by adults. It was also in the early 1920s that he remembered that Cleveland had in 1916 pinned numbers onto the backs of uniforms for home games. He had it done for the Cardinals too, but abandoned the practice after the season.

One of his first significant player moves was to plead with Breadon to buy an untried minor league knuckleball pitcher for $10,000. Breadon was skeptical but, like Hedges and Ball, respected Rickey's intuitive taste and feel for playing talent, and he borrowed the money from a local bank to pay for Jesse Haines's contract. The next year, rookie Haines led the league with 47 appearances and posted a 2.99 ERA, with a 13–20 record for a sixth-place club. Haines was the last nonfarm player the Cardinals bought until the mid–1940s.

Rickey drew a different lesson from the Haines deal, recognizing Breadon's disinclination to lay out too much cash for ballplayers. With this in mind he set out exploring alternative sources of financing. Breadon clearly outfoxed Ball by getting the Browns' owner to allow the Cardinals to rent Sportsman's Park for only $20,000 annually. Then, as a result, he sold obsolete Federal Park to the city for $200,000 and a quarter of the plot on which the field stood to a streetcar company for $75,000. At last Rickey had ample funds for player development.

But how to proceed? He returned to Hedges' old scheme of multiple ownership.

What Rickey was about to propose was revolutionary. He was going to build a network of affiliated minor league teams, a development with such far-reaching implications that it ultimately and dramatically changed St. Louis and, later, all of baseball.

He had been mulling over this strategy since returning from France, but without the wherewithal it had been an academic exercise. Occasionally he dabbled, buying several shares in the Texas League Houston Buffs (and seeing to it that old friend Al Bridewell of the Portsmouth Navvies was installed as manager and Fred Ankenman as business manager; loyalty and close ties were to be the glue that would keep the system working).

Then he invested in 50 percent of the Fort Smith, Arkansas, club, of the Western League. Breadon's financial instincts sensed a gold mine in the offing, and he handed Rickey $25,000 to do whatever he wished. And taken together with the National Agreement of 1921, which permitted minor league ownership by major league ball clubs, Rickey had all he needed.

As his elaborate design evolved it was first met with derision and scorn, called the "farm system," "chain store baseball," and "Rickey's plantation" (with its connotation that players were slaves). Caricaturists drew sketches of young athletes in striped prison garments fettered with ball and chains.

No matter how he might deny it, Rickey was ultrasensitive to the criticism and deeply resented it. "I was all the time cartooned with chalk on my hands and a blackboard and holding meetings, lecturing," he complained bitterly. Yet measured by the profits it engendered, the triumphs it produced, and how it saved minor league baseball during the depression and war decade and after, with the onslaught of television, the system worked extraordinarily well.

"Starting the Cardinal farm system was no sudden stroke of genius," he explained early in the 1920s. "It was a case of necessity being the mother of invention. We lived a precarious existence. Other clubs would outbid us; they had the money and the superior scouting system. We had to take the leavings, or nothing at all."

In February 1921 the Cardinals bought 50 percent of the Syracuse club of the International League from E.C. Landgraf for $20,000. Still, Rickey felt dissatisfied. If, he reasoned, moral agreements were often ignored by minor league owners then half-ownership was nearly as ineffective in getting prime players onto his big league roster. He was proven correct when Sunny Jim Bottomley was called up from Syracuse. Landgraf—who was still serving as Syracuse's president—phoned Rickey and after a good deal of hesitation told him that many other clubs wanted the big young first baseman, so many in fact that he was thinking of holding an auction.

Rickey was disappointed at the turn of events. If Syracuse could back out, he might have to face Breadon's sharp questions about the economic validity of the whole scheme, since the purchase of Syracuse was specifically designed to avoid exactly what Landgraf now proposed to do.

He drove to the airport. Once in Syracuse, he locked himself in with Landgraf for several hours. At last, they emerged, smiling and posing for photos. Bottomley, the press was informed, now was a Cardinal. How did Rickey accomplish that, he was asked. "By persuasion," he said, laughing. To another questioner in St. Louis, he answered, "By logic." And later, to a third reporter, he said, "By appealing to his sense of integrity." Years later he let the cat out of the bag: "By more money."

Whatever the technique used, the deal was now consummated and the system had overcome a serious hurdle. Breadon was so pleased he bought the remaining half interest in the Syracuse club—that, probably, was the payoff to Landgraf—picked up a greater portion of Fort Smith in the Western League, and added more shares of Houston to his portfolio.

Rickey was now off and running. In 1925 he started his tryout camps, at first in Danville, Illinois, and afterward, through the 1920s and 1930s, throughout the Midwest and South. Jim Bottomley had first drawn his attention when the Nokomis, Illinois, boy sent him a penciled, badly written letter, asking for a tryout in his Danville camp. At another camp Rickey spied a young Mount Vernon, Illinois, athlete named Ray Blades, who "ran like a deer." John Martin, later dubbed "Pepper," first showed up at the Greenville, Texas, camp. By 1928, the Cardinals had established dozens of such organized camps, owned seven minor league farm clubs, and controlled 203 minor league players. The consequences were as he hoped they would be: so many talented players developed that not only would the parent club be amply stocked, but surplus players would be produced in such abundance they could be sold to other teams at premium prices.

The more complex the organization became, the more he seemed to be ever present. When he spotted Blades, for example, his "Bible" told him that, as a guest umpire, he had observed the boy in a grade school game in St. Louis. He had also watched him play for the Lafayette Park Methodist Church Sunday School team, as well as for a local high school when once again Rickey umpired. Finally, Rickey saw him play for a Mount Vernon, Illinois, pickup team that challenged his Cardinals in 1920.

At another practice game he was seated alongside Joe Sugden watching as a farmhand smashed a pitch over the left field fence.

"Judas Priest, Joe, who hit that ball?"

"That," said the veteran catcher he had just hired as a scout, "was a boy named Hafey, from California. He's a pitcher."

"A pitcher?" Rickey's voice boomed through the rickety stands.

"A pitcher?" His cigar waved wildly in the air. "You mean he *was* a pitcher. Tell him he's no longer one. He's an outfielder. Throw away his toe plate and buy him a pair of glasses."

Within one year the farm system brought forth Taylor Douthit, Watty Holm, Art Reinhart, and Tommy Thevenow as well as Jim Bottomley and Chick Hafey, all of whom went on to star with St. Louis.

By 1922 Breadon had paid off his debt to the previous owners; six years later the club was earning a handsome profit, thanks to the farm system and the mushrooming sales of players. "They were a rich club in a poor town," wrote Sid Keener of the *Star-Times*. By Keener's estimate, a once bankrupt organization earned more than $2 million on player sales alone between 1922 and 1942, a generous proportion of which went into Rickey's pocket.

Before long, Rickey's radical and revolutionary operation ran afoul of Commissioner Kenesaw Mountain Landis. Rickey had found a young first baseman named Phil Todt on a local sandlot. Driving across town to scout Todt personally, he stood behind the catcher for an hour before returning to his office. Taking the phone in one hand and jiggling his cigar in the other, he told an aide to sign Todt.

Once signed, the boy was released and shipped to one Cardinal farm team after another. Irked by the practice, someone informed Rickey's enemy Phil Ball, who promptly signed Todt as a free agent. Which, of course, brought Landis into the case, his first involving Rickey. The Judge ruled against the Cardinals, declaring that Rickey had a secret agreement with Sherman (Texas) of the Western Association and Houston of the Texas League to hide the player in the minors. "The various transfers to which player Todt had been subjected were ... void," he stated. Todt became a free agent, and now Rickey knew he would have to take great pains not to offend the powerful Commissioner too much and too often.

If Breadon was overjoyed with the benefits received from Rickey's farms, Landis despised its coming and its growth. Landis' hates were famous and legion; some, like gamblers and crooked players, were deserving of his abhorrence. But many others, such as liberals and radicals, labor unions, other judges, and off-season black versus white barnstorming games, were not.

Landis, a doughty, wiry man, was the son of a Union Army surgeon who lost his leg at the Battle of Kennesaw Mountain (the proper spelling, unlike the Judge's given name). Landis believed the farm system caused irreparable harm to local ownership of minor league clubs and, as he so often put it, "the free market in players." Throughout the 1920s and well into the following decade he argued publicly, and privately to owners and general managers, that it was legally and morally wrong to hide players in the minors, and thereby deny them the chance to play in the majors. He also added a warning that if the farm system flourished then only the rich clubs would benefit while the poor would be reduced to scratching among the leavings for an occasional player.

Such was Landis' authority—in Federal Judge Walter Lindley's memorable phrase, "a benevolent but absolute despot"—that when he excoriated the farm system Rickey retreated into virtual silence even as he continued to develop his network, fearful lest he overstep the limits of behavior set by the Judge.

Meanwhile, Breadon's knowledge and enthusiasm for the game was growing. He still remained behind the scenes but his diffidence was wearing off. He proposed the league establish a publicity office to help spread the word about the sport's new era of superstars. He suggested an award of $1,000 in gold be granted annually for the "most valuable player." A Cardinal decal decorated each panel of his office doors, as it did Rickey's. But where Rickey's office was one of several along a narrow corridor, Breadon's took on the appearance of a man who enjoyed dealing as an authority. He installed wall-to-wall carpeting, a brown leather sofa (Rickey had only chairs and a room-size rug), an ornate desk with a bizarre statue of a batter with an interior gold clock set into its marble base, plus an ordinary alarm clock with which he liked rousing too-talkative visitors. On his walls were framed photos of Cardinal stars.

Breadon continued to marvel at the scouting staff Rickey had assembled, old and dear friends who trusted one another. They were part of Rickey's generation, his peers really, who still called him "Branch" while younger men were already beginning to speak to and of him as "Mr. Rickey." Charlie Barrett was, of course, an essential part of that staff, "a matrimonial coward" Rickey once dubbed him because Barrett never married, a Roman Catholic who revered Rickey, a regular visitor to the Rickey home. If Rickey had an equal competitor in detecting raw athletic talent, it was Barrett.

The others included Joe Sugden, Jack Ryan, Fred Hunter, Wid Matthews, Joe McDermott, Walter Shannon, Joe Mathes, Charley and Jay Kelchner, Gordon Maguire, and in time, Branch's younger brother Frank, who scouted the most rural backwater areas and managed to find a large number of prospects, including Enos Slaughter.

Rickey's network of part-time scouts and bird dogs was large and trustworthy and often exceeded his budget. "Large staff?" asked Sugden. *"It's everywhere.* It's the way he approached his problems, listening to his network of trusted people, asking for their advice, and generally accepting their judgment but also reserving the right to say 'no.' A combination of native intelligence, a keen willingness to move by instinct, and an understanding of his men added to his effectiveness in the front office."

By contrast, he was only a mediocre manager on the field.

In 1921 he asked Breadon if he should quit as manager, but Breadon turned him down. That year they had finished in third place, an improvement; the next year they slipped back one notch, and the year after that, fell into the second division. On the field Rickey wore street clothing and remained too much the talker and intellectual, holding forth daily at 11 A.M., asking questions about the previous game, giving pointers on the forthcoming game. "He was very strict on being on time for his lectures and always on time and he expected all of us to be there at eleven sharp. This went on as long as he managed," said Burt Shotton.

As manager, Rickey took a special delight in Heinie Mueller, his erratic outfielder. In a game against the Cubs, Rickey told him: "Son, when you see that our pitcher has been signaled to throw a slow ball, move in twenty feet. Go back to the fence when a fast ball is called for."

Mueller complied, coming in on slow pitches and moving back on fast balls. Soon, the bleacher fans grew wise to what was happening. "Slow ball," they shouted in unison as Heinie moved in. "Fast ball," and back he went. The chanting made Mueller nervous and, to Rickey's chagrin, he reversed himself, advancing when he should have been retreating and allowing a fly ball to go over his head and bounce against the wall, thereby losing the game.

Rickey was flabbergasted. "Son," he said in a soft tone, unwilling to hurt Mueller, "what went wrong? Didn't you get the fast-ball sign?"

"Sure I did," answered Mueller. "I got the sign all right. But I just thought I'd cross up those wise guys in the bleachers."

By 1925 Breadon decided the team should be doing much better and that Rickey would have to go as manager. When, during spring training, Coach Red Barrett told Rogers Hornsby—the hero of St. Louis, having hit .424 the year before—that Rickey was on the way out, the second baseman went up to his manager.

"I asked Branch if it was true and he said that it was. He asked me to speak to Breadon and see what I could do to patch things up between them. I said I would. I thought that Rickey was a fine manager"—this in spite of his and Rickey's having had a fistfight years before in the Polo Grounds clubhouse and a series of constant disagreements. They had learned to work together, although Hornsby disliked Rickey's penchant for switching positions and batting styles and Rickey thought Hornsby's tendency to arrive late for games (and on one occasion, his failure to show up at all) merited stiff fines.

There was no managerial change until the Cardinals slumped as the season progressed. With the approach of the Memorial Day weekend— two games in Pittsburgh and a single against the Reds in St. Louis were scheduled—the team was in the cellar and advance ticket sales poor.

"I was sitting in the lobby of the Hotel Schenley in Pittsburgh, the morning of May 29," said Hornsby, "when Rickey, looking very low, came over and told me that Breadon was firing him and making me the manager."

"Do you want the job?" asked Rickey, dismayed. Hornsby shook his head vigorously. He was only twenty-nine years old, and everybody respected his fielding ("The best double play man I ever saw," said Rickey) as well as his sensational hitting.

"Good, then," answered Rickey. "Then would you go upstairs to his room and tell Breadon to give me another chance?"

"I'll do my best," answered Hornsby.

"Rogers," Rickey called after him, "and if not me, see if you can get him to let Burt Shotton manage the club."

Hornsby told the strong-willed owner he would not accept the job. Breadon was just as forceful. "I won't have any goddamned Sunday School teacher running my team," he screamed. *"You're going to run it!"*

"No, I'm not," Hornsby shot back.

Later, Hornsby repeated the conversation to his manager. "Judas Priest," Rickey exploded, "the man is stabbing me in the back." Badly hurt and filled with anger, Rickey felt betrayed. "Clumsily brutal," was the way he described Breadon's action. "I had told him often that I did not want to manage and we had discussions who should take my place. But when the dismissal came, just at that moment, it was quite abrupt and surprising. I was knocked out."

He sold his stock to Hornsby out of pique and turned exclusively to being a salaried administrator.

Just the same, the change hurt him deeply and many times in his later life he referred to the "brutality" and "callousness" of Breadon's act, even if his managing had been less than perfect.

His resentment turned to escapism after receiving an offer from Northwestern University to become its athletic director. He was greatly tempted and called it "the greatest and most pleasing of surprises." Even so, Jane talked him out of it. Their fifth and sixth children, Sue and Elizabeth, had been born in 1922 and 1924, and Jane was reluctant to move again. Moreover, she surely must have told him, as she did countless other times in their lives, not to surrender to passing moments of despair so easily nor allow the disappointments of the day to so mar his life.

Yet his resentment of Breadon smoldered. When someone suggested that Breadon deserved a share of credit for the Cardinal farm system, he blew up in exasperation.

"Sam Breadon never in his entire lifetime discussed with me anything along the lines of baseball having to do, for example, with the farm system. He wouldn't venture an opinion about it. He might in the later days of his lifetime venture an opinion that the putting of new seats in Rochester (which replaced Syracuse in the farm network in 1928) or Columbus was advisable or inadvisable. Oh, that sort of thing, but the idea of his having an original idea about the so-called farm system is nonsense."

The Rickey-Hornsby team finished fourth in 1925, but around Cardinal headquarters there was a sense of excitement as people sensed their time had finally arrived. One or two more players, Rickey told Breadon and Hornsby, would make the difference. He traded his favorite Heinie Mueller to the New York Giants for Billy Southworth (McGraw's "worst deal," said a New York writer, and it may well have been: Southworth hit .317 that year and was the Cardinals' leader on the field). Sending Mueller away bothered Rickey, but he had decided never to let sentiment sway him in trades, a principle he raised to a way of life over the next four decades. "You must know ahead of time who is failing," he said to the press when queried for the reasoning behind the trade. "You must take risks."

Then, while Rickey was traveling, Breadon and Hornsby teamed up to buy Grover Cleveland Alexander from the Cubs for the $4,000 waiver price. Cub manager Joe McCarthy didn't mind that Alexander was a drunk, but he refused to put up with the fact that, drunk or sober, the veteran was a hard man to handle.

The result was that in 1926—for the first time since its American Association title in 1888—St. Louis, mostly Rickey's farmhands—Bottomley, Thevenow, Larry Bell, Douthit, Blades, Holm, Hafey, and Rhem, and specially selected players Sherdel, Southworth, Haines, Alexander, and catcher Bob O'Farrell, whom he acquired from the Cubs—won the pennant.

The city celebrated wildly and even more when the Cardinals beat the Yankees in the seventh game of the World Series. It was, Rickey recalled, Sunday and drizzling, and he and Jane were at home in St. Louis listening to the radio. In Yankee Stadium, the series was tied at three all and St. Louis was ahead 3–2 in the bottom of the seventh.

Haines was on the mound as Yankee outfielder Earle Combs opened the inning with a sharp single and moved to second on shortstop Mark Koenig's sacrifice bunt. Haines purposely walked Babe Ruth but Bob Meusel forced Ruth at second. Two men were out but then Lou Gehrig walked. The bases were loaded. By now Haines was utterly exhausted. He was a knuckleballer and his knuckles were rubbed raw and bleeding. The bases were loaded as Hornsby waved his right arm in the air for Alexander, the forty-year-old veteran who had won the opening game and pitched a nine-inning, 10–2 victory the day before and spent the night celebrating.

Hornsby strode toward the left field line to meet the older man. "You can do it, Pete," he said, slapping him on the back.

When Rickey later asked Hornsby why he had walked out to greet Alexander, Hornsby told him, "I wanted to find out if he could see. He recognized me alright, which was encouraging. He had been dozing in the bullpen, but his eyes were about open when he met me. So I told him we were ahead, but that the bases were filled, two out in the seventh inning, with Lazzeri at bat." During the season Lazzeri had driven in 114 runs, second only to Ruth.

"'Don't worry, Rog,' Alexander told me. 'I guess there's nothing to do but give Lazzeri a lot of trouble.' And so, after I saw that he could see and walk, and didn't have anything in his hip pocket, I told him to go in and pitch."

Alexander threw a quick strike. Lazzeri lined a foul past third base. And then, the old man struck him out. In the eighth he set down the Yankees, and in the bottom of the ninth, he held them as O'Farrell threw out Ruth trying to steal.

Back home, Rickey's radio had broken down, and he and Jane were in a neighbor's living room listening to the broadcast. They embraced at the end of the game.

The Cardinals were world champions.

Not long after, the honeymoon between Breadon and Hornsby ended, and Rickey found himself in the middle of a raging public storm. The Cardinals had experienced a curious financial record during the club's championship year: a profit was earned, but total attendance was only 681,575, nearly 200,000 fewer than that of the fourth-place Cubs and the same as the sixth place Brooklyn Dodgers. Thus when Hornsby abruptly complained that the president's eye was too much on profits and not enough on players, Breadon blew up.

"Such as?" he demanded.

"Such as scheduling too many exhibition games," replied the uninhibited Hornsby. "You're money hungry."

Rickey watched in barely concealed horror as the cooperation of the past several months disintegrated into mutual recriminations. When Rickey tried to mediate, Breadon told him that he could never forget nor forgive the public humiliation of Hornsby's throwing him out of the clubhouse last season in full view of the players; above all he wanted to trade him. Nor would Hornsby be pacified, confiding in Rickey that Breadon was not paying him enough money.

By December, Breadon had enough and he told Rickey that he proposed to trade Hornsby to the New York Giants. Rickey believed trading Hornsby was a mistake but since Breadon was adamant, he ought to ask for the young Giant second baseman, Frank Frisch, in return. But he asked Breadon to try once more to reconcile with Hornsby, arguing that the Cardinals could easily repeat the next year with him as player-manager.

The two men met alone on December 21 in Breadon's office. Rickey and the staff overheard raised voices interrupting one another and then Hornsby stormed out, slamming Breadon's glass doors in anger. Rickey rushed in and Breadon's hands shook as he reached for a scotch and then, having calmed himself, for the phone, asking to be put through to Charles Stoneham, owner of the Giants. Stoneham could not be located for hours while the agitated Cardinal owner walked the floor, nagged Rickey and other staff members, and drank himself into a sullen mood. At last at 6 P.M., Stoneham returned the call. Breadon said, "Well, Charles, you've wanted Hornsby for a long time. You can have him now for Frisch and [Jimmy] Ring."

On orders of Breadon, Rickey negotiated the trade. Stoneham, who called Rickey "Major" in deference to his army days, had five years earlier unsuccessfully proposed a swap for Hornsby to which Rickey responded: "Forget Hornsby, he's the only star we've got." But he had offered Stoneham $150,000—which, of course, he did not have—for a ballplayer "you have had for two or three days, just out of school, never has played professional baseball, and is on your team. I'll give you $150,000 for Frank Frisch."

News of the trade threw sports-loving fans in St. Louis into turmoil. If they failed to fill Sportsman's Park they remained passionate about their team and their heroes. The Chamber of Commerce issued an official proclamation condemning the move and demanded Landis intervene. The mayor protested. Organizations of businessmen and workingmen castigated Breadon. A *Star* reporter began a boycott movement so long as Breadon remained in charge. Hornsby added to the hate Breadon sentiment by adding personal arguments to the bitterness. "You know," he told the press, "you [Breadon] have not even congratulated your players in person for winning the pennant and the World Series."

For Breadon the ugly reaction was startling and frightening, although he never gave way. The venomous calls he received at home forced him to disconnect his phone. He and his wife stopped appearing in public. His office calls were carefully screened.

"I'll never forget it," he told Rickey. "I was in the lobby of the Jefferson Hotel a day or two after the deal. People I'd known for years passed by without saying a word. Others stopped to call me every name under the sun."

Rickey was spared withering criticism, but many people felt he should have raised stronger objections. When a reporter interviewed him he was vague, saying only, "I understand it," adding only that had he been running the club, Hornsby would have stayed.

The irony was that reporters, who tended to create the mood of the fans, forgave Breadon quickly, but not Rickey. Frisch performed well, the team came in second in 1927 and first in 1928. Breadon was right. "A good club makes fans forget what happened before." Although Breadon hired and fired managers with rapidity, he never put off reporters' questions with pompous and tortured words which fogged the issues, as they felt Rickey did. When Rickey meant to say that teams benefited by removing poor players he called it "addition by subtraction," an abstraction that infuriated some writers. When he intended to say a club could not have one star and expect a pennant, he described it as "quantitative quality." Most of all, many reporters hated his constant use of quotations, feeling he was condescending toward them and trying to intellectualize a business that was basically very simple. Before long, he was portrayed as a masterly and clever manipulator, a wheeler-dealer, an evader who couldn't tell the truth.

When the local Baseball Writers' Association gathered at their favorite watering hole for an annual meeting soon after the Hornsby bombshell, Breadon was invited but not Rickey. The Cardinal president asked the chairman to include his vice-president too, but John E. Ray of the *Post-Dispatch* complained, "Jeez, Sam, he's a teetotaler," acceding reluctantly to Breadon's request.

When Rickey rose to speak, he began: "I never told a sportswriter a lie."

"Now *that's* a lie," Ray shouted, drunk.

Sid Keener was also drunk and shouted to Ray, "You're a liar. You can't talk to my friend Branch that way."

With that, a drunken mob of sportswriters started a small-scale riot, heaving curses, blows, glasses, and plates at one another. Above the bedlam Ray was heard shouting, "He always lies," in what proved to be the association's last dinner until 1948.

All the same, Keener knew something that Ray did not: Rickey indeed tried to manipulate the press when it suited him; yet Keener and others throughout the country were fascinated by his extraordinary stories and analytic ability. They considered him great copy, a never-ending source of news who could always be parodied should the need arise.

Another veteran writer, J. Roy Stockton, who could take Rickey or leave him, felt the press owed him recognition for his serious contributions to the sport, especially the way his farm system strengthened minor league teams. "The far-sighted Rickey realized that without the minor leagues, baseball would soon dry up at the roots and die. With no grade or high school, there would be no use for a university, and much of Rickey's Cardinals attention has been devoted to the Class D and C leagues, the grade schools of baseball training."

The end of the twenties saw Rickey a success in his profession, prosperous on the eve of the Great Depression, a middle-aged man with six children. The family lived outside the city limits seventeen miles from his office, on a twenty-three-acre estate he called Country Life Acres, in a setting that must, in his mind, have resembled Duck Run.

There were horses, cows, chickens; dogs and cats were everywhere, including a dachshund puppy named Branch; a goat and sheep, both pets; a pair of peacocks, many ducks and geese; turkey and pheasants; wheat, corn, and Jane's vegetable garden guarded by a possessive bantam hen; a grape arbor; apple and cherry orchards; and especially for his children, a lake with an island that could be reached by a small bridge.

Nightly, he stormed into the Tudor house alone or with a bevy of friends, shouting "News, news" as all the household gathered about him at the front door. His children worshiped him. Sundays they joined him and visitors in hide and seek, cops and robbers, kick the can. They were a "game" family, and Rickey never tired of devising new ways to delight his young.

Looking back at the seventeen years he had spent in St. Louis since his departure from the University of Michigan, he sought to summarize his life. "Change is good," he wrote on a sheet of yellow legal paper at the age of forty-seven in the middle of 1929. "And baseball is good, an honorable profession, a great challenge. It has blessed me, I blessed it, and it has blessed our country."

# Chapter Six

THE 1930s STARTED OUT WELL. Phil Ball apologized for accusing him of breaking his contract when he left the Browns for the Cardinals:

> My Dear Rickey:
>
> Not being the silver-tongued orator that you are, I am unable to couch my thought in soft spoken words—but I shall be very glad to resume the amicable relations which existed before our agreement.

Rickey was overjoyed since few of his arguments in public life had caused him as much anguish. In his own hand he wrote Ball:

> Your vocabulary in soft spoken words never was very good but your letter was the best thrill I had in 1930.
>
> Life's sufficiently full of disagreeable things that we cannot help—so I feel a lot better to get rid of all I can.
>
> I, too, can forget and from now on, your letter and this one will be to me the beginning of a new and lasting friendship.

The club won the pennant that year and while turnstile receipts continued to remain low (though total income was soaring) St. Louis fans greeted the team after its defeat to the Athletics in the World Series "from curb to curb, amid shouts of acclaim and adulation, through blizzards of falling paper," commented the *Globe-Democrat*.

Meanwhile throughout the 1930s his reputation as the sharpest of traders, bargainers, and talent judges was unrivaled. "He'd go into the vault to get a nickel change," said the young Enos Slaughter after a negotiating session with Rickey. Slaughter batted .273 with Martinsville (Virginia) in 1935 and struck out more than one hundred times, yet Rickey noticed what everybody else in the organization had failed to see: half of Slaughter's hits had been for extra bases. "Rickey noticed that," said Slaughter. "He noticed everything, that son of a gun." Rickey promoted Slaughter to the Columbus, Georgia, team the next year, a B league and a step up.

Seated in his Sportsman's Park box in the steam heat of the city one day, he turned to his son-in-law John Eckler. "Look how quick, how fast he moves," he said after weeks of criticism of a player. "Look, John, see how quick and agile he is." "Then you've decided to trade him?" asked Eckler. His father-in-law smiled, sat back easily, and puffed at his cigar. "Yes indeed, son, yes indeed."

It was his trademark: the sweeping praise and unequivocal raves about ballplayers he wanted to send away. Tom Winsett, for example. A twenty-six-year-old Tennessean, Winsett had been a minor league star and his 6'2", 190-lb. frame and perfect swing belied a devastating flaw—he was an awful hitter.

"Watch that beautiful swing, my boy. Mr. Winsett sweeps that bat in the same plane every time, no matter where the ball is pitched." When he chose to let him go after only seven games with the Cardinals, Rickey told the press Winsett was the "coming Babe Ruth," although why he would want to ship off the future Sultan of Swat was left unasked. "Woe unto the pitcher who throws the ball where the Winsett bat is functioning," he told everyone in earshot. Privately, he added, "But throwing it almost anywhere else in the general area of home plate is safe." Shipped to Brooklyn, Winsett hit seven homers in three seasons at Ebbets Field.

Rickey ran virtually every phase of the business. He appointed Ray Blades the Columbus manager and also hired Larry MacPhail as the club's president. Soon, however, he was exasperated at MacPhail's approach to administration. In the summer of 1933 he phoned Blades at two-thirty in the morning.

"It was Mr. Rickey and he wanted to see me. I went to his hotel room and I could see something was really bothering him. 'Ray, he's got to go,' he said. I really didn't know who he meant until he said Larry was spending more money than we're making." Not long after, Blades heard that Rickey had recommended the Cincinnati Reds take on MacPhail as their president.

"Rickey also engineered all the minor league player movement," said Arthur Fetzner, who served for years as one of his secretaries. "This was a man-sized job. He alone moved the players around the system, authorized unconditional releases, and guided the progress and advancement of the players to the big leagues. Often, after a day's observation in a training camp, analyzing the verbal reports and recommendations of the managers and other camp personnel, and an all-night player distribution meeting, he set the clubs for the start of the season." Another Cardinal employee also noted that "once weekly" Rickey wrote "long, very detailed and very warm letters" to Breadon describing what he was doing, why, and what he believed were the implications of his many maneuvers.

By 1938, the Cardinals had thirty-two farm clubs, some wholly owned and others tied by working agreements. The Rickey principle for locating prospects was producing. ("He had a formula," said Bob Clements, his secretary, driver, and traveling companion in 1937 and 1938: "running speed, a good throwing arm, and a strong bat, essential ingredients Rickey believed simply could not be taught. Every pitcher had to have an adequate fastball. Simple things, really, but it was amazing how many teams overlooked them.") That winter the Cardinals reserved twenty-seven rooms for a minor league meeting in Louisville's Brown Hotel while Clements counted "a line of seven men in the lobby waiting to see him."

By now he had also developed the art of selling off local heroes when he thought they were nearing the end of their careers. He traded Bottomley to the Reds in 1933, where Bottomley performed modestly well, and then without apologies to the fans and columnists who criticized him for sending Sunny Jim away in the first place, brought him back to replace Ripper Collins, the man who had replaced him. After Chick Hafey demanded more money, Rickey unceremoniously exiled him to the last-place Reds despite the fact that Hafey had lost none of his skills. Once done, Rickey called up Houston farmhand Joe Medwick as a replacement. He sold farm star Johnny Rizzo to the Pirates for $25,000 because he had spied a serious defect in his fielding and running, but kept Enos Slaughter in spite of Pirate bids to buy him too.

Yet if there was no sentiment in baseball, occasional exceptions were made. He brought Rogers Hornsby home again after persuading Breadon to forgive and forget. Hornsby, who fought with nearly everybody during his long career, was then with the Cubs. He hated Cub manager Charlie Grimm and Grimm returned the compliment. The Cub pilot appealed to Rickey (for whom he had played in 1918) and the Cardinals took him back. The grateful if aging slugger hit .325 in 46 games.

Rickey's calendars indicated constant travel. Once he had his daughter Mary accompany him as chauffeur-secretary on a moment's notice. When she complained she had no luggage he waved aside her objections. Clothes, he told her as they sped to a waiting automobile, could always be bought in the nearest store. He hated driving and always seemed to have a legion of drivers at his beck and call. Without notice he took his two teenage daughters, Alice and Jane, along with Arthur Fetzner as driver, on a trip to New York. Driving through Illinois, Rickey asked Fetzner, "What's the trouble?" since they were moving too dangerously to suit him. "I'm just getting the feel of the car," answered Fetzner, hours after they left St. Louis. "Pooh," answered Rickey. Turning to one of his children he ordered, "Jane, you drive." She was sixteen and she drove all night as her father slept in the back seat, occasionally waking and issuing directions to "Gun and shoot it"—his pet phrase for accelerating and passing another car—and then returning to sleep. Since he rarely carried any money or wore a watch, he seemed to require an army of aides to pay his bills. It was routine for him to race for a train and not have the cash to buy a ticket. Or to arrive at an air terminal without his suitcase. In one widely told but probably apocryphal tale, he departed Grand Central Terminal and only when his train pulled into Newark did he remember he had left his wife in the Grand Central waiting room. But if that story may not be true, this one is. Driving to Hannibal, Missouri, one frigid wintry day with Mel Jones at the wheel, he scribbled notes for a speech on the back of an envelope as he simultaneously urged Jones to "step on it." When they had to pause for gas he jumped out, broke the ice on a can of water alongside the pump, washed his face, and then returned to the car to shave, reaching matter-of-factly into the glove compartment for his razor. Jones was not surprised at all.

One fall day he and Arthur Fetzner traveled to Springfield to speak on behalf of Jesse Barrett's campaign for governor. A black button was all he had in his pockets as he raced out of his office barely in time to catch the afternoon Frisco train to the state's capital. Moments later, they walked into the dining car. Fetzner had only thirty-five cents; he had learned only moments before of the trip. He managed to pay the check and tip with the thirty-five cents. Just as they were to leave the dining car, Barrett joined them. "How about some lunch, Jesse. Mine was great," said the hospitable Rickey. Barrett demurred but then sat down. "I'll take a baked apple," he told the waiter. The apple cost thirty-five cents. Fetzner paled.

"After talking politics for an hour or so, Rickey and Barrett rose from the table and started to leave the car, leaving me 'holding the bag' for the check. Rushing up to Rickey, I whispered my plight to him.

"'Things always have a way of working out,' Rickey said calmly, smiling. 'Go along with Jesse. I'll take care of it.'"

Later, as the train pulled into Springfield, Fetzner asked what had happened with the check.

"'Wasn't nothing to it,' Rickey shrugged. 'It was easy. I just talked the waiter into paying for the check out of the tip we gave him.'"

Scout George Silvey watched in amazement as Rickey observed twelve minor league clubs simultaneously in their Albany, Georgia, complex, then "we would go into meetings that would last until four in the morning making up all twelve clubs and then he would be on his way again"—fortified only by a fifteen-minute catnap on the most convenient couch or floor.

When Silvey wired him for a pitcher for his Class D team, Rickey wired back: "Am sending you pitcher Roland Van Slate." Silvey, though, had heard rumors—unfounded as it turned out—that Van Slate was a troublemaker, and he questioned his boss's choice. Within hours another telegram arrived from Rickey: "When I was a little boy I did not like Calomel. My father made me take Calomel. You take Van Slate."

But at the heart of this frantic pace was his strong sense of loyalty.

When the Depression ruined his Ohio Wesleyan classmate Don Beach's bank in St. Petersburg, Rickey wired: "I need you in St. Louis. How soon can you come?" He hired him at Columbus and later found him a job as the Dodger and Pirate auditor. In fact, when Beach's daughter was unable to attend college because of lack of funds, Rickey turned over his own daughters' scholarship awards to the Beach girl.

He reached into Washington University's athletic department for Bob Finch because he liked the school's attitude toward the Cardinals in their poverty-stricken years. When Bert Shotton and Ray Blades' playing days were over, he saw to it they had jobs in the Cardinal system. But he also took on people instinctively, when it seemed capricious to others.

"We were working late one evening at old Sportsman's Park," said Arthur Fetzner. As usual Rickey had a tremendous pile of mail in front of him. He came across a well-written letter applying for a job in the publicity department. It was from Tom Doherty of Chicago. "'This chap is really a gifted writer,' remarked Rickey. 'Suppose you get him on the phone.' I reached Tom in a few minutes. After a brief conversation, Rickey told Tom to take the midnight train for St. Louis and see him in the morning. Tom was on hand bright and early and after talking with Rickey a few minutes he was hired and reported to the publicity department."

Always, he maintained a serious interest in the lives of many of the young men who worked for him. "I offered mill hands, plowboys, high school kids a better way of life. They rose on sandlots to big city diamonds. In a month they earned more than they could have earned in a year. And no young man who signed a contract with me has ever suffered—educationally or morally. If he chose to remain in school, I helped him. When he quit the Cardinal chain, he had learned the lesson 'clean living' and moral stamina."

When the gifted catcher Bill DeLancey was struck down by tuberculosis in 1936, Rickey refused to cut off his salary and instead organized a Cardinal affiliate in Arizona so DeLancey could work as manager. When DeLancey's wife wanted to become a nurse, it was Rickey who contacted associates in Phoenix. Before DeLancey died at the age of thirty-six in 1946, he told people that Rickey had acted as if he were his caring and loving father.

Branch Jr. turned twenty in 1934—it was doubtless his father's dream to have the boy serve alongside him so that he could teach him all he knew and one day, perhaps, be his successor when he retired.

The sole male child, Branch Jr. was called "Boy" all his life by his sisters, a name given him by one of the girls when very young because of an inability to pronounce Branch. Like his father before him and his slightly older sister Mary, he studied at the fashionable nonsectarian private John Burroughs School outside of St. Louis and afterwards at OWU. He was sturdy and muscular, his massive shoulders and huge chest making him seem shorter than he actually was. At college he majored in European history, caught for the baseball team, became a guard on the football team, and then abruptly quit after the Delaware newspaper described him as "Branch Rickey's son." Instead, he sought out athletic activities his father had never participated in, such as track and wrestling.

He received his degree in 1935 and married Mary Iams, a fellow OWU graduate. Like his father, he matriculated at the University of Michigan Law School. But soon his father intervened in his life, urging young Branch to leave law school. "He pulled him out for a baseball job in St. Louis," says William Turner, who grew up with Branch Jr.

Adds Mary Iams Rickey: "He would have loved to have been a doctor, but he felt his father wanted him to be a lawyer. But Mr. Rickey wanted Branch to travel with him as a secretary, and he left law school and went instead to secretarial school. Mr. Rickey was very possessive about his son. He had to have somebody with him all the time, to talk things over. Mr. Rickey loved his son deeply and vice versa. He wanted his son to learn everything he knew and more, but about baseball, not law."

Newly married, Branch Jr. and his bride spent their honeymoon on the road for his father, traveling an estimated 27,000 miles in three months. "He's just like his father," marveled Mary to J. G. Taylor Spink of the *Sporting News*. "We were in twenty-eight states and we had a swim in the Pacific at San Francisco and in the Atlantic at Jacksonville, Florida, before it was over." By mid–1939 they had lived in twelve locales, Branch Jr. having served as business manager of the Cardinals' Albany (Georgia) and Asheville (North Carolina) farms, as well as roamed the countryside setting up his father's pioneering tryout camps.

He and Mary drove into small cities and towns and they issued press releases he had composed and she typed to local papers and radio stations within a hundred-mile radius. For three days he and the scouts then watched the farm boys and smalltown hopefuls throw, run, field, and hit. Evenings, Mary typed long reports sent to Rickey.

They traveled as much as three hundred miles daily, driving all night and setting up camps during the day. But they were young, in love, and heady with the illusion of freedom travel brought them. On one trip they held tryouts in St. Louis, Laramie (Wyoming), Falstaff (Arizona), Sacramento, and several Florida towns. Rickey occasionally flew in, was briefed by his son and the assigned scout, wandered among the young players asking questions, and then flew on to somewhere else.

Rickey also sent daughter Mary and her husband, John Eckler, to work with tryout camps. "Our first camp was Petersburg, Virginia," said Eckler. "I would drive all over the area speaking with Sunday school teachers, coaches, and high school superintendents about Mr. Rickey's tryouts. 'Bring your own glove, shoes, and uniforms,' we'd tell them, 'and we'll supply bats and balls.'"

Thoroughness and organization were the key to the system, and each player was card-indexed, screened, and evaluated carefully by Rickey's team of professionals. A reporter dubbed the system "Rickey's dragnet," and another called it a "sweep" camp.

Occasionally, mistakes were made. He nearly committed a major blunder when he forgot to exercise his option for slugger Taylor Douthit with the St. Joseph (Missouri) club of the Western League. The Pirates offered $35,000 for Douthit, but St. Joseph president Warren Giles had been hired thanks to Rickey and he saved Douthit for the Cardinals. Then, too, Arkansas fastball pitcher Lon Warneke was signed to a Laurel (Mississippi) farm contract but received a bad report from the Laurel manager, although the raves on the Cardinal card index contradicted his judgment. Still, several officials approved his release. Rickey was apprised of this while scanning a roster list; he had stood for nearly an hour behind the catcher and watched Warneke pitch and he blew up, calling the release a terrible mistake.

His own marginal notations about players, the rookies, and minor leagues were pithy, acute, but at times also inaccurate:

- About a catcher—"Great prospect but a bum."
- A left-handed pitcher—"More stuff than I have seen. No sense. No control. Prospect de luxe nevertheless." (He failed.)

- Rocky Nelson, first baseman—"Can do everything." (In nine years of major league ball, Nelson hit .249.)
- Del Rice, catcher—"Fine prospect." (Rice spent eleven years with the Cardinals and another six years in the majors.)

Another scout, Joe Mathes, marveled that Rickey "visited every club I ever operated for the Cardinals to check on the ability of the players." Rickey had handpicked Mathes as he had Silvey, and they reported personally to him. "With his tenacious memory, he knew many of the kids by their first names and he had the uncanny ability to recognize a 'diamond-in-the-rough.'"

In the spring of 1937, a first child, Carolyn, was born to Branch Jr. and Mary. Rickey was so excited at becoming a grandfather that he and Fetzner drove all night from Washington to Asheville to see the infant. Listening to her cry, he stared at the baby "minutely from head to toe" (said Fetzner) and then broke into a smile. "Yes sir, folks! She's got the Rickey chest."

Two years later a second daughter, Nancy, was born, and Branch Jr. tried to resume his legal studies evenings at Washington University in St. Louis. But his workaday world and the obligations of his family made it hard to concentrate on the abstractions of the law, and he settled instead on learning the business of baseball.

The Gas House Gang tended to swagger and strut on and off the field; their exaggerated sense of theatrics lent them an air of excitement and personality that stamped them as special, despite the fact they won but one pennant—in 1934—and World Series. Very quickly they became the media and the fans' darlings. They helped define baseball's depression decade—the insouciance of Dizzy Dean, the grace of manager–second baseman Frankie Frisch, the idiosyncrasies of Pepper Martin, the aggression of Joe Medwick. Frank Graham of the New York *Sun* said he named them the Gas House Gang, but Frisch credited Leo Durocher. What was incontestable was that they were Rickey's singular creation—not only the players, but also their glamour, flamboyance, and eccentricities, many of which were planned and stage-managed by him at the beginning.

"It was a high class team, with nine heavy drinkers who were paid more money over a period of ten years than any other club in the National League, excluding their World Series take," boasted Rickey. "They were the best team I ever had."

Added Frisch: "It was Rickey who first brought to St. Louis the colorful stories of Pepper Martin—dubbed with joy the 'Wild Hoss of the

The stars of the famous St. Louis Cardinal Gashouse gang, Dizzy Dean (left) and the "Fordham Flash" Frankie Frisch with Rickey, in 1938. (Courtesy Branch B. Rickey)

Osage' by reporters—Dizzy Dean, Ernie 'Showboat' Orsatti, and Joe Medwick." Frisch watched Rickey seek out reporters in every National League city, regaling them with stories of his players' exploits. One of his favorite writers, Bill Corum of the New York *Journal-American,* grew up in Missouri and never tired of recording the deeds of his beloved Cardinals. In story after story he amplified on Rickey's tales. Soon the players were acting out his and their fantasies. John Martin should properly be called "Pepper," he told the press, as he spread Charlie Barrett's apocryphal story of driving 60 mph in Oklahoma and suddenly looking up to see a jackrabbit run by his car pursued by Martin. "Anyone who can run that fast can play baseball," Barrett was supposed to have said, according to Rickey. "Someone," Rickey later told Frisch, "has to give this team color."

Soon Pepper Martin stories flooded the local and, later, national sport pages. Once he struck out swinging and stormed back into the dugout shouting his frustrations loud enough for all nearby fans to hear.

Then he sat down and, smiling, said to his teammates: "Someone has to give this team color." Martin was so taken by the educated Rickey and so pleased at the attention he had given him he had started patterning his speech after Rickey's.

Rickey returned the compliment. Martin's dash and elan were the epitome of what he most admired, in and outside of baseball. "Pepper Martin," he told Arthur Daley of *The New York Times,* "is the most genuine person I've ever met in my life. There never was an ounce of pretense in the man." When Judge Landis sought to compliment Martin by saying, "Young man, I'd give anything to change places with you tonight," the unflappable Pepper answered, "It's agreeable to me, Judge, salaries and all."

The stories kept reaching the desks of writers, their arrival often prompted by Rickey and his staff. During one game Martin's wife delivered their third child in a neighboring hospital. Pepper played the game and then raced to the maternity ward, bursting into her room, saying, "Darling, great news, we won a doubleheader." That too was told and retold by Rickey to everyone who would listen.

He also took pains to point out to reporters that outfielder Ernie Orsatti was "a stand-in stuntman for Buster Keaton." It was Rickey who spread the tale of the girl seated in the Houston stands declaiming that Medwick walked so much like a duck he was "ducky wucky"—a name the often bad-tempered outfielder from Carteret, New Jersey, hated, but which accompanied him throughout his major league career.

Dean always claimed Rickey encouraged his antics, although like Martin and the others, he had a zaniness all his own. From the day he was signed by Houston and he asked permission to marry at home plate— which was denied—through his other nationally publicized antics, Dizzy was a shrewd and clever bargainer, certainly one of the few ballplayers who were Rickey's equal.

He was always on stage, telling interviewers he hailed from Lucas, Arkansas, or Bond, Mississippi, or Holdenville, Oklahoma; that he was named Jay Hanna or Jerome Herman. Rickey called him Jerome, and Dean responded by calling him Branch, a clear breach of the pecking order in the Cardinal organization.

"There were things in heaven and on earth not dreamed of then in Dizzy's philosophy, things like charge accounts and bank checks, whose existence he discovered after joining the Cardinals," wrote Red Smith. "He found that if he signed a check, a man would give him money and later Mr. Rickey would take care of the man. If he bought something and said, 'Charge it,' Mr. Rickey would take care of that."

Most of all Dean liked to drop into Rickey's office unannounced, place his huge feet on the boss's desk, lean back and talk countrystyle.

One cold December day he stopped by and then left by the back door as the exhausted Rickey walked into the main room to meet the press, out of character—his jacket off, tie hanging loosely, his collar unbuttoned, his hair rumpled, and a ring of sweat on his forehead. "By Judas Priest!" he began. "By Judas Priest! If there were more like him in baseball, just one, as God is my judge, I'd get out of the game." And to his family at dinner he confided in exasperation that he often asked himself what a lawyer and educated man was doing dealing with the likes of a Dizzy Dean.

The Gang won the pennant in 1934, beating Bill Terry's Giants by one game. (This was the year Terry asked a reporter, "Is Brooklyn still in the league?" and thereby roused the Dodgers to win several crucial games against his team.) Dean, more than any other Cardinal, was "King of St. Louis." "They can talk of Grove and Hubbell," went an anonymous ditty of those days, "But when the team's in deep-down trouble, you're a better man than they are, Dizzy Dean." In florid prose the *Globe-Democrat* exuded poems of praise: "Never before did King Arthur and his knights of the round table, even in their quest for the Grail, bring forth the popular acclaim that befell King Dizzy and his eight colleagues. As he struck out the last Red to win the pennant flag, 37,402 people, their eyes moist, their voices made hoarse by the cowbells, whistles and shouts, struck a wondrous note."

In spite of the emotion and a monster parade down Lindell Boulevard, Breadon remained worried by the long-term financial prospects of his club. The Depression had hit the city hard as it had every other place, and attendance dipped badly. St. Louis's population was one of the smallest in the big leagues, yet the city was home to two ballclubs. From 600,000 fans in 1931 the number of paying customers fell to 268,000 in 1933; in 1934 only 335,000 people paid their way into the park.

Breadon searched for a remedy and instructed Rickey to try to negotiate a sale of the Cardinals to Lew Wentz, a Ponca City, Oklahoma, oil man. Breadon wanted $1,100,000 and the oil man wanted to bargain. Breadon grew annoyed and told him he had half an hour to decide. After thirty minutes, he rose and told Wentz, "Sorry, time's up." When the deal collapsed, Breadon moved to have the team shifted to Detroit, but that was blunted by the opposition of the Tigers.

Still and all, the club was doing well financially by virtue of its seemingly unlimited supply of surplus players. During the following years Rickey sold Johnny Mize ($52,000 plus two pitchers), Bob Bowman

($35,000 plus one player), Bob Worthington and Charlie Wilson ($60,000 plus a player), Nate Andrews ($7,500), Johnny Chambers ($6,000), Don Padgett ($35,000), Lew Riggs ( $20,000), Jimmy Jordan ($20,000), Frank Melton ($30,000), and many others. The biggest sale of all was when he shipped Dean to an obliging Philip K. Wrigley in Chicago for $185,000 and pitchers Curt Davis and Clyde Shoun.

"Rickey Sells Dean for Cash and 2 Hamburgers" one of Rickey's daughters remembers reading in a St. Louis newspaper headline. Rickey had gone out of his way to warn Wrigley that the Great One's arm was damaged but if he still wanted him the price was $185,000. Wrigley, however, went along with the deal, explaining—or so rumors had it—that Dean would sell a lot of chewing gum for him, good arm or not.

A few months later he traded Leo Durocher to Brooklyn because he could not get along with Frisch. With Durocher gone, Rickey's farms produced Marty Marion as his new shortstop.

All this activity kept Breadon reasonably content and willing to continue operating in St. Louis. It was also very profitable for Rickey, for while his salary sagged during the Depression from $51,470 in 1934 to $40,000 in 1937 (then leveled off at $50,000 annually), he was still granted 10 percent of the sale price of players.

The farm system was taking hold. If it made the Cardinals and the other teams happy, it always agitated Landis. As far back as the 1920s he had forced through a measure at the Major League Steering Committee outlawing the ownership of stock in more than one club in the same league. In the late twenties, Barney Dreyfuss—who was still smarting at Rickey for "stealing" George Sisler in 1915—informed Landis that his information indicated Rickey and the Cardinals had violated this rule. Dreyfuss' facts were premature (dual ownership within one league would arrive several years *after* Dreyfuss went to the commissioner) but Landis distrusted the St. Louis operation and began to carp.

At the annual baseball session in late 1929 in Chattanooga, Tennessee, Landis denounced the entire concept and proclaimed his intention of destroying it. Breadon exploded with indignation and said he had five statements from minor league clubs favoring the system. To Landis, he shrieked, "You've gone out of your way to hurt my business." The Judge's response was that he and Rickey were the damagers. He accused them of robbing small-town America of its precious heritage of independent minor league baseball. "You are both guilty of raping the minors," he told Breadon, who shook with rage at the charge.

The guerrilla warfare between Landis and St. Louis dragged on, each side provoking the other into further allegations and statements.

Privately, Landis started referring to Rickey as "that sanctimonious so-and-so" while Rickey made another effort to defend the system at the Minor League Meeting in Montreal in December 1930. Staring ahead at Landis seated in the front row before him, Rickey defended the system as a means of insuring the health of the minors. In an allegory, he suggested the minors were ill and while one doctor (Landis) was not prepared to offer any remedy the other (the Cardinals) was. The minors, he went on, were ill—from mismanagement, undercapitalization, other interests capturing more mobile fans, and the onset of bad times. The Cardinals now had eight minor league affiliates who would survive as others died. According to Mann, he then looked directly at the Judge and challenged him: "Baseball is bigger than any one club. It is bigger than I am. It is bigger than any one man."

In 1931, Herschel Bennett, a Brown farmhand, charged his career was being ruined because his parent club kept shuffling him between farm clubs in Tulsa, Wichita Falls, and Milwaukee. Bennett told Landis he wanted a chance to be a major leaguer and be rid of the yo-yo treatment. Although Landis' claim to fame was the way he dealt with gambling, often denying suspected players basic constitutional rights, he was generally on the ballplayer's side and opposed almost every owner at one time or another. Now he directed Phil Ball to place Bennett on the Browns roster or sell him. The irascible Ball refused and, instead, filed suit in federal court charging interference with private property. Federal Judge Walter Lindley heard the case and backed Landis. But he also went much further—in a direction Landis did not like—and recognized the legitimacy of the farm system provided players were not treated unfairly. Landis had won the battle, but he had lost the war. Now all that was left was to police the game for illegalities.

Which is precisely what he did. He was especially interested in curtailing Rickey, for whom he had developed a massive dislike. Landis was especially upset that St. Louis controlled teams in six leagues from Florida to the west coast and that it owned the rights to hundreds of minor league players, in addition to working agreements with nearly thirty additional minor league clubs. In 1938, Rickey was called in to see Landis at the Judge's winter home in Belleair, near St. Petersburg, Florida. Rumors flew that a major development was about to explode, but Rickey returned from the meeting untypically silent but exuding confidence without revealing anything. Once alone, he phoned Breadon in St. Louis. Whatever passed between the two will never be really known, but Landis' biographer, J. G. Taylor Spink, who was also the editor of the *Sporting News,* insisted Breadon asked Rickey if anything in their minor league operation was outside the law. "I'm absolutely in the clear, Sam," Rickey answered. "I've kept within all the rules and regulations. Landis has nothing on me."

In the third week of March the bomb finally exploded. Following weeks of investigation by his chief aide, Leslie O'Connor, Judge Landis announced that seventy-four Cardinal minor leaguers were to be freed, including Pete Reiser (who later won the National League batting title in 1941) and Skeeter Webb (who played shortstop for the 1945 World Champion Detroit Tigers). In what came to be known as the Cedar Rapids case, Landis charged that Rickey and Breadon had tried to obtain "complete control of the lower classification clubs through secret understandings," had broken the law banning a club from contracting away "its right and obligation to get competitive playing strength as needed and whenever obtainable," and had violated the order not to have any working agreement with more than one team in anyone league. Donald Ray Andersen, who wrote a doctoral dissertation on the Cardinal farm system, noted that "further investigation by the Commissioner's office revealed that Rickey and the Cardinals even controlled entire leagues."

Landis then fined Sacramento of the Pacific Coast League—which was run by Rickey's very close friend Phil Bartelme—Springfield of the Western Association, and Cedar Rapids of the Western League, for bargaining away their right "to get competitive playing strength as needed and whenever obtainable." The commissioner then released the text of Rickey's remarks in Florida. His sins, Landis publicly concluded, were as "big as the universe."

At first, Breadon rushed to Rickey's defense, charging Landis with selective discrimination because the Cardinals had started a system Landis had always opposed and was pledged to destroy. ( Yet Landis also freed ninety-one Detroit farmhands in January 1940.) Rickey, rather than Landis and other "do-nothings," was the true defender of the minors, Breadon insisted.

Still, the findings stunned and frightened Rickey. He knew that given the capriciousness and vindictiveness of the Judge's moods, it was even possible that he could be barred from baseball. He sought therefore to present his case to the public, declaring that the Cardinals had no legal connection with Cedar Rapids. But his rationalizations seemed lame in the face of the undisputed fact that the owner of that club was his personal friend and that another club in the same league was a Cardinal farm, thereby giving him illegal control of two teams. When Landis' investigators discovered Rickey's friend had panicked and altered checks and ledgers to conceal the relationship with the Cardinals, Landis' case seemed incontrovertible.

Rickey nevertheless contended he had done nothing wrong. But the more he tried to defend himself the more Breadon came to believe there was an ambiguity and therefore possible guilt in his protestations of innocence. Breadon stopped defending him and started confiding to close friends that Rickey had betrayed his trust. When Rickey protested that having a friend in the right place was hardly a crime and no collusion had been proven, Breadon would not be won over. He insisted his reputation had been stained, his honesty questioned. And to have the stigma broadcast by Landis, whom he loathed, was simply too much for Breadon to bear. Closeted in Breadon's office a week after the ruling, Rickey urged Breadon to sue Landis and try to have the decision revoked. J. Roy Stockton was present that morning and listened as Breadon rose from his desk chair, flushed with barely concealed anger. His business was endangered, he shouted at Rickey. "Breadon was a proud man," Stockton later wrote of that meeting, "a man of integrity. He was ashamed that the Cardinals had been caught cheating. We were present when Rickey was pleading that the Cardinals fight back at Landis. Breadon refused. He recalled that he had told Rickey the Cedar Rapids situation was wrong and had urged that it be cleared up."

Landis' verdict, though, was never really proven. Neither Rickey nor Breadon ever received a formal statement of charges. Nor were they permitted to present their side of the case and offer evidence, the right to witnesses, counsel, and cross-examination. Most significantly, the far from impartial Landis served as judge and jury, and was beyond the mere right of appeal. Again, as in so many of his previous decisions, the decision might have been different had the Cardinals or any of the other major or minor league clubs affected challenged him in the courts. But no one dared.

Enter Dizzy Dean again, who had only recently joined the Cubs. He visited Landis to complain he had signed his original contract without his parents' approval, hoping no doubt to sign with another club at a higher salary. Branch Rickey was to blame, he charged.

Rickey was appalled when told of Dean's allegation and probably believed a plot was developing to drive him out of baseball. Phoning Fred Ankenman in Houston, he asked for assistance. "Mr. Rickey called and said he needed proof that Dizzy was not under age when we signed him. I agreed to help."

Called to Chicago for a hearing, Judge Landis told Rickey, "Dean's charges sound rather conclusive," at which point Rickey pulled from his inner jacket pocket a copy of Dean's marriage license that Ankenman had found in the Harris County Courthouse, proving Dean had lied about his age.

When Landis showed the license to Dean, Dizzy broke into the boyish grin he affected and answered, "You got me, Judge."

In 1939, Branch Jr. received a surprising invitation from Larry MacPhail, who had recently become president of the bankrupt Brooklyn Dodgers. MacPhail offered him a role in the new farm system he said he was devising. Young Branch never hesitated. It may have been MacPhail's way of repaying Rickey for the Columbus and Cincinnati jobs. He really had nothing specific in mind for Branch Jr. but to MacPhail, an old debt was canceled. "I was in Brooklyn for a month," young Rickey said, "before I knew what my job was to be. Or even what my salary was."

At least, he and Mary were now independent. "He never wanted to hurt Daddy," says his sister Jane Rickey Jones, "but in St. Louis he had no sense of accomplishment, nothing really to do." In Brooklyn, it might be different, or so he hoped. Free of his father's domination, he and newly hired Mickey McConnell ran a small but healthy farm network with eleven clubs stretched from New York State to Arkansas and Santa Barbara in California.

They rented a rambling and comfortable house in Richmond Hill, about thirty minutes' drive from Dodger offices at 215 Montague Street in downtown Brooklyn. In the spring of 1941 he flew nine thousand miles in a two-week inspection tour of their minor league clubs.

MacPhail, however, was a difficult man to work with, his booming voice often humiliating his employees and his bouts of drunkenness making him mean and surly and irritable. The freedom Branch Jr. dreamed of was turning into an illusion. He complained to a friend that MacPhail made deals involving their minor leagues without ever asking him. Before long, he told one friend he "hated to enter the office every morning." Another friend wrote a confidential letter to his father describing MacPhail's mistreatment and saying how Branch Jr. "is really getting himself worked up more and more about the thought of quitting the Brooklyn organization immediately."

The father bided his time, kept in close touch with his son, and went out of his way to cross paths with him in his travels. His own rift with Breadon was now irreparable. Beginning in 1939, Breadon was traveling with the club, feeling more certain of himself, inviting friends and reporters into his suite for a drink, and then afterward often joining them in harmony. He no longer felt he needed Rickey to guide him through baseball's maze.

Rickey was quite aware of Breadon's ongoing resentment of him for the Cedar Rapids decision. He knew too that Breadon had been angered when he sent Medwick to the Dodgers and when Ray Blades, his personal choice, failed as Cardinal manager. He understood how proud and sensitive Breadon was and how his accumulated enmity had led him to challenge Rickey's contractual right to earn a percentage on every player sale. Breadon had even questioned the propriety of Rickey's serving as middleman—and picking up $25,000 for his trouble—in the sale some years earlier of the Browns. But Rickey too had his grievances. A few months earlier, smarting at Breadon's 10 percent wage reduction of employees not under contract, Rickey exploded in anger:

"Sam, I will dig ditches at a dollar a day rather than work for you one minute beyond the expiration of my contract."

It all came to a head when Rickey insisted that neither Hyde Park Beer nor any other beer company ought to be allowed to sponsor their radio games. Breadon put his foot down. It was past time (Rickey later told Warren Giles, then running Cincinnati) for Sam Breadon to run the Cardinals on his own. The signal was clear and Rickey made plans to leave at the expiration of his contract.

For several weeks after he chose to leave, he thought about quitting baseball. A moderately active member of Missouri's Republican Party, he had campaigned in the 1920s for a losing senatorial candidate; in the 1930s he had been offered the jobs of St. Louis fire and police commissioner, the chance to run for the Senate (he proposed instead that Arthur Hyde run; he did, and lost to Harry Truman) and for governor, which he also rejected. He supported Herbert Hoover, Alf Landon, Wendell Willkie, and Thomas E. Dewey in their quests for the presidency; Franklin Delano Roosevelt was his pet peeve, and he defined the New Deal as "the Dole System, something for nothing ... inflation, repudiation, and chaos." When FDR tried to pack the Supreme Court with more sympathetic jurists, Rickey went on the public speaking trail to denounce the action before Republican audiences. But in 1941 he broke with isolationists in foreign policy and signed an "Open Letter to Congress" for aid to Great Britain. When a Republican congressman from St. Louis objected that aid would be a step toward Roosevelt's dictatorship, Rickey answered that lend-lease aid did not go far enough. "I prefer a dangerous freedom to a peaceful, international permanent slavery," he told a rally.

Politics was, however, out of the question now. He had turned down his opportunities and besides, he was past sixty. He leaned toward a business career and seriously considered joining Mutual Benefit Life as vice-president for public relations. On the day set for his interview, Mutual's president—himself already past retirement age—balked at the entry of Rickey since it would threaten his status. When Rickey reached the firm's office in Newark the next morning, a friend informed him he had been rejected.

A few days later he accepted an offer to speak to the membership of the Agonis Club in Columbus. That morning, he told the five hundred people seated in front of him, he had read the *Dispatch* and its coverage of the war then under way in Europe. "Many countries are gone. I see my home and look at my table. My children. My neighbors and those who play bridge with me. Look at today's headlines."

He paused and there was complete silence in the vast room. He continued: "I was traveling in a plane yesterday when an editor who said he was not a religious man asked me: 'Mr. Rickey, what will abide?'"

Raising a Bible he had brought with him in his right hand, Rickey told his listeners, "This will abide."

He opened the book and leafing through its pages stopped at Matthew 5, the Sermon on the Mount. Reading aloud, he said, "Blessed are the poor in spirit; for theirs is the kingdom of heaven"; "Blessed are they who mourn, for they shall be comforted."

On October 19, 1942, he resigned. Soon after, he accepted a job as Larry MacPhail's successor with the Brooklyn Dodgers, mainly, as he explained decades after, because he wanted to be with his son.

# Chapter Seven

MacPhail was a hard act to follow. If the St. Louis press had been increasingly critical of Rickey, especially during his last years, New York newspapers alternately praised and mocked Leland Stanford MacPhail, one writer puckishly repeating Durocher's assessment of him as "half madman and half genius." Like Rickey (said another columnist), MacPhail "could deliver a few thousand words, out of which the following brief facts were winnowed." But unlike his onetime mentor, patron, and now successor, MacPhail was explosive, petulant, pugnacious, a nagging and frequent scold with a prickly temper, his face commonly beet red with anger, most notably after his many drinking bouts.

The two men shared one significant trait: a restless penchant for change and experimentation. MacPhail introduced night baseball in 1935 in Cincinnati; three years later he brought it to Ebbets Field. He used a yellow baseball for two games to try to improve the batter's perception. He placed a hidden microphone under home plate so radio audiences could hear arguments with the umpire—that lasted but one game. He broke the New York City baseball ban against play-by-play broadcasts. He imported Red Barber from Cincinnati (he had originally brought him to Ohio from a Florida station) and even put the team on experimental television. He signed Babe Ruth and Jesse Haines as coaches in 1938 to stimulate attendance. And he served free whiskey to the press, designed new green uniforms for ball-park attendants, and repainted aging Ebbets Field. Before he departed to join the army in 1942, MacPhail had initiated an early version of Old Timer ceremonies, begun a pension plan for office employees, had the club travel by air, and even tried to persuade players to wear batting helmets. He fired managers and assistants innumerable times, his temper tantrums magnified by his hoarse and ear-splitting voice, which a *New Yorker* writer compared to the bray of "an adult male moose." Rickey considered him a brilliant and daring risk taker and entrepreneur.

From the day they first met, Rickey had been drawn to MacPhail, as he was to so many similarly uninhibited men. He liked the idea that the redhead came from an industrious small-town Michigan family and had attended the University of Michigan Law School. And when the Cardinals' Columbus farm team sought a president in 1932, Rickey nominated MacPhail.

With Columbus, MacPhail had been no different from what he would be years later in the majors. Impetuously, he phoned a local furniture store one morning complaining about a delay in delivery. Told of a further delay, he burst into a fit of screaming and slammed the receiver down. Within seconds, his phone rang. It was Jane Ann Jones, the store secretary he had just insulted.

Larry MacPhail (left) and Rickey embracing. Rickey once recommended the Cincinnati Reds hire MacPhail as its president. MacPhail later ran the Brooklyn Dodgers. Rickey and MacPhail shared one significant trait: they both had a penchant for change and experimentation. When MacPhail resigned his Brooklyn post to join the Army during World War II, Rickey accepted the job as head of the Dodgers. (Courtesy of the Los Angeles Dodgers)

"No one speaks to me that way, or hangs up on me," she snarled back, hanging up just as abruptly. MacPhail was so impressed with her spirit he dropped everything and rushed to the store, first mollifying the young woman and then hiring her as his secretary. In 1938, she followed him to Brooklyn.

MacPhail was aware of his debt to Rickey. All the same, business was conducted as usual between the Cardinals and Dodgers, culminating in the trade for Joe Medwick in 1940, which MacPhail hoped would bring Brooklyn the pennant. Medwick, though, was beginning to fade. Still, MacPhail believed he had outsmarted the old man, which partly explains his hysterical reaction to the beaning of Medwick by Cardinal pitcher Bob Bowman shortly after he put on a Dodger uniform. By all contemporary press accounts, the Dodger president was in the press box, hardly able to see all the action on the field below; but shrieking curses, he raced down the aisles of the box seats onto the playing field, and later called for a criminal investigation, charging the beaning deliberate. The next morning his passion spilled over when he saw Bowman on the Hotel New Yorker elevator. Pursuing the hapless pitcher into the sprawling lobby and onto Eighth Avenue, he denounced him as an assassin and criminal. "He's so paranoiac he even thinks Rickey put the kid up to it," said one reporter who followed the cursing MacPhail into the street.

When the Dodger board of directors decided they had had enough of MacPhail's theatrics, despite the capture of the 1941 pennant—their first in twenty-one years—they happily accepted his announcement that he wanted to join Major General Brehon Somervell's staff in the Army Services of Supply unit. Their subsequent talent search finally turned to Rickey (whose 1942 Cardinals had just beaten the Dodgers by two games, St. Louis ending up with an incredible 106 victories and the Dodgers with an almost equally remarkable 104 wins), whose name had been broached to the board in 1935 by board member Jim Mulvey. For all his idiosyncrasies MacPhail had done very well for the organization. But as National League president Ford Frick confided to Mulvey: "MacPhail stirred things up; now Branch will be the one to restore quiet."

Only Branch Jr. was puzzled by the arrival of his father. "I don't know why Dad came over here. He could've gone to Philadelphia or the Browns," he told scout Howie Haak.

Within weeks after being hired, Rickey and Jane arrived with her sister Mabel and Jane's mother to take up residence in Bronxville. (Soon, though, they rented an apartment near the Dodger office and ballpark and later a home in Forest Hills Gardens in Queens.) They were grandparents for the third time, daughter Mary having given birth to a boy the year before. Almost immediately, Rickey became fascinated by Brooklyn's "fierce local nationalism—with distinct neighborhoods and distinct loyalties, each to his own neighborhood—a community of communities, an intelligent, proud, and ambitious city."

He was overjoyed to be head man again, free at last of Breadon's domination. Toward the end of his contract period in St. Louis, he and Singing Sam hardly talked to one another. Breadon was eager to rid himself of Rickey's influence, and he began to purge his loyalists in the front office. Most of the exiles followed Rickey to Brooklyn, where his spacious office at 215 Montague Street reflected his full control. The chairs were large and roomy, upholstered in soft leather, a huge sofa set against the wall for the legion of men who regularly trooped in to see him. Rickey sat at a mahogany double desk, which filled one corner of the room. Behind, on the wall, hung photographs of his family and of Leo Durocher, his arm cocked, ready to throw.

Typically his day at work ran very long, often from 8 A.M. until seven or eight in the evening; frequently he stayed until midnight, ignoring meals and impatiently and insensitively calling late night staff sessions or rousing people out of their beds at 6 A.M. to talk shop. Staff meetings concerned with the farm network's young players were the most arduous of all. No two meetings were alike, but Rickey leaned heavily on the analytic assessments of his staff plus his own uncanny ability to judge athletes. Every such meeting had a large blackboard as backdrop, and each player in the system was discussed and rated. And no session ended until every farmhand had been assessed. Often the meetings lasted long into the early morning hours so that speech became blurred and memories clouded—all except Rickey's. He stood alert, in the front of them, chalk in hand, and urged them on.

He took dozens of phone calls, read mountains of literature, league memorandums and staff reports and maintained a huge correspondence. Each morning a secretary pasted up the box scores of the preceding evening's farm team games for him to scrutinize. Budgetary analyses took much of his time. Would-be friends, job hunters, unsolicited dispensers of advice and criticism and assorted politicians sought

Rickey at work in the Dodger offices at 215 Montague Street in Brooklyn. (National Baseball Hall of Fame Library, Cooperstown, NY)

to be close to the team, many of them pleading for free passes and caps and jackets for their children.

"Once," said Barbara Buhler, who worked seven years in the Dodger office, "he ordered all of us to the Dodger private plane at six in the morning."

Occasionally he confided to Jane Ann Jones, his personal secretary now that MacPhail was gone, that the workload was too much for him, a protestation she took with a large dose of skepticism. He was an inveterate catnapper who would awaken alert and vigorous after a ten-minute doze. He often slept in the car on the way to the ballpark, a ten-minute drive from the office. Winters he napped on the sofa after lunch and even on the carpeted floor. As a boy, he once told her, he had learned to lie on the ground with other field workers after a heavy noon meal and he was entirely at ease—in spite of Jane Ann's complaints that it was beneath his dignity.

But she knew that when a doctor had recently told him to slow down, he had grinned and responded, "I certainly expect my funeral cortege to move at a dignified pace." More seriously, she recognized that when office affairs grew too restricting or exhausting he would order the club's five-seat Beechcraft aloft to satisfy his unquenchable urge to look at a center fielder in Elmira, watch a left-handed pitcher in Fort Worth, inspect the outfield grass in Durham, chat with manager Jake Pitler in Newport News. He was driven, as he had always been, by the ethic of work for work's sake, and also by his passionate faith in detailed and meticulous planning. "Luck," as he so often informed everyone within earshot, "is the residue of design."

It wasn't very long before sportswriters gave him the full New York media treatment. He was good news and good copy. Tom Meany of Marshall Field's newspaper *PM* christened him "Mahatma" after he read John Gunther's description of Gandhi in *Inside Asia* as "a combination of your father and Tammany Hall." Then he crowned Branch Jr. as "Twig." The press helped whet the appetites of Brooklyn fans for winning ballclubs.

Still, it was wartime. All baseball executives could do was wait out the war. But not Rickey. Not long after he arrived he set out to expand the club's scouting and farm system while every other club was cutting back drastically. His idea was to find and sign as many young and gifted athletes as possible so that when the war ended their pool of talent would be the largest in the sport.

Within three years he had amassed twenty-seven farm clubs, a greater number than any other team, including the Cardinals and Yankees. To Rickey, the clubs in the Class D leagues were as important as those in

AAA ball. Pitler's Piedmont League Newport News club, for example, had fifteen boys, seventeen years old or younger, including outfielder Edwin Snider, nicknamed Duke, and pitcher Clem Labine. Pitler, an instinctive and methodical teacher, was charmed with his adolescent charges. "When we took off in our bus on a road trip we were loaded with comic books and candy bars, but we carried practically no shaving cream."

The fans were patient until 1943, when he sold first-base hero slugger Dolph Camilli to the hated Giants. Rickey was hung in effigy in the stands behind third base, but the protest was mild compared with the firestorms following the Hornsby, Dean, and Medwick deals in St. Louis. For Rickey had detected a fatal flaw in Camilli everyone else had missed: the left-handed Camilli was hitting the ball to left field, "an indication that he was slipping. He hit the ball hard but didn't pull it to his power." Camilli, who refused to report to the Giants, played one more year with the Red Sox, batted .212, hit two home runs, and then departed.

The Camilli flap was nothing compared to the irrepressible Durocher's ability to provoke constant turmoil. "Leo was Dad's pet reclamation project," explained Branch Jr.

The Dodger manager was accused of loving gambling and gamblers. Reporters started complaining to Rickey and his staff that while they were often barred from the clubhouse, bookies and touts and assorted gambling celebrities were not. Ford Frick had gone to Rickey with the identical complaint. Rickey did nothing until at last word reached him that Durocher was gambling with his players in the clubhouse before games. Rickey summoned him to his office. Poker soothed their tensions, Durocher argued in his defense; besides, he went on, when he won he returned the money to players who performed well. "It was Leo's idea of an incentive plan," said Harold Roettger, one of Rickey's aides in the Dodger front office, laughing. Quite un–Mahatma-like, Rickey put his foot down. "From now on, there will be no poker with a higher limit than fifteen cents," he ordered.

Durocher, Rickey's darling, got off scot-free. But not shrill-whistling, insecure coach Charlie Dressen, an uncontrollable gambler on horseracing. Wishing to set an example, Rickey unexpectedly and unfairly fired the popular Dressen. Once done, he recognized it had been a mistake, since Dressen, by far the more vulnerable of the two men, had been made to shoulder Durocher's guilt. Inviting the cowed Dressen in for a meeting, Rickey made him pledge to end his gambling. A few months later, assured by Dressen the conversion was genuine, Rickey rehired him, but for $1,500 less. Cries of "slave owner" appeared in the press, but Tommy Holmes, who was covering the team's affairs for the *Brooklyn Eagle,* learned that Rickey had placed a blank check before Dressen with instructions to fill in the salary figure himself. "I needed the job," the intimidated Dressen said in explanation. "And I felt that's what Rickey wanted me to get."

If Dressen returned to the club humiliated and silently unhappy, Durocher blithely continued to carry on as he always had. In a 1943 game, Durocher confronted pitcher Bobo Newsom and accused him of throwing a spitter to embarrass catcher Bobby Bragan. The much traveled Newsom hotly denied the accusation. Durocher then petulantly turned to veteran reporter Tim Cohane of the *World-Telegram* and said, "Well, as far as I'm concerned—and you better check with Mr. Rickey—this guy is suspended indefinitely."

Sensing a good story, Cohane raced back to the press box and spread the word among his colleagues. When their pieces appeared that evening and in the next day's Saturday morning papers, shortstop Arky Vaughan, who nursed large grievances against Durocher, read the articles and, turning to his manager, accused him of making a scapegoat of Newsom. Throwing parts of his uniform in disgust at Durocher's feet, he announced he was quitting, a sentiment echoed by the very popular outfielder Dixie Walker.

When he read the newspaper stories in his Brooklyn apartment, Rickey told Jane he feared a mutiny. It may be justifiable, he mused, but it was a mutiny nonetheless. "It is very threatening to my administration and my authority," he told Roettger later that morning.

The phone rang and it was Cohane. An angry, nearly sputtering Cohane. Durocher had denied the veracity of his report, thus calling into question Cohane's reputation as a journalist. Rickey tried to assuage the furious reporter, but Cohane would have none of it. What he wanted, he said, was a full-scale meeting in the clubhouse at which he, Cohane, would be permitted to question Durocher and the players involved. "We'll see who's lying," he shouted over the phone. Rickey blinked. He shifted his argument, trying to delay the inevitable. "Well, Mr. Cohane, you know I never visit ballparks on Sunday." When the maneuver failed, he acceded only after Cohane pleaded his personal integrity and reputation for honesty were at stake. "Now *that* is a different story," answered Rickey. "I'll be there."

The next day, a few hours before a Sunday game, Rickey perched on a large trunk, the players at the edge of the room, listening to Cohane speak. Frank Graham of the *Sun* was also there and he observed Durocher "white with rage and shaken by the hostility of his players, who glared at him from every corner of the clubhouse, all the time saying he had been misquoted." As Cohane talked, Rickey held a cigar tightly in his right hand, whispering from time to time to Branch Jr., seated alongside him.

Cohane resembled a district attorney. Repeatedly he destroyed Durocher's credibility until, finally, his case was set down—the manager had lied. All eyes spontaneously turned to Rickey: What was he going to do now with his troublemaker? Rickey flicked the ashes from his cigar and left, silent and shaking his head. The next day, accounts in the press speculated that Durocher's days were numbered.

But he survived. Newsom was sold to the Browns, Vaughan and Walker went unpunished, and the insurrection fizzled out. Privately, Rickey met with Durocher and warned him—as he would do often in the years ahead—that his uncontrolled temper and would-be friends would surely lead him into trouble, trouble even he, Rickey, would not be able to rescue him from. Act like a leader of men, Leo, he advised.

Publicly, though, he declared, "No player or players, no president, no public, nobody, can run a club for a manager. Durocher will have my undivided loyalty and support."

Like most Americans, Rickey was affected by the war. All his sons-in-law were in uniform. His daughter Alice had qualified as an aviator in the Women's Air Service Pilots. Breaking his life pattern, he attended two Sunday games on behalf of the Red Cross and war bond drives, answering those who once again raised the hoary issue of hypocrisy: "I would do whatever is necessary and my personal reasons would not be violated either." He traveled throughout the country to sell war bonds for the Treasury Department and even filed an application with the United States Civil Service Commission, hoping to be placed somewhere on a full-time basis. "He is war-conscious, more than any other man in the national pastime," wrote an adoring midwestern columnist who had heard him speak in Peoria, Illinois.

For the Rickeys, the years following the surrender of Germany and Japan were among their happiest of times. In 1946 he ordered his farm department employees to spend as much of the season as need be finding and acquiring minor league clubs to accommodate the many young veterans they had signed during the war. He was $300,000 in debt, but his income and reputation continued to soar. He was running the Dodgers with a free hand, and when John Smith, president of Pfizer Chemical Corporation, and his wife increased their ownership to 50 percent of the club after World War II, he was overjoyed; the rest of his working days, he must have surely believed, would be spent with Brooklyn.

**Leo Durocher, left, Dodger manager, smiles at Rickey in the Dodgers' clubhouse at Ebbets Field after the game with Cincinnati on September 28, 1944, when Rickey announced that Durocher had signed a one year contract to pilot the club again in 1945. (AP/Wide World Photos)**

Sundays, he and Jane often drove north to Quaker Hill in exurban Pawling, New York, to visit with OWU alumni Pherbia and Pinky Thornberg. He loved walking the rustic countryside filled with working farms and attending their lovely nondenominational church nearby. Afternoons he enjoyed the restfulness of their home with its comfortable chairs, oversized brass candlesticks, cabinets filled with Chinese dishware and artifacts gathered from Thornberg's many years spent in China. Often he read in their spacious library, preferring technical books on farming but on one afternoon becoming absorbed with Viktor Kravchenko's *I Chose Freedom,* a story of Soviet espionage. On other occasions he visited with Pherbia's brother, Lowell Thomas, who lived close by, or with other neighbors—newsman Ed Murrow, the Reverend Norman Vincent Peale, Governor Thomas E. Dewey. Arthur Flemming, then president of OWU, liked to stop by to talk politics. But on other Sundays he would perform and entertain, Pherbia Thornberg recalled, once balancing three baseballs one on top of the other to the enormous glee of the children present and another time devising dining table games such as one where guests had to answer deliberately inane questions with equally foolish responses.

The Dodgers, meanwhile, showed a net profit of $451,000 in 1946, a dramatic improvement over past years. Paid attendance was more than 1.7 million, but more than half the profit, $239,000, came from selling surplus farm players to postwar big league clubs hungry for talent. Rickey's formula for success was still the same—discovering and developing latent talent. When, for example, pitcher Carl Erskine left the navy in 1946 and became a free agent, Rickey brought his parents to the Kenmore Hotel in Boston to talk about their son's future.

"My father had been a farm boy in Boone County, Indiana, and Mr. Rickey spoke feelingly of his own farm boy days in southern Ohio and the values it had given him," said Erskine. "Mr. Rickey then added: 'I understand the Braves want to sign Carl. But they've never beaten us in a deal I wanted to make. What do you want?'

"I wasn't much of a pitcher, even with those school no-hitters and an 18–3 record in the navy. I had a fastball, but not much of a curve, and no change of pace. After the season [at Danville in the Three-I League] ended, Bob Finch asked me to play in Cuba that winter. I told him I couldn't. I was planning to marry Betty that November and we wanted to start a home of our own in Anderson.

"A few days later Mr. Rickey himself called me. 'Carl,' he said, 'you have the aptitude and temperament to be a big league star. But you haven't much of a curve and no change of pace. We need young men like you as quickly as possible. You'll gain a full year's experience by pitching in Cuba next winter.'

"'But I want to get married in November,' I said.

"'Move the date up to October,' Mr. Rickey suggested. 'And remember this—you'll be doing more for your bride if you pitch this winter. You'll make good money and be worth more next year.'"

Erskine gave in, married in October, and pitched under the tutelage of Lefty Gomez of the Cienfuegos club in a four-team Cuban league. "The experience and conditioning did more for me than anything else," he said.

Ironically, the more profits the club earned and the better the team performed on the field, the more harshly Rickey was attacked. The *World-Telegram* columnist Joe Williams turned sharply anti–Rickey in 1946, charging that Rickey had foolishly lost the pennant with injudicious trades.

Williams' criticisms were mild in contrast to the six-year effort of *Daily News* sports editor Jimmy Powers to bring down the Dodger president. Rickey, his family, and staff were accustomed to his being lampooned and caricatured by cartoonists, but Powers' ceaseless and humorless barbs nagged at him emotionally until his staff could take no more. From 1943 until 1949, when it abruptly stopped, Powers' column "The Powerhouse," published in the most widely read newspaper in the country, poured out his venom. Arthur Mann calculated that between June and December 1946, eighty columns blasted Rickey and seventy-four others contained passing insults. Powers charged that Rickey's blasts at the Mexican League's player raids in 1946 were simply his way of keeping salaries low; that Rickey hated Jim Mulvey; that he was really trying to move to the Yankees; that he buried players in the minors. Powers dubbed him "El Cheapo," describing him as a "tight-fisted man who paid his players coolie salaries." Calling on the club to fire him, Powers sponsored a contest and asked, "Shall we send him over Niagara Falls in a barrel? Shall we maroon him on a Bikini atoll?"

He and Jane were stunned at the incessant bombardment, with its inexplicable hatred and encouragement of public contempt. He had never even met Powers. "Describe what he's wearing," he said to Harold Parrott at an exhibition game at Yankee Stadium, "so I can turn and see what he looks like."

Unable to contain himself any longer, he finally ordered his staff to prepare a detailed rebuttal. What emerged was a thirty-seven-page document "designed to confront him [Powers] with the truth." By late July 1946, the report declared "it was apparent that the Powers smear campaign was deleteriously affecting the operations of the Dodger organization. Players were disturbed; business personnel wondered if matters were as they seemed or as Powers described them. Potential recruits veered away from Dodger scouts to sign contracts with other, supposedly more trustworthy, clubs. Fans, other sports writers, picked up Powers' phrases and used them in conversation and in print." Rickey's presence was everywhere and his handwritten comments are scattered throughout the memo. It was circulated to John Smith and Walter O'Malley, Roettger, Mickey McConnell, Parrott, and Branch Jr., asking for their comments and whether they thought legal action was desirable. "Mr. Rickey charges us all to absolute silence with respect to this document," Finch wrote. "It must be held in the strictest confidence."

The document rejected Powers' El Cheapo crusade, citing Dodger bonus payments and salaries as among the highest in the league. The salaries of Dixie Walker, Augie Galan, Peewee Reese, Peter Reiser, and Ed Head were offered as examples.

The conclusion was vintage Rickey: Powers' charges were "poisonous smokescreens, personal vilifications, innuendoes, colored exaggerations, half-truths, untruths, flat lies, a disgrace to the sports writing profession."

Luckily, cooler heads prevailed. Smith told him, "Your mode of refuting Powers' assertions dignifies them and adds weight to them." Instead, he proposed leaking favorable material to sympathetic newspapermen.

Harold Roettger counseled legal action but was reluctant to open the Dodgers' books to public scrutiny. McConnell favored a defamation suit but also worried about making salaries public. Parrott and Branch Jr. both warned against doing anything to alienate the press, who would clearly interpret any suit as a threat against the First Amendment and rally around Powers. And Walter O'Malley cautioned against any hasty action, telling Rickey: "Laugh it off, roll with the punches. You see, a suit will mean that every newspaper will turn against you."

Faced with the conflicting advice, Rickey retreated, still furious at Powers but saying nothing publicly. Nothing more was heard until early in 1949 when an anonymous correspondent sent Rickey a copy of a letter Powers had written.

"I talked to the captain last night [publisher of the *News*] and he told me not to worry over latrine gossip picked up by the FBI. That if Winchell and the rest of the Jews had their way America would be a vast concentration camp from Maine to California. There wouldn't be enough barbed wire to hold back all the decent Christians maligned by the Jews and those who run with them. In short, I was in pretty good company with him, Col. McCormick, Joe Kennedy and several other decent family men.... How in hell can I be termed 'pro–Nazi' simply because I don't happen to like certain crackpot politicians and Jews?"

At last, he had Powers. The release of the letter so soon after the annihilation of six million European Jews would have ruined Powers in New York. Rickey's aides gloated and urged him to release it quickly. Yet he refused to do so, recognizing that the Powers plague was finally over and done with. To Arthur Mann he confessed, "I've never sunk low enough to do a thing like this and I should never have taken him seriously. Now we can forget him." Later, to Parrott, he confessed, "I've never met him, you know. But I thought he was a responsible person. We should never have taken him seriously."

Someone in the front office called Powers, however, and informed him that Rickey held his letter. Immediately, without a word of explanation ever, Powers stopped writing negatively about Rickey.

Not long after Rickey sent the silent Powers and his family free passes. Responding in a letter, his erstwhile inquisitor wrote: "I appreciate your thoughtfulness very much. I too wish you a lot of luck, and if there is anything I can do for you during the season I will be glad to do all I can to help you."

Powers' "El Cheapo," however, became part of folklore and even took roots within his official family. When Bob Cobb arrived with a delegation from the west coast to negotiate a working agreement between Brooklyn and their Hollywood Stars of the Pacific Coast League, the cab driver at LaGuardia Airport raised his eyebrows when told to drive to 215 Montague Street.

"Why there?" he asked Cobb, who was in the taxi with two of his co-owners and scout Howie Haak.

"Why, to see Branch Rickey," answered the startled Cobb. "Then, Mister, you better sew up your pants pockets or he'll have your money before you leave."

In another story, most likely apocryphal, Rickey rejected an aide's request for a raise but tried to soften the blow with advice on the virtues of poverty. "Remember," he informed the disconsolate man, "happiness always lurks close to a poor man."

"Hmph," the aide responded. "That's the trouble, Mr. Rickey. It lurks and lurks and lurks."

In spite of these widely repeated tales, the 1946 Dodgers spontaneously presented him in late September with a Chris-Craft boat they named "Dodger," each player paying about $300 toward the gift. When Dixie Walker approached the microphone at home plate for the presentation, the *Times* reported that "Rickey was almost overcome by the gesture and found it difficult to speak." Said Walker, afterward: "Everybody on the team contributed on an equal-share basis. We thought he deserved it."

On the same day, Carl Furillo received a gift too, a gold lapel pin from the 77th Division Association, his service unit during the war, together with a watch from admiring neighbors in Reading, Pennsylvania, where he had been born and reared. "I was especially glad of what we did for Mr. Rickey," he said. "One thing I always liked about him. When he gave his word, that was it. And he had promised me a raise. When the season was over, he called me in and I got it. Of course, I think I deserved it. I was making $5,000 at the time."

The 1946 pennant race ended in a dead heat with the St. Louis team he had assembled. In their first playoff game, Ralph Branca was beaten 4–2 on the hitting of catcher Joe Garagiola. The second game was played in Ebbets Field and the Cardinals won that too, 8–4, and then went on to beat the Red Sox in a seven-game World Series.

Once the Series was finished, Rickey sat with a reporter and peered into the future. "The Cardinals deserved to win this one, and they did. But it will be a long time before St. Louis finishes ahead of Brooklyn again."

Two years later St. Louis finished in second place, ahead of the third-place Dodgers. Nevertheless, he was essentially correct: not until 1964 would another St. Louis team win the pennant, while Brooklyn became one of the powers of the National League.

# Chapter Eight

In the years after, Rickey boasted of his "glue man," as he referred to Eddie Stanky. He had the incomparable Reese at shortstop, whom he presented with a copy of Dwight Eisenhower's *Crusade in Europe* "so Harold may develop into a leader of men." There were a long list of promising youngsters on the farms. And, at last, Rickey the teacher had fashioned the training facility he had long dreamed of in Vero Beach, Florida.

He learned of the site's availability from a local Florida businessman who'd heard the navy was about to close down its air station. His interest aroused, he dispatched Mickey McConnell and Buzzie Bavasi, who worked for Rickey in the front office specializing in the Dodger farm club operation.

"We found barracks large enough to house all our players (a total of 480 to populate twenty-four teams at the peak of our expansion), hangars for indoor workouts in inclement weather, furnished cottages for married players and staff members, several playing fields, a swimming pool and a lake for fishing. Office space, a dining hall, and a recreation area, dressing and training rooms, a theater for lectures and movies, also were available. It wasn't the Waldorf, but it was more than adequate," said McConnell.

There was also an excellent air strip for the Dodger plane. Rickey flew to Vero Beach to see for himself. It was, he decided, perfect, although when he reported to the board of directors, Walter O'Malley said the expense was too great and the idea frivolous. Just the same, Rickey was in command, and his word was to proceed. It was for him a dream come true, the kind of training facility in which his teaching practices could be applied and the most outlandish experiments tested. It was, by far, the most comprehensive and scientific training camp in all athletic history.

# Chapter Eight

One week before the scheduled opening in 1947, he summoned all the managers, coaches, and scouts from the vast and sprawling system to Vero Beach, where he personally instructed them in basic precepts underlying Vero Beach: everyone in the organization was to teach fundamentals and handle strategy in the same way so players could easily move between teams and assignments. To determine what would be taught and how, he named special instructors. George Sisler would lecture on batting, scout Wid Matthews on bunting, Pepper Martin on base running, Clyde Sukeworth on catching, Sisler on first-base play, Fresco Thompson on second base, Durocher on shortstop, Dressen on third base and signals, Ray Blades on the outfield, Burt Shotton on managerial strategy, and, finally, Rickey himself on pitching.

That first March he seemed to be everywhere in his baggy old khaki trousers, a flopping hat or baseball cap perched on his head. Mornings he lectured on baseball techniques, morality, courage, and religious faith as he had to his earlier Ohio Wesleyan, Allegheny, Michigan, Brown, and Cardinal teams; later, at work in the camp office, he plotted trades and transfers of players, haggled over contracts, fussed over a myriad of details associated with running a baseball empire, huddled with his aides. Afternoons he was back out on the playing fields.

On one occasion that spring a coach at Hastings College in Nebraska asked why baseball didn't employ track coaches to teach sprinting since so much running in baseball was the sprint, the longest being slightly more than 120 yards if an inside-the-park home run was hit. When Mickey McConnell passed the suggestion to him he barely paused. "The man is right. We'll hire a track coach, build a running track, and teach sprinting at Dodgertown," the name he had given the new complex. Soon after he installed a batting tee with instructions it be used as an integral part of the batting program.

In that same year MacPhail was president of the Yankees. Among his first acts was raiding his former ball club, luring away coaches Charlie Dressen and Red Corriden and scout Ted McGrew. Rickey had released Corriden and McGrew, and they were, of course, free to go. But when he learned Dressen was leaving, he hit the ceiling. Only a few days before they had reached an agreement. According to notes dictated after Dressen left his office that day, the coach was "very happy with it [the contract]." Rickey had confided in Dressen—again, according to his notes—that should he be offered a managerial slot "I would not only be willing to let him go but ... I would help him get the job." He had even phoned the Pirates in Dressen's presence but they were uninterested. Then he turned to Dressen and asked, "Do we have an agreement?" And, said Rickey afterward, still seething at what he considered to be an act of disloyalty, Dressen answered, "We certainly do." "Let's state it again," Rickey went on. "Your salary is to be $12,500 and you are to receive an additional $2,500 if the attendance equals or exceeds 1,250,000. Is that correct?"

Dressen nodded. An agreement.

"Then this is a definite agreement and you are not to consider a coaching job or management of any minor league club. Do we understand each other very clearly that you are not to consider any job in baseball other than a major league management job?"

He was insistent on reaching an understanding with Dressen, a weak and easily influenced man who he believed "was an easy mark for MacPhail, for whom a public fight was meat and drink."

MacPhail refused to retreat, sneering at Rickey's complaint and going to great pains to explain to five different writers in the Yankee press box one day that the men he sought to hire were free agents. Why, he told Dan Parker of the *Mirror,* just working for the "miserly" Rickey meant a $14,000 loss in salary for Dressen. And then he dropped his bombshell. Dressen had come to him for a job, but so had Durocher.

To Rickey, the insertion of Durocher's name was another matter entirely. But why, Rickey wondered, was MacPhail acting so badly? His manager, Joe McCarthy, had quit him and former Yankee star catcher Bill Dickey also left quickly. Was a reunion with his onetime Dodger manager in his mind? Or, asked Rickey of his staff, was he up to something else, something Rickey couldn't yet understand?

Years later Durocher wrote that MacPhail had phoned Joe Trimble of the *Daily News* to say that Walter O'Malley and John Smith had told him "in confidence" it was all right to deal with Durocher, an obvious tactic—if true—to embarrass Rickey.

But Byzantine plots on the Dodger board were far from Rickey's mind and he turned to confront the specter of Durocher *and* MacPhail. To him, one was tempestuous, belligerent, but utterly charming when he had to be; the other was growing nasty and unpredictable.

Durocher's gambling friends still troubled him. Not long before, he had been barred from the Dodger clubhouse by a burly man. "You can't go in, Pop," said the guardian of the door. Huffing with anger, he turned to Parrott and Tommy Holmes of the *Brooklyn Eagle.* "Harold, Tommy, who is that man?" "Why he's George Raft's bodyguard, Mr. Rickey," answered Parrott.

Judge Landis, who died in January 1944, had always liked the rascal in Durocher and winked at his activities on and off the field but nevertheless compiled an extensive file on his associations. When Landis' close friend Westbrook Pegler concocted a series of vile and untrue columns associating Durocher with organized crime and a major check-cashing swindle, Rickey paled. He didn't like Pegler's poison-pen articles any more than he had Powers', but there was a whiff of corruption in the air. Gamblers had already penetrated some minor leagues. Boxing champ Rocky Graziano had failed to report a bribery offer. And the college basketball scene was filled with rumors of "fix."

Something had to give. Calling in Arthur Mann, the freelance writer who also served as his personal troubleshooter, he told him to visit the new commissioner, Albert "Happy" Chandler, and ask him to give Durocher a warning.

Mann flew to Cincinnati where Chandler had his office. A warm and affectionate man, Chandler had been a good governor of Kentucky who had opened the state's first psychiatric hospital and had built its initial four-lane highway.

"I read Landis' file on Durocher. So I knew who I was up against," he announced to Mann.

Armed with Rickey's request, he called Durocher several weeks later while he was on the West Coast; Durocher was in Hollywood rehearsing for the *Jack Benny Program*. Pegler had recently published a column charging that Raft had held a marathon crap game in the Dodger manager's apartment, neglecting to mention that Durocher was away and had not given his permission. Chandler met a frightened Durocher on the golf course of the Claremont Country Club in Berkeley in December and bluntly threatened to suspend him if he didn't avoid associating with gamblers. "This is the last warning," he said. "The last one."

The issue seemed forgotten until the morning MacPhail was shown a ghosted "Durocher Says" column from the *Brooklyn Eagle*. "This is a declaration of war," said Harold Parrott, putting words into Durocher's mouth. "I want to wallop them Yankees because of MacPhail and Dressen. [I] regard Branch Rickey as my father."

Parrott was working for the Dodgers, and it was a typical piece of puff during the preseason lull. MacPhail blamed Rickey for the column and denounced him as "that Brooklyn hymn singer." Before long, events were beyond anyone's control.

In an exhibition game between the two teams in Havana's Gran Stadium, Durocher informed Rickey he had seen MacPhail and his assistant Arthur "Red" Patterson seated in the Yankee box separated by a rail from two alleged members of organized crime—Connie Immerman, who had once run New York's Cotton Club then left to manage Connie's Inn in Havana, and Memphis Engelberg, one of the few World War II GIs who described his civilian occupation as "handicapper."

Durocher knew them both very well but he fumed at the scene. Was there a dual standard of behavior, he asked Rickey? Weren't the four men in the Yankee box? Why wasn't Chandler as interested in MacPhail as he was in him?

Rickey agreed.

"I fired Charley Dressen once because of his association with one of those gamblers. If I saw these men in the Brooklyn ball park, I would have them thrown out. Yet there they are as guests of the president of the Yankees. Why, my own manager can't even say hello to this actor, George what's-his-name. He won't have anything to do with these gamblers. But apparently there are different rules for Durocher and other rules for the rest of baseball."

When the enterprising Dick Young of the *Daily News* heard the remarks, he visited MacPhail's box and asked for his version. MacPhail refused to answer and, reported Tom Meany of *PM* the next day, "invited Dick to get the hell out of his box."

Later, MacPhail denied the two were present as his guests but added: "As for myself, I'd much rather have Engelberg as my guest at a ball game than Rickey. Judge Landis told me his one mistake as baseball commissioner was in not barring Rickey from the game as a result of that Cedar Rapids deal where he was covering up players. Landis told me he never encountered anything to equal this case for brazen contempt of baseball law."

But it was Durocher's, and not MacPhail's, conduct that continued to arouse hostility.

The Catholic Youth Organization and the National Catholic Welfare Conference condemned Durocher for his conduct "both on and off" the field. The CYO withdrew from the Dodger Knothole Club, since the Dodger manager was "undermining the moral and spiritual training of our young boys."

Rickey moved to try to head off impending disaster. Chandler was a "sincere" man but had somehow gone off "the deep end somewhere on this thing." In a "personal and confidential" letter to the commissioner, he wrote in urgent tones, defending his manager and asking him to reduce the pressure.

> Confirming my telephone conversation with you, the names of the parties referred to are Max Engelberg, known generally as "Memphis," and Conrad Immerman, known as "Connie." Connie is the boss man of the Casino in Havana. Memphis is alleged to be the odds-fixer, the top man of the fra-

ternity around New York. You will undoubtedly find Memphis and Dressen et al. together very frequently.

It is not easy for Leo to understand that he cannot say, "Hello, George," to a person he has known for many years and a person, too, who has never bet on a baseball game and does not frequent race tracks nor bet on horses—an acquaintance that dates back many years—and at the same time find that the President of one of our great baseball clubs and other officials are in intimate relationship with men like Connie and Memphis. All this, too, without apparent criticism.

It is my opinion that Leo has completely cut acquaintanceship with "George" and he has avoided as best he could, I am sure, any contact whatever with such persons as Connie and Memphis and I don't believe that at any future time he will renew a speaking acquaintanceship with men of that type. I resent the criticism of persons who will say to you, as was said to me, that ... Leo Durocher [has] done more to hurt baseball in the past few weeks than has been done to build it up in forty years when such persons, at the same time, were living in glass houses so vulnerable. Besides, I think something ought to be done about it and I know that you will take proper steps.

Chandler claims he answered Rickey by phone.

"Can you handle Leo Durocher?" he asked rhetorically. "Well, I don't believe you can."

When Rickey appealed for time and patience, Chandler said there was an accumulation of evidence against Durocher that compelled him to act. "I've given you your chance, Branch. Now I'll handle him." Actually, Chandler was under heavy press criticism for behaving as a do-nothing commissioner when compared to Landis, and as if in reply he told a Cincinnati reporter just after the conversation with Rickey that someone important soon would be kicked out of baseball.

Chandler called a hearing in Sarasota on March 24, but Jane's brother died and Rickey left for the funeral, leaving O'Malley in charge of Brooklyn's and Durocher's defense. This worried him. Two days before the hearing he wrote ex–Senator George Williams of Missouri, a close friend he had also asked to be present at the hearing, "I don't believe Walter O'Malley regards the hearing as serious." So concerned was he that in outlining the entire case on the back of an advertisement for women's nylons, he asked himself: "O'Malley Friendly to MacPhail?"

When the rivals to the dispute gathered they tried to back away from the heat of the dispute, which by then seemed more inane than ever. Durocher explained his ghosted column was "just another rhubarb" and offered to apologize. He and MacPhail shook hands, O'Malley beamed and reported optimistically to Rickey the feud had been amicably muted and the turmoil was over.

Chandler, though, was of a different mind.

He fined the Yankee and Dodger clubs $2,000 each, and Parrott $500. (When Parrott protested he had wronged no one, he was forgiven and the money returned.) And Chandler suspended Durocher for one year.

When the news arrived Durocher was seated with Rickey in his Brooklyn office.

"What for?" screamed the outraged manager, jumping up. *"What for?"*

His new wife, the actress Laraine Day, was so upset she immediately blamed Rickey, hanging his photo on their bathroom wall. Unknown to her, Rickey had already decided to pay Durocher for his year of non-managing.

MacPhail was astounded to learn that his resentment of Rickey had gotten badly out of hand. The last thing he ever wanted was to have Durocher banned. When he heard the news he called a press conference and announced: "Commissioner Chandler didn't have sufficient grounds on which to hang a five-minute suspension on Durocher."

Red Smith was there for the *Herald-Tribune* and in his next day's column he described the Yankee boss as a "clown and a mountebank."

Parrott, who despised O'Malley, believed—though without substantial evidence—O'Malley had masterminded the whole affair. "Rickey had reason to wonder who had put the churchmen up to this," said Parrott, considering O'Malley's considerable influence with the Catholic Church. "The Catholics had never boycotted Hitler or Mussolini the way they went after Leo." And both Tommy Holmes and Arthur Mann were so incensed that they later wrote extensively about the suspension, Holmes devoting a large portion of his history of the Dodgers to it while Mann considered it worth an entire book.

Durocher was understandably angry and hurt and came to believe he was the victim of a power struggle in which Rickey's opponents had laid plans to take control of the Dodgers. As Rickey's man he had been caught in the crossfire and made to pay for it.

Rickey's attitude varied, but he was increasingly uneasy with O'Malley's tactics. After the Los Angeles *Herald-Examiner* headlined: DUROCHER BRANDED LOVE THIEF, when he and actress Laraine Day eloped to Mexico in defiance of a California court's divorce decree, Rickey mournfully read the accompanying story and turned to Parrott, saying, "This should make great ammunition for Jimmy Powers, Joe Williams—and of course, O'Malley."

When Durocher's suspension was announced, Rickey flew to visit

Chandler at his home in Versailles, Kentucky. He appealed to Chandler's
sense of decency and justice.

"I believe MacPhail and others may have misled you badly," he said
as they sat in the large annex behind the main house, Chandler at his
huge desk, Rickey in a comfortable black leather chair, surrounded by
photographs of Gandhi, Franklin Delano Roosevelt, David Ben Gurion,
and dozens of other world figures Chandler had met while a senator.

Chandler was adamant. "I was right, Branch. Absolutely, positively
right. The suspension was just an accumulation of things." Durocher, he
continued, pressing his case on Rickey, was "amoral," and an "associate
of known and notorious gamblers."

Yet, Rickey wasn't convinced, and like the lawyer he still was, he
fenced with his witness, looking for an opening.

"And MacPhail? Do you believe *him*? Does he *ever* tell the truth?"

"Aw, Branch," Chandler drawled, "sober, he's just about the sweet-
est man in baseball. Drunk, though, he's a mean bastard. Maybe you all
caught him on the down side."

"Besides," and he leaned forward in confidence, his voice hushed
as if someone were listening, "I'm sure MacPhail will not be in baseball
for very much longer."

"Lift the suspension, Albert. As a personal favor, if need be. You
have no real case, anyway."

Chandler took a deep puff of his cigar. "I'll mull it over, Branch, I
sure will."

Rickey rose to leave and Chandler handed him a smoked Kentucky
ham and then drove him back to the airport, waving to him continuously
until Rickey could no longer see him from the air.

He had to find a manager.

"I am falling out of a window," he shouted to his staff of aides and
scouts gathered in his Brooklyn office. "I am on the ledge and on the
verge of going over. The sidewalk is twenty feet below. One name—one
name can save me."

In the wake of the suspension he had called them in. Seated in his
swivel chair, waving his ragged cigar in the air as if he were dropping
through the sky and trying to save himself, holding in his other hand a
sheet of yellow legal paper, he proclaimed, "There are eight names in
this paper. One of them can save me—save you—one of them can manage the Dodgers this year. You have got to help me pick the right man.
Or down I go." It was a splendid performance, one which he loved performing and they watching.

Rickey wanted Joe McCarthy. Old Marse Joe, the former Cub and Yankee manager, a quiet and thoughtful man, was in Rickey's mind a winner. But McCarthy was feeling poorly after having left MacPhail in anger, and decided baseball could do without him for a while. Other names were proposed but the only one on the list all agreed could do the job and fit Rickey's requirements was Burt Shotton, the Brownheim, Ohio, native who had first played for him with the 1913 Browns. After first meeting Rickey, Shotton had quickly concluded that the quizzical, quick-thinking thirty-two-year-old manager just fresh from law school and the University of Michigan campus was the brightest man he had ever encountered in the game. "Rickey," he told his teammates, "was the first manager I ever knew who even pretended that ballplayers had brains." Rickey returned the compliment and made the dignified Shotton his main "Sunday manager." And when Breadon fired him in 1925, Rickey recommended that Shotton be his successor rather than the hot-tempered Hornsby. Rickey never again lost contact with him. In 1928 Shotton managed the Phillies because Rickey recommended him for the job. Seven years later he was leading the Rochester Red Wings, a top Cardinal farm, and between 1936 and 1941, he won two pennants for the Columbus Red Birds, another St. Louis farm team. For his last year at Columbus, the *Sporting News* named him Minor League Manager of the Year.

Shotton was living in partial retirement in Florida, scouting a bit and fishing. One morning, as he was leaving for a ballfield in Miami, a telegram arrived, which he placed in his pocket. Hours later, his wife at his side, he tore open the envelope. "Be in Brooklyn tomorrow morning," it read. "See nobody. Say nothing. Rickey."

Shotton turned to his wife matter-of-factly. "Rick needs me." There was a pennant to be won and always, always in Rickey's thoughts was a young black ballplayer named Jackie Robinson, who needed to be shepherded through his pioneering season.

# Chapter Nine

"The very first thing I did when I came into Brooklyn in late 1942 was to investigate the approval of ownership for a Negro player. There was a timeliness about the notion. The Negro in America was legally but never morally free. I thought: if the right man with control of himself could be found..."

On a cold January morning in 1943—his notes indicate the appointment was for 9:45 A.M.—Rickey walked into George V. McLaughlin's office at the Brooklyn Trust Company. His goal was to obtain McLaughlin's acquiescence in what was then widely believed an impossible and madcap scheme.

McLaughlin's bank controlled the Dodgers by virtue of a 50-percent trusteeship of the Ebbets family stock. McLaughlin was a onetime police commissioner, a power in Brooklyn's not inconsiderable Roman Catholic–dominated Democratic Party and among the borough's dominant Irish population. His approval counted, very much.

Only he and Rickey were present at that meeting, but in later years both agreed with the published reports of what had taken place. (Several years later, Rickey also told Arthur Mann—who was writing a book on Jackie Robinson's coming—what had happened that morning.) Rickey began by explaining that the 1941 pennant winner of the MacPhail era was decimated by the military draft and age. Dolph Camilli, the Most Valuable Player in 1941, Whitlow Wyatt, Billy Herman, and the others would simply be unable to perform as well after demobilization. The Cardinals had beaten the Yankees in the World Series and would dominate the league for years to come unless Brooklyn acted now.

McLaughlin lifted his eyebrows and sat back in silence as Rickey went on.

Given the war and its inevitable drain on men and resources, he said, slowly leading to his point, all ballclubs had been cutting back on their scouting and player development expenses until the war was ended. What he was now proposing was that Brooklyn commit themselves to exactly the opposite tactic. Let us, he urged McLaughlin, enlarge our scouting staff and seek out and sign as many young players as possible. Let us be ready for the end of the war. "We are hoping to beat the bushes," he ended up, *"and that might include a Negro player or two."*

McLaughlin was hardly surprised at the man's nerve. That, of course, was why he had been selected after MacPhail left to join the army. Once Rickey took hold of an idea—however brilliant or mad it might be—he couldn't abandon it, dragging people into his scheme as confidants and conspirators, talking incessantly about its formulation, overpowering his listeners, trying to maintain a God-like mastery over people and circumstances. But what McLaughlin liked most about Rickey was that he was smart and very clever. Attendance at Ebbets Field was falling. Blacks were clamoring for entry into the game. New York City was a liberal town. Rickey's plan just might work, he concluded.

"If you're doing this to improve the ball club, go ahead," he finally answered. "But if you're doing it for the emancipation of the Negro, then forget it."

Rickey nodded, inwardly pleased. McLaughlin was unsparing of himself and others, he thought, but fair. He pushed his chair forward and leaned over. Could McLaughlin then arrange a formal session with the full board of directors soon? He would like their approval on record, too. A week later four directors and Rickey gathered for a luncheon meeting at the New York Athletic Club. McLaughlin and his crony George Barnewell were there, as were Joseph Gilleaudeau for the Ebbets family interests and James Mulvey for their rival family, McKeever. The talk was strained, especially between the latter two men, until Rickey lit a cigar and began to speak, repeating his conversation with McLaughlin and asking for their approval. Profit rather than social justice was most likely on their minds and after Barnewell said, "We probably haven't tapped the Negro market enough," the others agreed Rickey could proceed.

Yet he had to move cautiously lest he threaten the Dodgers' economic interests in southern states or arouse the hostility of baseball's owners. He remembered an incident in the 1930s when he had tentatively raised the issue of desegregating Sportsman's Park with Breadon. "I had made that effort in St. Louis only to find effective opposition on the part of ownership and on the part of the public-press-everybody." Forget it, ordered the Cardinal owner and president. The white fans would never sit in the stands to watch blacks perform, he insisted. Well, Rickey persisted, would Breadon permit black customers to sit anywhere they chose in Sportsman's Park without making any formal announcement? Breadon said he personally didn't give a damn about desegregating seating but the fans would never allow such liberties. Business, he said, was business. Rickey later discovered after questioning a municipal official that no city ordinance demanded black fans be seated apart from white fans. Even so, he backed away, unwilling to offend Breadon or white customers. Yet he had struck a responsive chord in the New York–born Breadon. Soon after, at the league's 1936 meeting, Breadon and John Shibe of the Philadelphia Athletics urged Landis to meet a delegation led by the singer-actor Paul Robeson but the Judge wasn't interested.

Rickey opened his talent search in the Caribbean. In 1943 he asked Jose Seda, the University of Puerto Rico's athletic director (they had met when Seda was a student at New York University; Rickey liked and respected Seda and paid his tuition in return for future scouting services), to watch for prospects. The next year Seda accompanied a Dodger scout to Mexico to observe Negro players. Rickey also leaned on his bird dogs, the amateurs and buffs who might turn up a lead. Professor Robert M. Haig of Columbia University, for example, a fraternity brother and OWU alumnus, visited Cuba on several occasions and reported to Rickey. And Walter F. O'Malley, whom McLaughlin had brought into the Dodger organization as its counsel and, later, as a limited partner, went to Cuba with a letter of credit for $25,000 with instructions from Rickey to sign Silvio Garcia, a black player, only to learn that Garcia had been drafted into the Cuban army.

Rickey, meanwhile, was trying to think through the question of race in America, and he began now to read extensively about slavery. He read over and over again his treasured volumes of Lincolniana in the late evenings and on Sunday, marking passages and pages he considered central in black-white relationships. He discovered Gunnar Myrdal's *An American Dilemma,* a Swedish socialist's examination of the gap between democratic pretensions and the treatment accorded blacks. He made long lists of books to be read. He read Gilberto Freyre's account of slavery in Brazil. "Eminently useful," he noted in its margins. When J. Saunders Redding, a black historian at Hampton Institute, published *No Day of Triumph* in 1942, Rickey spontaneously wrote and thanked him for his contribution. In his letter he attacked an anthropologist's alleged lack of sympathy for blacks. "I intend to attack him plenty," wrote the aroused Rickey. "I simply mean that I [am] going to quote him to show him up. Please give me your views in the greatest confidence."

Reading constantly, but now looking for explicit evidence to support his powerful feelings, he rediscovered Papini's *Life of Christ,* a book he had read years before. He marveled at the Italian writer's moving characterization of Jesus' nonviolent nature, a trait he believed necessary for the first black player. And as he put down his book in the late evening he must have mused on his own experiences—as a teacher in Turkey Creek, Bishop Welch and his visions of equality, Charles Thomas at OWU. Perhaps he recalled Thomas' visit to Sportsman's Park in the 1930s and his inability to seat him among white fans in the field boxes or grandstand because of Jim Crow rules.

In these early years it was impossible for him to state openly that sooner or later he would dare to defy baseball's segregated tradition. When Arthur Mann suggested years later that not until two years after his meeting with McLaughlin did he seriously dream of desegregating the ball club, he shouted "No!" and then scribbled a detailed memo explaining why Mann was entirely in error. But at the same time he asked in its margin, in pencil, "Why?" For it was to him a moral issue from the start. What needed to be worked out was a way to put it into practice. In December 1943 he celebrated his sixty-second birthday, and he found himself struggling seriously to unravel the tragedy of white supremacy in the country he so loved.

A few days after his birthday he attended baseball's annual winter meeting at the Commodore Hotel in Manhattan. Once more, Paul Robeson asked Landis for permission to address the owners. This time, Landis unexpectedly acceded to the pressure growing outside of baseball and he placed the famous actor on the agenda.

Robeson was then at the peak of his theatrical career, a one-time brilliant twelve-letter athlete at Rutgers University, Phi Beta Kappa and a lawyer, whose rich bass-baritone voice and acting talent brought him to a starring role in *Othello,* then on Broadway.

So it was that on a bleak and stormy day in December the brass of both leagues met to hear the black baritone. Just before he was ushered into the room, Landis arose and issued a stern warning:

"Don't interrupt Robeson. Let's not get into any discussion with him."

Robeson stood quietly, a practiced performer at ease before his audience, spoke for fifteen minutes on the need for allowing blacks into baseball, and awaited the questions and challenges. There were none; Landis' words had been obediently heeded. Then Robeson left and Landis matter-of-factly resumed the chair and continued to the next item on the agenda. No one in that room or outside in the corridors or hotel

# Chapter Nine

bar or restaurant, said Browns official William DeWitt, Rickey's former office boy, so much as mentioned what had been said. Inhibited by Landis, they themselves were equally against bringing blacks into baseball. It was as if Robeson had never been with them.

Rickey too said nothing. And certainly nothing about the fact that McLaughlin had already acquiesced in Rickey's looking for black players. His silence was uncharacteristic and, for him, somewhat uncomfortable. He was by nature demonstrative and voluble, a mover and shaper who did little in moderation and no doubt would have loved to overwhelm his audience of peers with words. But Landis' dislike for him dated back to the Cedar Rapids case and possibly even to the 1920s, with the coming of his farm system. Ever since then the Judge privately sneered at him as "that hypocritical preacher" whom he ought to have permanently barred from the game, or "that Protestant bastard [who's] always masquerading with a minister's robe." Nor had any of the owners ever expressed any sympathy for his activities. Most of them were pleased that Breadon had let him go the year before.

So he sat quietly, saying nothing, surprising even DeWitt. Yet he was still filled with misgivings. Given to scribbling private notes to himself as a way of thinking through problems and dilemmas, he wrote a few words in his large, rounded, almost incomprehensible scrawl.

"Robeson a Communist?"
"South"
"Negro leagues"
Alongside each entry he then wrote:
"Attendance"
"Jesus"
"America"

The next day Wendell Smith of the black newspaper the Pittsburgh *Courier* called Landis for a comment.

"Each club is entirely free to employ Negro players to any extent it pleases and the matter is solely for each club's decision without any restriction whatsoever," Landis told Smith.

Nat Low of the Communist *Daily Worker* interviewed Durocher and asked if he thought blacks were good enough to make the majors. "Hell," answered the onetime poor French Catholic kid from Springfield, Massachusetts, "I've seen a million good ones." Durocher also intimated that Landis, not players, was the real roadblock.

When the *Worker* ran the story the next day and word reached Landis in Chicago, he was thunderstruck. For one thing he simply did not see himself as standing in the way of the entry of blacks, and for another he resented Durocher's public criticism. The Dodger manager was then ordered to fly to Chicago, where, behind closed doors, the Judge read him the riot act. The following day Landis' office released a statement insisting that he was not excluding blacks "and never have been during the twenty-one years I have served as Commissioner."

In truth he had, although often it was hard to say whether he was leading or following the owners and public opinion. In any event, by now Sam Breadon had lost his slight interest in desegregation and Tom Yawkey of Boston was always considered unsympathetic to eliminating the racial barriers. In New York too, the Yankee and Giant ownership and management opposed blacks in baseball.

Seated at his desk in the *Courier* office in Pittsburgh, Smith kept hammering away, trying to keep the question of baseball integration alive. Perhaps more than any other sportswriter, he had dedicated himself to opening the game to members of his race. On the day after Landis' statement absolving himself and baseball from any responsibility for the color bar, Smith sent letters to all twenty-six owners and managers asking for their reaction to the commissioner's release. Six replied. Three backed Landis, but offered no concrete idea how the sport could desegregate. Two vaguely hoped for changes after the end of the war. Only Clark Griffith, Rickey's former New York Highlander manager, had a specific alternative to propose. "My idea," he wrote Smith, "is that the Negro leagues should develop to the place where ... someday the teams could play our top clubs for the world championship and thus have a chance to really prove their caliber."

Baseball continued to resist. J. G. Taylor Spink, Landis' biographer and editor and publisher of the *Sporting News*, refused until the very end to concede the right of blacks to play. "Because of the obvious reason they [Negroes] prefer to draw their talent from their own ranks because the leaders of both groups [white and black] know their crowd psychology and do not care to run the risk of damaging their own game."

And there was even more, Spink added, as if in code language to his readers. Let them into baseball, he warned, and racial problems would tear teams apart and hurt Negro leagues badly at the gate. Besides, only "agitators" wanted integration. Among baseball people and right-minded Negroes, he concluded, that demand was never expressed.

Throughout World War II there were sporadic if abortive efforts to break baseball's color barrier. In 1943 two Pacific Coast League owners, Clarence (Pants) Rowland of the Los Angeles Angels and Vince De Vencenzi of the Oakland Oaks, held tryouts but stopped short of signing anyone. Not long after, Jimmy Dykes of the Chicago White Sox conducted a workout in Comiskey Park (named, ironically, after Charles Comiskey, who as a turn-of-the-century St. Louis Brown once refused to join in a player strike against black players). Two players were scheduled to perform. One of them, Nate Moreland, a war veteran, was visibly upset. "I can play in Mexico but I have to fight for America where I can't play," he complained. The second player never appeared because he was nursing a charley horse. But Dykes, a shrewd judge of baseball talent, told the press later: "I'd hate to see him on two good legs. He's worth $50,000 of anybody's money."

He was talking about Jackie Robinson.

Nineteen forty-three saw still another abortive attempt to desegregate. Bill Veeck, Jr., tried to buy the perennially last place Philadelphia Phillies and "stock it with Negro players." The rosters were going to be chosen by Abe Saperstein, the sports promoter, and by A. S. "Doc" Young, sports editor of the black Chicago *Defender.* They had in mind Roy Campanella, Monte Irvin, Luke Easter, and other players deferred from the military. Veeck was so sure he was going to win the 1944 pennant with such a club that he contacted a black jazz band to play at the World Series. Ready to buy, and asserting—but never proving—he had the backing of an anonymous CIO official, Veeck said he visited Landis, an old friend of his father, and apprised him of what he was trying to do. Landis' initial response was that Veeck was pulling his leg. When, however, Landis realized Veeck was serious he said nothing. "The next thing I knew," said Veeck, the bankrupt Philly owner had "turned the team back to the league," thus forcing him to negotiate with Ford Frick, who immediately told him the Phillies had been sold to William Cox, a sports buff who had made millions in the lumber business. In retrospect, Veeck commented that his courtesy call had been a "terrible mistake."

In early 1944 the *Courier* and *Defender* both reported that black sluggers Josh Gibson and Buck Leonard were to be tested by the Pirates. William Benswanger, the club president, a well-meaning racial moderate and liberal in a hard-boiled and racist city, was furious at the game's unwritten code. "Colored men are American citizens with American rights," he declared publicly, trying desperately to pave the way for baseball's local acceptance. "I know there are many problems connected with the question, but after all, somebody has to make the first move."

For all his sentiments, Benswanger backed down after protests poured into his Forbes Field office. After that, he gave up the idea.

By the end of 1944, the outlines of a campaign to introduce a black player had taken shape in Rickey's mind. It included:

- Support of the Brooklyn Dodger board of directors.
- Choosing a black who knew how to behave on and off the field.
- Winning a favorable reaction from the press and the fans.
- Working with important local blacks to avoid any white backlash.
- Getting the player accepted by his teammates.

The first step had been achieved. The arrival of a new owner, John L. Smith, president of the Charles Pfizer Chemical Corporation, made some of the others easier for him.

That year Smith, Rickey, and a new director—Walter F. O'Malley, the McLaughlin protégé—bought 75 percent of the outstanding shares of the Dodgers. Each now owned one-third of the purchased stock, for which they paid $1,046,000; each made an $82,000 down payment. Rickey borrowed heavily on his life insurance policies for the cash, but Smith and O'Malley were wealthy enough to buy them outright. The remaining $800,000 was financed by $75,000 paid by Smith, a like amount by O'Malley (although he was to advance nothing of his own until the club returned a profit), and the balance a loan granted by the Brooklyn Trust Company. Dearie Mulvey, Steve McKeever's daughter and Jim's wife, retained her 25 percent interest, but Smith's coming broke a 50-50 ownership split between the warring Ebbets and McKeever families. The new triumvirate was now in full control.

What was most significant about the move was that Smith initially welcomed Rickey's approach. He and the Dodger president struck it off well from the start, and Smith admired and enjoyed the company of the baseball man. Unlike Rickey, he was a "meticulous man, neat, orderly and impeccably dressed." But as Rickey noted, Smith was intimately involved in everything the Pfizer Company did. He loved to pay daily visits to his factory, roll up his sleeves, doff his tie, open his collar, call workmen by their first names and even ask after their families. He worked long hours and weekends and was inordinately pleased—he told Rickey— to learn that his peers thought of him as a thoroughly able scientist, fair in his dealings with employees, but always a hard driver with often impossible goals. Each year he dictated individual letters to employees evaluating and grading their work. One year he stopped the sale of beer during working hours not because he was a "dry"—as was Rickey—but because someone made off with the beer money.

Smith was a fanatic about sports who delighted in boxing, boating, and watching baseball—in that order—and in fact met Rickey (who first pushed the idea with Smith of buying control of the club) at the Brooklyn Crescent Club's pep rally for promoting sports among young people. Saturdays he arrived in his private box overlooking first base. On several occasions he brought Sir Alexander Fleming, whose discovery of penicillin had made millions for Pfizer and Smith. The Briton was fascinated by the game and Rickey, and each time he visited Ebbets Field he spent the time collecting signed balls and souvenir caps and pennants and asking questions of Rickey.

Rickey and Smith were both self-made men, rough-hewn individualists and fervent Christians. Eventually, when Smith lay dying of cancer, O'Malley would wean him away and turn him against Rickey, but in their early relationship Smith admired Rickey's creativity and intensity and inexhaustible energy; Rickey's respect for the corporate head often approached reverence. But there was more. When he learned of Smith's passionate wish "to do something" for blacks, he happily revealed his secret. Pfizer in fact had been the first New York corporation of its size to integrate its employee teams in softball, bowling, and basketball.

The demand to desegregate baseball was most intense in New York City. Starting in April, the "End Jim Crow in Baseball Committee" threatened to picket the city's three ballparks and City Hall. To relieve the pressure and try to score some political points against Governor Dewey, Mayor Fiorello LaGuardia persuaded the two league presidents to merge two study groups mandated to examine the subject with his Anti-Discrimination Committee and named Rickey and Larry MacPhail as their representatives.

When the announcement was made, Rickey cringed. LaGuardia's committee was dominated by anti–Dewey Democrats and he told the mayor heatedly he would have no part in such tactics. But more important was the fact that the committee's previous sessions had been aimless. He was afraid his appointment would only flush out the bigots, rendering the signing of a black even more difficult.

It developed that LaGuardia took most of the heat as letters of protest poured into City Hall, one of them typically blasting him as "part Jew and part Dago; but we did not know you are part Nigger." Ignoring the extremists on his right, the mayor turned instead to the left and asked the Jim Crow Committee to call off their picketing "otherwise all we have done to date is to be destroyed."

At the same time, Red Sox owner Tom Yawkey abruptly arranged for three players to try out in Fenway Park because a Jewish Boston councilman named Isadore Muchnick threatened to push through a blue law forbidding baseball on Sunday unless he did so. Sam Jethroe of the Cleveland Buckeyes, Marvin Williams of the Philadelphia Stars, and Jackie Robinson of the Kansas City Monarchs were invited to appear.

Leo Durocher and Rickey, most likely during wartime spring training in 1945 in Bear Mountain, N.Y., when all teams during the Second World War had to forgo training in warmer climates and instead stay close to home. (Courtesy Branch B. Rickey)

"Black players," said Robinson later, "were familiar with hypocrisy. Not for one minute did we believe the tryout was sincere. The Boston club officials praised our performance, let us fill out application cards, and said 'so long.' We were fairly certain they wouldn't call us and we had no intention of calling them."

The wartime 1945 Dodgers, who had languished in seventh place the year before, were on the playing field in Bear Mountain State Park, situated in the gently rising highlands thirty miles up the Hudson River from Manhattan. It was April 7, and before he died in 1944 Judge Landis had decreed that for the duration of the war, baseball teams must eliminate southern spring training bases and stay as close to home as possible.

Not that training in warmer climates would have meant much to Rickey's assortment of itinerant 4Fs, older castoffs, and adolescents who gathered that morning under Durocher's tutelage. With the exception of the Cardinals, wartime baseball players were a poor lot and clubs were only marking time until the real players returned from military service.

The sun was shining and the morning cool and brisk as Rickey sat in the rickety wooden bleachers alongside Jane, playing host to another of his legion of ex–OWU fraternity brothers, Herbert McCracken and McCracken's ten-year-old son, George. McCracken had once coached Allegheny College's football team (as Rickey had) and was now working for *Scholastic Coach*. He and young George had driven up for the day to be with the Rickeys and spent almost an hour sitting on the crude wooden slats leisurely observing infield practice and listening to Rickey's ceaseless chatter.

"Watch that boy bunt, Herbert. He'd hit thirty points higher if he knew how to use his feet."

"Motion, son, motion," he called out, "it's all in the motion." "He can't run or throw but that boy's an inspiration to his teammates, a fine family man."

"If his pants came up two inches higher, he'd look better."

Or to himself, but still loud enough for everyone to overhear: "Don't hold the ball, son. Pretend it's absolutely red hot. Then see how fast you'd get rid of it."

Rickey found it hard to sit in one place and every few minutes he rose and walked about, often positioning himself behind the catcher, where he observed everyone on the field. Durocher and his coaches were nearby and Rickey said little to the players directly or to his manager, but his presence was felt. At one point the old Brown catcher leaned over

Mike Sandlock's shoulder and whispered to the Dodger catcher as he squatted behind the plate. Sandlock then raised himself, removed his mask and grinned, as did Rickey, who started back to the bleachers, stopping again to speak with sidearm pitcher Curt Davis.

Returning to his seat, he spied four men approaching from the third base side, about fifty yards away. One was white, he noticed, and held a large camera. The others were black.

"Branch seemed to sense immediately what was going to take place," said McCracken. "Within a few minutes they were standing in front of us."

Rickey knew two of the visitors, the *Daily Worker* sportswriter Nat Low and Joe Bostic of the left-wing black weekly, *People's Voice,* both of whom had been campaigning for years for the entry of blacks into baseball. Rickey thought they had come for a statement on Mayor LaGuardia's new Anti-Discrimination Committee, of which Rickey had been named co-chairman. The two other men, he soon learned, were ballplayers: thirty-four-year-old first baseman Dave ("Showboat") Thomas and thirty-two-year-old hurler Terris McDuffie, both veterans of the Negro leagues.

Quickly Low, who had engineered the visit, explained why they had come. Surely the Brooklyn club knew of the widespread demands for breaking the color bar, he began. And just as surely Mr. Rickey knew of the recent enactment by the state legislature of the Ives-Quinn Law, aimed at reducing racial discrimination in hiring. They wanted to test that law there and then with the Dodgers.

Rickey, of course, knew of the law. He and Governor Thomas E. Dewey were friends and Republican Party allies who spent occasional Sundays together in Pawling, New York, where Dewey owned a farm and Rickey's close friends the Thornbergs resided. It was likely they had talked about the bill and its impact on baseball while it was still pending in Albany.

But a tryout? It was apparent to Rickey that Thomas and McDuffie, over-the-hill and getting on in years, were hardly an improvement over the discards, rejects, and adolescents practicing a few yards from him.

"Mr. Rickey explained that the Dodgers were engaged in a workout," said McCracken, "and he would like to concentrate his attention on that and instead invited all four men to take seats a little further down in the bleachers and following practice he would gladly talk with them."

The four nodded, and moved away, for the moment satisfied while Rickey turned to McCracken and said quietly, "Herbert, I am now representing all of organized baseball, not just the Dodgers."

The four men were invited to join Rickey and Jane at lunch in the inn. Rickey, as usual, dominated the table and peppered the players with questions about their personal lives. Were they married, did they have children and homes, were they religious, certain the answers would give him a clue into their character. Most of his attention was directed at McDuffie, to whom he took an instant personal liking. "The spiritual life," he told them, as he had so many others who craved entry into the game, "cannot go too deep." And he repeated yet another pet maxim: "A good home life should never be abandoned because it will hold the athlete in a steady course." Baseball, he knew so well, was filled with snares and traps and marked by a competition so relentless it often overwhelmed weak and rudderless men.

No doubt Low and Bostic had heard this before. But they were glad for the attention accorded them even though they must have seriously doubted the outcome. Rickey, however, resented their presence. To be sure, they did not know, and most certainly he would not tell them, that the club had been looking for black players since 1943. And for another, he thought their interest insincere and even a Communist ploy to win new adherents. He was especially annoyed with the cynical Bostic, whose columns asserted that tryouts were a sham, yet another ruse to lock out the all-too-trusting black player. What could Mr. Rickey do, Bostic asked him, to assure them he would not merely go through the motions as had Pittsburgh, Philadelphia, and two Pacific Coast teams in recent years, only to crumble in fear at the first sign of opposition?

Rickey sat up straight, his face ashen white, his hand shaking with anger.

"You know, gentlemen, I am more for your cause than anybody else you know, but you are making a mistake using force. You are defeating your own aims."

It was a gratuitous and ingenuous remark, but the four men let it pass, more concerned with the tryout than starting an argument with the obviously furious Rickey. At last, Rickey rose. He would, he conceded, watch Thomas and McDuffie perform the next morning at the indoor field in nearby West Point.

McCracken then walked up to Rickey.

"I believe Branch felt in advance of the workout that those two men were not big league quality—and that proved true the next day. But he said to me before we separated: 'Now more than ever I must start my search for the right colored man to enter organized baseball.'"

The day after he turned down the two black players, Rickey drove to his office in Brooklyn. He was warned by his staff that a group of black reporters were lying in wait for him, furious that once again a white man had given a tryout to black players and cynically refused to allow them to play ball. To blunt their charges, he arranged a formal press conference so that white reporters could also ask questions.

Before the questions began he opened with a formal statement, ignoring Thomas and McDuffie, and instead took an entirely unexpected tack, hoping therefore to direct and dominate the conference and thus distract the angry black writers. Reading from notes placed on his desk, he denounced the two Negro baseball leagues as corrupt and inefficient.

His contempt for the Negro leagues was boundless, and he described them as a "front for a monopolistic game-booking business, controlled by booking agents in Chicago, Philadelphia, and New York." He ended the conference by denouncing Communists for trying to "use" blacks and mentioned his notion of forming "a well-organized, legitimate Negro league."

Ludlow Werner of the black *New York Age* was in a rage when it was over. "My aching back! Did you ever hear such double talk from a big pompous ass in your life? I predict that it'll be a cold day in hell when that big windbag puts a Negro into a Brooklyn uniform."

Harold Roettger was also concerned over Rickey's intemperate and unexpected conference, but for different reasons. Roettger, a cautious, somber, and taciturn man, believed greater care should have been exercised before attacking the powerful men who ran Negro baseball. Someday the Dodgers might need their cooperation. It was one thing to call for a third black league, but it was quite another to impugn the honesty of the people who owned the two existing leagues.

Rickey heard the same worried concern from one of his front office assistants, Bob Finch. Uneasy with Rickey's sharp words, Finch reminded him that the Yankees had earned $100,000 in 1943 for renting the Stadium to Negro teams. Why, he asked, weren't the Dodgers in the market for such lucrative business, too?

Rickey heard them out and probably thought them both correct, but only in a lily-white setting. Neither Roettger nor Finch knew of his agreement with the Brooklyn board, and he was not about to tell them yet. It was April 1945, and he felt he could turn only to his son for the support he desperately needed. Branch Jr. was no rubber stamp and often was the sole "no" man to confront him. Rickey was afraid that when he revealed his plan to bring in a black player, Branch Jr. would object because of the impact such a move might have on their farm system. Instead, his son was pleased with the idea. Bringing blacks in, he said, would mean a fresh and larger source of players to be mined.

That was all Rickey needed to hear. The day after a press release was issued:

"They [the Negro leagues] are the poorest excuse for the word league and by comparison with organized baseball, which they understandably try to copy. They are not leagues at all. I failed to find a constitution or a set of bylaws. I failed to find a single player under contract, and learned that players of all teams became free agents at the end of each season."

The booking agents and owners bristled but there was little they could do. Agent William Leuschner charged Rickey's proposed United States League and Brooklyn Brown Dodgers were a trick to fill Ebbets Field while the white Dodgers were away. A black owner denounced Rickey as a "carpetbagger" and another declared he was trying to steal their players.

But now with his call for a third Negro league and the theoretical Brown Dodgers, Rickey had what he badly needed—an excuse to send Wid Matthews, George Sisler, Clyde Sukeforth, and Tom Greenwade, the club's superscouts, into the bushes to search openly for black players. His orders were clear and explicit: no place was off limits. Go everywhere, talk to everyone, watch anyone worth watching. All the scouts thought they were looking for future Brown Dodgers and despite Greenwade's later claim that he knew, there is no evidence that any of them ever did. Certainly, if Rickey had confided in anyone it would have been George Sisler.

Their reports arrived at 215 Montague Street regularly, screened by Branch Jr. and then passed on to his father. Exceptional players were diligently observed and carefully assessed—Buck Leonard, the hard-hitting first baseman of the Homestead Grays; Cool Papa Bell, the Grays' swift, sure-handed outfielder; the great catcher Josh Gibson; the second baseman Marvin Williams; outfielder Sam Jethroe; shortstop Piper Davis; catcher Roy Campanella; and shortstop Jackie Robinson.

At that very moment, while his scouts were looking for an athlete, Rickey was looking for a man. "I had to get a man," he explained, "who would carry the burden on the field. I needed a man to carry the badge of martyrdom. The press had to accept him. He had to stimulate a good reaction of the Negro race itself, for an unfortunate one might have solidified the antagonism of other colors. And, I had to consider the attitude of the man's teammates." Rickey was in his office following another press conference when Branch Jr. told him about the charade at Fenway Park. His son thought the gesture cruel and mentioned things had come to a pretty pass when genuinely fine prospects could be toyed with and then ignored, simply because of color.

Although the other newsmen had left, Wendell Smith of the Pittsburgh *Courier,* who was depressed at the turn of events in Bear Mountain and Boston, still needed some newsworthy quotes and headed for Rickey. He was surprised as the Dodger president took him aside, placed his arm around his shoulders, and asked, "Wendell, tell me about the Fenway Park workout."

Would Smith care to recommend to the Dodgers a player genuinely capable of playing in the major leagues?

The so-called United States League with the Brooklyn Brown Dodgers had just been announced, and Smith was skeptical. "If you aren't serious about this thing, Mr. Rickey, I'd rather not waste our time in discussing it," said Smith. "But if you are serious, I do know of a player who could make it. His name is Jackie Robinson."

"It seems to me," answered Rickey, his encyclopedic mind riffling through the thousands of scouting reports he had cataloged in his brain, "I've heard of that fellow before."

In August 1945 Rickey sent Clyde Sukeforth, who had been a part-time catcher for ten years with the Reds and Dodgers and since 1943 a Dodger coach and scout, to Comiskey Park in Chicago to observe Robinson during a Kansas City–Chicago Friday night game.

By now, Rickey knew Robinson was a Georgia-born, California-reared brilliant four-sport college athlete whose mother had instilled in him a self-reliance and fierce independence along with a deep reverence for Christian ideals. Rickey knew also he was a pigeon-toed, 9.8-second runner in the 100-yard dash, a young man his UCLA basketball coach had praised for having perfect timing and unmatched grace. And most important of all, he knew that Robinson had been charged with conduct unbecoming an army officer because he had refused to move to the rear of a segregated bus on an army base in Texas. When Rickey was informed of his court battle for vindication he became excited. "A man of ideals," he said, shaking his head. "A battler."

"I want you to see that game," he told Sukeforth (and directed him afterwards to keep a written record of the entire search for Robinson), "and especially do I want you to see a shortstop named Robinson. I would like you to see Robinson before the game. There is some doubt as to whether he really has a good arm. I would like you to speak to Robinson and ask him if he will throw the ball overhand from the hole, his right, in practice. Ask him to do that for you."

"I went to the park early," Sukeforth reported in confidence to Rickey, thinking he was scouting the black player for the Brown Dodgers. "When the gates opened, I bought a box seat ticket near the Kansas City dugout and waited for the club to come out. I had purchased a scorecard and got Robinson's number—but they were sometimes incorrect, so I waited until some guy called Robinson by name and gave me my cue.

"I called him over and introduced myself. I told him you had sent me out there and I was very much interested in his arm. I explained to him there was not much doubt about the rest of his ability—he could run and hit, but there was disagreement as to his arm." (Buck Leonard of the Homestead Grays had said, "We didn't think too much of Robinson.... He was a hustler but other than that he wasn't a top shortstop. We said, 'I don't see how he can make it.'")

"I asked if, during the practice, he would go to his right and throw the ball overhand with something on it; and to have somebody hit him balls over there. He said he would be very glad to, except for the fact that he was not playing. He said, 'I fell on my shoulder several days ago and won't be able to play for probably a week.' I then asked him if he would come down to the Stevens [Hotel] and meet me after the game.

"[We] knew he was discharged from the army and we did not know why.... I asked him why he was discharged and a number of other questions I thought you would want to know about. It seemed an old football ankle injury had brought about his discharge but, as it proved, it did not bother him. I reasoned that, if he was not going to play for a week, it would be an ideal time to bring him in to Brooklyn. A great time to make the trip. I had him make a few plays from the hole in the room. His moves were good.

"I had to stop in Toledo on Sunday and see if Bobby Rhawn could throw. I made a date with Robinson to meet me at the Toledo park. So, he met me ... and I had arranged transportation in the meantime and brought him into Brooklyn that night. I wired you that I was bringing the player with the sore arm in and you told me to come ahead.

"We arrived in New York Monday afternoon and Robinson went to the Theresa Hotel up in Harlem, and I arranged with you to see Robinson early Tuesday morning."

It was August 28 and Sukeforth introduced the two men. Later Robinson described the man who dramatically altered his life: "Square, heavy-set man of about 5'8", a cigar clenched between his teeth, advancing toward me with the rolling gait of a catcher going after a pop foul. His summer suit was shapeless and wrinkled. Blue eyes peered up at me from behind the silver spectacles as he held out a massive hand."

He looked fatherly, but for all his graciousness and the aura of caring he imparted there was something in his manner—a bite, a sharpness perhaps, that set Rickey apart from other baseball people—that indicated, as his critics suspected, that he was hardly as innocent and kindly as he looked. Robinson, he thought at that very moment, "had somewhat halfheartedly" agreed to the interview and was eyeing him suspiciously.

Rickey's office overlooked Court Street and across the street Robinson could see a small park and, beyond, a large court building. Off to the right, a mid–nineteenth-century structure housed the borough's president. Rickey stopped at an illuminated fish tank and sat down in his large, leathery chair, pushing a massive, unabridged dictionary away to make room on his cluttered desk. He reached into a humidor for a fresh cigar and Robinson noticed a globe behind him and on the wall photographs of a family and Leo Durocher.

"Do you have a girl, Jackie?" he asked, unsmiling but not unkindly, chewing on his unlit cigar, his thick eyebrows arched.

He had been carefully preparing for the session, knowing he soon had to reach a decision. Two other players had been under serious consideration by the Dodgers shortly before Robinson's name had cropped up. But Josh Gibson was ill. From 1943 on, his enormous talent had eroded swiftly, he had several nervous breakdowns and had been institutionalized twice in Washington, D.C.'s St. Elizabeth Hospital for mental patients. Even now as they sat together, Dodger scouts reported that the man who hit about 75 home runs in 1931, when he was

The great day: After the famous signing of Jackie Robinson to a Brooklyn Dodger contract, here they are in the Dodgers' offices in 1946 at 215 Montague Street, Brooklyn. Note Lincoln's photograph on the wall. (National Baseball Hall of Fame Library, Cooperstown, NY)

nineteen (no reliable records were kept), and who had smashed an estimated 800 homers in little more than a decade, was suffering from undiagnosed blackouts and serious and painful headaches. The second player had been dismissed quickly from Rickey's mind when he learned the man was suffering from syphilis.

Robinson shifted uneasily in his chair. There was a girl, he said with diffidence. Her name was Rachel and she was a nurse and they intended to marry. "Wonderful!" Rickey's voice rose, his face now beaming.

Sukeforth sat silently on the couch, the only witness to the interview.

"Do you know why you are here, Jackie?" Rickey asked suddenly.

Robinson started shaking his head, but stopped. What did he really know about all this? Only that Sukeforth had urged him to come, saying he thought it was important.

"Well," Rickey continued, now softly pronouncing his words ever so carefully, "I am interested in bringing you into the Dodger system. I don't know how you play but my scouts do. If Sukeforth says you're a good player, I'll take his word for it."

There was not a sound in the room.

Could Robinson stay out of fights, on and off the field? Could he behave and not arouse or instigate black fans? Could he avoid as much as possible openly antagonizing the southern white players?

"I remember one thing you told him," Sukeforth quoted Rickey afterward. "You said that if you could get your hands on a great colored ball player, you would be tempted to put him in Montreal or even Brooklyn, providing he was the right temperament, had poise, and was the type of fellow who could take insults and carry a flag for his race. You said, 'I don't think you are that fellow. If somebody called you a black so-and-so, you would start a fight and that would set the cause back one hundred years.'"

Rickey's words continued to pour out ceaselessly, making and remaking the same points over and over again. His voice rose and fell depending on the emphasis he wished to give those words. His soft tone turned harsh and dramatic and then soft again and then, in high emotion, to a shout.

Standing, he demanded: "What I'm saying to you, Jackie, is that you will have to be more than a good player."

He waited, while Sukeforth watched, astonished, at the incredible scene unfolding before him. Robinson sat, as if deep in thought. Minutes seemed to pass and at last, he crossed his legs and spoke. "Mr. Rickey, I think I can play ball, but I promise you that I will do the second part of the job although I can't be an obsequious, cringing fellow."

"Obsequious" and "cringing"—the very words sent Rickey into raptures. Robinson was obviously a well-schooled, well-read young man. A combative man and, it appeared, a gentleman, with good breeding. The very man. By Judas Priest, he had at long last found the right man.

Was he under contract with the Kansas City Monarchs?

"No, sir," answered Robinson, "we don't have contracts."

But did he have any oral agreements with the two owners? Again, he said he did not. "I just work from pay day to pay day."

Still, Rickey was not fully satisfied. Once more he returned to the question of the first black entering baseball. He began speaking of the Eighteenth Amendment, the ill-fated prohibition clause he had once favored and campaigned for passionately. Had Robinson heard of it? (He had.) At last, Rickey approached his point: The amendment was a mistake. Not because the cause was wrong; it was not. But it was poorly timed and as a consequence had done fatal harm to prohibitionism. And finally he reached his moral: If Robinson created an explosive or irreparable incident on or off the field, then the cause of "the Negro race" would be seriously set back.

He paused and replaced the well-chewed cigar in his mouth. He then leaned back in his swivel chair and removed the cigar, still staring at the befuddled Robinson, his tone somber but sympathetic. "You will be carrying a tremendous load."

Reaching for a book under the mountainous mass of papers on his desk, he shuffled impatiently through its pages and then stopped. "It's Giovanni Papini's *The Life of Christ*, son. Ever hear of it?"

Robinson shook his head.

Rickey barely looked up at him and began to read aloud. First, he quoted:

"Ye have heard that it hath been said, An eye for an eye, and a tooth for a tooth: But I say unto you, that ye resist not evil: But whosoever shall smite thee on the right cheek, turn to him the other also...."

And then, he read, with excitement and feeling:

"For an infinite number of believers this principle of not resisting evil had been the unendurable and acceptable scandal of Christianity. There are three answers men can make to violence: revenge, flight, turning the other cheek. The first is the barbarous principle of retaliation.... Flight is no better than retaliation.... The man who takes Right invites pursuit. Turning the other cheek means not receiving the second blow. It means cutting the chains of the inevitable wrongs at the first link. Your adversary is ready for anything but this.... Every man has an obscure respect for courage in others, especially if it is moral courage, the rarest and most difficult sort of bravery. It makes the very brute understand that this man is more than a man ... the results of nonresistance, even if they are not always perfect, are certainly superior to those of resistance or flight.... To answer blows with blows, evil deeds with evil deeds, is to meet the attacker on his own ground, to proclaim oneself as low as he.... Only he who has conquered himself can conquer his enemies."

He placed the book down.

"Now," he said softly to Robinson, *"can you do it?* You will have to promise that for the first three years in baseball you will turn your other cheek. I know you are naturally combative. But for three years—three years—you will have to do it the only way it can be done. Three years— can *you do it?"*

Robinson was an intense Christian, but Rickey also described him later as excessively competitive, "instantly violent by natural disposition, immediately ready to counterattack, relishing physical involvement and capable of dealing physically with anyone he encountered."

*Can you do it?*

What will you do, Rickey stood again and demanded, shouting, what will you do when they call you a black son of a bitch? When they not only turn you down for a hotel room but also curse you out?

*Can you do it?*

Rickey was perspiring, despite the whirring of an electric fan. His brow and shirt were damp.

Nervously, Rickey sat and then, just as quickly rose again, walking to the front of the desk to where Robinson sat. Robinson was tense and involuntarily clenched his fists. Abruptly, Rickey swung his bulky fist at Robinson's jaw.

*"What do you do?"* he screamed.

"Mr. Rickey," the young black man whispered hoarsely, "I've got two cheeks. Is that it?"

Sukeforth, who had been sitting silently on the couch, almost invisible to the two men, now grinned with relief as he watched Rickey's expression. He was purring with pleasure, he thought, exhilarated, almost intoxicated.

Then Rickey sat down, exhausted, breathing deeply, perspiring. He told Robinson he would be offered a contract with the Montreal Royals, the Dodgers' flagship farm club. He would receive a bonus of $3,500 and $600 monthly wages. But for the time being, Rickey warned both Robinson and Sukeforth, no one else was to learn of the meeting.

He placed his unlit cigar in his mouth and looked at his watch. Sukeforth rose and checked his too. The session had lasted three hours.

In the weeks after meeting with Robinson, Rickey shared the news with his wife and children to win their support. He had Branch Jr. on his side. Now he turned to Jane.

"Why you, Branch?" she asked one evening in their Forest Hills home during a visit by Harold Parrott and his wife. Parrott, a former *Brooklyn Eagle* sportswriter who had been hired as road secretary on Branch Jr.'s recommendation, was visibly upset. Trouble ahead was all he could think about—in travel arrangements, scheduling, housing, eating. But to Rickey, Jane was the key to his elaborate scheme and he desperately needed her approval.

"Haven't you taken enough abuse about being 'El Cheapo,' about the 'chain gang' and all that? This will be more slander on your name," she argued. He was nearly sixty-four, had had several serious illnesses, and was now suffering increasingly from sickening waves of dizziness.

Yet once she had expressed her initial worry for his health and his reputation she never opposed his plan and quickly passed from mere acceptance to far more active support. Never for a moment did Rickey doubt she would. And once she had met the handsome Robinson and his lovely fiancée, he told Parrott later, her heart would quickly go out to the beleaguered couple.

Nor did any of his daughters feel differently. Though each reflected their mother's concern for their father, they all rallied behind him, in part because early on he took them into his confidence in long, wide-ranging talks. In the end there was a family sense of shared risks and pending excitement, of new and different challenges, of history-in-the-making. He had a unanimous family behind him.

Later he invited Robinson and his fiancée to his home, and a group of the Rickeys piled into a station wagon with them and drove off for a picnic. On another occasion in October, Jane and her husband Bob (a play-by-play broadcaster for the Fort Worth Cats) spent the afternoon with Jackie and Rachel at Baker Field in the northern reaches of Manhattan, watching Rickey's friend Lou Little lead his Columbia football team against Cornell.

Rickey was so exultant with their backing he sent each of his children a copy of a book he had recently read and profoundly admired. It was Frank Tannenbaum's *Slave and Citizen* and he added an aside to one of his daughters: "We're going to indulge in what most people would call a social experiment." And at that he laughed aloud with pleasure at the very idea of it.

He was so excited about discovering Tannenbaum's book he wrote Arthur Mann: "Arthur—This is it!" It seemed to be the central key he had been searching for, the thread that tied it all together. "An essay with good research on the effect of slavery on Western Hemisphere history—on culture—on social relations—on whatever you wish to care to call it—'The Negro!'"

Tannenbaum fascinated Rickey, for he was the sort of man whom Rickey admired most of all, a generalist who was as concerned with race relations as he was with prison reform, labor unions, and politics. They differed sharply in their political sympathies, one a left-wing socialist and the other an upholder of conservative and religious values, but they were also alike in many ways. Tannenbaum, a professor at Columbia University, was unhappy with the division of knowledge and experience into separate disciplines. Like Rickey, he sought to create a synthesis to cope with life's riddles.

When they could, they would meet and talk about Tannenbaum's thesis and its relationship to Robinson. Rickey was captivated by the professor's history of the development of human slavery and how its vestiges might be erased. He found support for his growing faith in evolutionary and nonviolent racial progress. "Force," said Rickey at this time, "has no place in the picture." Time, and Tannenbaum's "proximity"—which Rickey first uttered in mid–1946 and thereafter for years—did, and stood a far better chance of bringing equality to black Americans than legislation and court decrees.

"The last paragraph," he wrote to Arthur Mann on the flyleaf of the book, "could well be memorized." Days later he told Mann to think about Tannenbaum's words; once understood, Robinson's coming would not seem so surprising.

And Rickey read aloud to him:

> Physical proximity, slow cultural intertwining ... the slow process of moral identification work their way against all seemingly absolute systems of values and prejudices.... Time—the long time—will draw a veil over the white and black in this hemisphere, and future generations will look back upon the record of strife as it stands revealed in the history of the people of this New World of ours with wonder and incredulity. For they will not understand the issues that the quarrel was about.

Rickey now moved for fan acceptance. What better way, he reasoned, than to win over to his side Mississippi-born radio announcer Red Barber? If Barber would go along, so would the vast numbers of Dodger fans. From the time he arrived in Brooklyn, Barber's self-proclaimed "catbird seat"—only a box suspended from the upper stands behind home plate—was the focus of an attention rivaled only by a cult leader. Whether he was "recreating" games based on the information gleaned from Western Union's ticker tape or really present at the ball park, Barber's moral sway was considerable. If a black athlete was to join the club in peace, his backing was essential.

Rickey approached Barber with the hoary "you're-the-only-one-I've-told-this-to" technique he had used so often with his children. Asking Barber to lunch, they sat in Joe's Restaurant on Montague Street. Watching him break the Italian bread into small pieces and carefully butter each of them, Barber thought the old man looked tense.

"Listen, Walter," said Rickey, leaning toward him, as if in the deepest confidence. "I'm going to tell you something. I'm going to tell you something that even my board of directors doesn't know. Nobody knows outside my family."

Barber was shocked, although he soon accepted the idea enthusiastically. Rickey pressed on, stretching the truth when necessary to score his point.

"They [his family] say I'm too old to get involved in such a battle. They say my health is uncertain. They say I don't have to do it. But I'm going to do it. I don't know who he is or where he is, but I'm going to put a Negro ballplayer on the Brooklyn Dodgers. I don't know when—but he is coming."

He related the story of Charles Thomas to the announcer, and then rose to leave. "I've made up my mind, Walter, before I pass on I'm going to do something about it."

Meanwhile, into the summer and early fall, LaGuardia's Anti-Discrimination Committee finally published its "tentative proposal submitted purely as a basis for discussion." At first, it seemed to support Rickey's opponents. "Consider," it asked, "the possibilities ... where a Negro player slides into second base and spikes a Southern white boy or vice versa." It dealt with spring training in the South ("he would not be accommodated"), team spirit ("could morale be maintained if a Negro joined a club?"), and the border cities ("The Negro would have to understand and make his adjustments" if as expected hotels in St. Louis, Washington, and Cincinnati refused to house him).

Still, in the end, the committee timidly called for desegregation, arguing "that where management took a firm stand and went about the process of integration correctly, very few problems resulted."

Concluding, they expressed "little doubt that New York City's baseball public would certainly support the integration of Negroes on the basis of their abilities. There was never a more propitious moment than the present, when we are just concluding a terrible World War to suppress the theory of racial superiority, to put our house in order."

As cautious and hesitant as the document was, it nevertheless offended MacPhail. Years earlier he had expressed opposition to the barring of black players; now in October 1945 he led those opposed to their entry. Acting apart from the committee, he publicly blasted the Negro leagues and dared them to set their house in order before any black player tried to enter the big leagues.

Since he returned from military service, MacPhail had been nursing a giant-sized inferiority complex, fed by what he perceived to be Rickey's colossal egotism and unbearable condescension toward him. The rift developing (in his mind) was based on their rivalry as successful entrepreneurs, the records they had built as daring innovators, the Medwick beaning which he could not easily dismiss from his memory, the resentment he felt for the man who first brought him into baseball and who succeeded him in Brooklyn. MacPhail decided that if Rickey was (as he thought) for desegregation, he was against it.

LaGuardia was incensed at MacPhail and he turned to Rickey. It was mid–October and elections were ahead. The Mayor asked Rickey if he could announce that "baseball would shortly begin signing Negro players and that it was the direct result of the Mayor's Committee on Anti-Discrimination." Committee member and friend Judge Edward Lazansky was alarmed and took Rickey and Mann aside at a Bossert Hotel dinner meeting. "I feel I must tell you, Branch," he warned, "our committee's an election football."

Worried that the efforts to sign a black player would get entangled with politics, Rickey promptly called Dan Dodson, a New York University sociology professor and LaGuardia's intermediary on the committee, and suggested a delay. Paralyzed suddenly with nagging personal doubts about his course of action, he recognized that if he was ever to act it would have to be soon. But he annoyingly insisted on weighing all the imponderables.

"Dad," his son impatiently snapped at him, "we've *got* to make the decision *now.*" That did it. Turning to Bob Finch, he told him to wire Robinson and ask him to fly to Montreal. There, on Tuesday afternoon, October 23, 1945, Jackie Robinson signed a contract with the Montreal Royals as Royals president Hector Racine, vice-president Romeo Gauvreau, and farm director Branch Rickey, Jr., witnessed the event.

Then, in an uncompromising statement to the press young Rickey added his own feelings:

> Mr. Racine and my father undoubtedly will be criticized in some sections of the United States where racial prejudice is rampant. They are not asking for trouble, but they won't avoid it if it comes. Jack Robinson is a fine type of young man, intelligent and college-bred, and I think he can take it, too.

It may cost the Brooklyn organization a number of ballplayers. Some of them, particularly if they come from certain sections of the South, will steer away from a club with Negro players on its roster. Some players now with us may even quit, but they'll be back in baseball after they work a year or two in a cotton mill.

The next day he and his father were bitterly denounced in many newspapers and baseball clubhouses and offices. Judge William Bramham, the minor league czar, a onetime Rickey protégé, denounced the signing. "Father Divine will have to look to his laurels, for we can expect a Rickey Temple to be in the course of construction in Harlem soon."
Now there were two Rickeys to attack.

Rickey called in the New York *Sun*'s baseball writer Frank Graham and asked him to conduct a survey of reaction to the signing in black newspapers. Graham admired and liked Rickey, who had provided him with reams of good copy and given his son, Frank Jr., a job in Dodger public relations, and he was happy to comply. A week later he reported to him that a delegation of black reporters had been to see Commissioner Chandler.
Among other characterizations, Chandler had a reputation as a clown and few of the owners took him seriously. "He loves sentimental ballads, the gloomier gospel hymns, white horses, parades, loud pajamas and, on all occasions, plenty of noise," went one description of him. And when Chandler told everyone:
"When I entered Transylvania College I had only a red sweater, a five-dollar bill, and a smile" they all laughed at the "blue-grass jackal" as one team president called him, but thought him a welcome relief from the imperious Landis. Rickey, though, told Mann he expected much from the down-home Kentucky politician. "He's like me, Arthur, a country boy with ambition and vision. I suspect he's got a few principles hidden away."
When black reporters visited Chandler in his Cincinnati office they asked him about the signing of Robinson.
"Once I tell you something, brother," he told them, "you can count on me."
Ric Roberts of the Pittsburgh *Courier* was present and he remembered Chandler grinning broadly, gripping his hands and arms, and proclaiming at the top of his voice for all the world to hear, "I'm for the Four Freedoms. If a black boy can make it on Okinawa and Guadalcanal, hell, he can make it in baseball."
Hearing the story related by Graham, Rickey chuckled aloud. "Wonderful wonderful," he repeated. "Just wonderful, Frank."

"Squire," Graham continued, "even Ludlow Werner, who called you a 'pompous ass who would never hire a black player' six months ago did a turnabout, although he's still worried about what it may mean to Robinson.

"'I'm happy over the event [Graham read aloud] but I'm sorry for Jackie. He will be haunted by the expectations of his race. To 15,000,000 Negroes he will symbolize not only their prowess in baseball, but their ability to rise to an opportunity. And Lord help him with his fellow Negroes if he should fail them.'"

Later Graham amplified on his findings to Rickey in his memorandum, concluding that black press comments were "jubilantly reserved."

Black objections arose mainly from owners. Because the twenty teams in both leagues had no reserve clause and a shoddy contract system, Rickey had no qualms in signing black players without compensation to their former teams. Bill Veeck set a better example a few months later when he signed Larry Doby to a contract and paid owner Effa Manley of the Newark Eagles $15,000. Indeed, Mrs. Manley was so incensed at Rickey she told everyone who would listen:

"Mr. Rickey tried to take our parks, but he couldn't take them. I begged the owners of the Negro leagues to try to find out what was on his mind. I felt he was too smart to ignore. He couldn't take our parks, but he did take our ballplayers. He outmaneuvered us completely and the fans deserted us." The anti–Robinson *Sporting News* added its support, appealing to Commissioner Happy Chandler to do something about Rickey's "piracy."

The owners of the Monarchs were equally indignant at the "theft" of Robinson. But there was little they could do to press their case since the overwhelming majority of black fans wanted Robinson to play big league ball. When the Monarch owners raised objections to signing Robinson without compensation, Kansas City black ministers, newspapers, and fans sent them an unsubtle message: Don't ruin Jackie's chances. Retreating, co-owner J. L. Wilkinson rationalized: "Whether we get any recognition for it may be considered beside the point. We want Jackie to have a chance."

Graham also handed Rickey summaries of white newspaper opinions. In general he found editorial comments were favorable; on many sport pages, though, he was attacked for "raiding" the Negro leagues.

The Negro leagues had no written contracts, only unenforceable and vague verbal agreements on a game-by-game or annual basis. Still, Rickey was stung by charges that his search for black players was a reflection of a plantation mentality. To blunt them he had his aides find out whether or not each player under consideration had a contract.

Don Newcombe wrote him: "I am not under any contract for my baseball services for any future time." He was therefore signed to a Nashua, New Hampshire, contract. Mrs. Manley heard the news and was astonished. "When Rickey took him," she said, "he saw something we didn't, I guess."

Roy Campanella, who joined Newcombe at Nashua, denied he had signed with the Baltimore Elite Giants for the 1946 season. Like many of the others queried by the Dodgers, he was excited about the prospect of entering the major leagues. From Venezuela, where he was playing winter ball, he wrote Rickey: "I want to thank you for giving me a chance in life. And I will do everything in my power to make you and my people proud of me. God is on my side and I am sure he will see me through because I have faith in him. I will close thanking you from the bottom of my heart." He added a postscript. "Jackie and I are roommates down here. He also sends his regards."

Campanella's turn came after a black-white barnstorming game on a cold night in Huppert Stadium in Newark, New Jersey, in October 1945, before Robinson had been formally signed. Dressen was coaching at third base and asked the young catcher to meet him when the game was finished.

Outside the ballpark, Dressen said Rickey wanted to see him the next morning.

"Ten o'clock okay?"

Dressen was simply the messenger, and if he speculated to anyone about the import of the meeting no one ever heard of it.

"Take an 'A' train of the Independent and get off at Borough Hall. Anybody'll tell you where Montague Street is. The number is 215," Dressen went on.

Unaware of the pending signing of Robinson, Campanella assumed Rickey would offer him a job with the Brown Dodgers. He was staying at the Woodside Hotel in Harlem and, unfamiliar with the New York subway system, he asked George Scales, a Negro league coach, to accompany him to Brooklyn. They arrived early, but Rickey called in the burly catcher. "Mr. Rickey did all the talking. He had a big looseleaf book in front of him, maybe two or three inches thick, all the scouting reports about me."

Campanella, though, wanted to play in Caracas in the Venezuela winter league and instead of signing a contract—which he still believed to be with the Brown Dodgers, a misunderstanding Rickey deliberately refused to clarify—he left his address with him and the mutual understanding that they would meet again and talk even more seriously about a contract.

A week later, Robinson told Campanella what Rickey had in mind. "I didn't sign with the Brown Dodgers," he told him. "I'm going to be the first Negro in organized baseball. I'm to be signed at a public ceremony in Montreal tomorrow. It means the end of Jim Crow in baseball."

Then, Campanella understood. Rickey wanted him to be the game's first black catcher.

# Chapter Ten

OCTOBER HAD FINALLY COME TO AN END. For ten months he had been laboring furiously from 8 A.M. until late evening hours, wandering the country, overtaxing his staff, pushing and driving everyone around him. There were few occasions to unwind, but when they could, he and Jane played bridge or chess; Sundays they sometimes drove north to Pawling to visit with the Thornbergs or Lowell Thomas. Periodically he left early on Friday to drive to his new farm in Chestertown, Maryland.

He remained consumed by his extraordinary restlessness, scrambling from airport to airport in search of whatever player or club took his fancy or aroused his curiosity. He marked his pocket calendar with scores of destinations that autumn and winter: St. Paul, Los Angeles, Fort Worth, Cincinnati, Chicago, and many other smaller, out-of-the-way places. In December he flew to Columbus, motored to Delaware for an OWU trustees meeting, and then returned to Columbus for the annual minor league session, stopping off to visit with Senator John Bricker and John Galbreath, later owner of the Pittsburgh Pirates. Then he flew on to Chicago, where the winter baseball meetings were being held at the Palmer House and where for hours he swapped stories with old friends and acquaintances about players dead or retired, trades, and gossip of the business.

The next afternoon at lunch he leaned across the table toward Bill DeWitt, who was representing the Browns.

"William," he whispered hoarsely, "I'm sick."

DeWitt was shaken. Rickey's mother had recently had a stroke and his elder brother, Orla, had died of a similar attack.

The room was turning and Rickey had lost his balance.

Leaning heavily against the burly DeWitt, Rickey staggered to the elevator, ashen-faced, unable to see clearly, his head spinning madly.

"William, I'm sick," he repeated.

The next morning Branch Jr. put him on the train for New York while the nausea and dizziness continued. Arriving at Grand Central Station, he was taken by chartered ambulance to the Jewish Hospital in Brooklyn and then to their emergency room, where he was registered under a pseudonym.

He was sent to Peck Memorial Hospital, where doctors could not determine the nature of his illness. He was now petrified with fear and convinced he had a brain tumor. But the disorder was finally diagnosed as Ménière's disease, an illness related to deafness, nervous tension, and loss of balance.

Rickey was hard of hearing in his left ear and was told that he was experiencing a disintegration of the auditory segment of one of his cranial nerves. A breakdown of the second branch caused his loss of balance and dizziness. The doctors advised that for the rest of his life he change course and begin to act like a sixty-four-year-old man—gradually easing into complete retirement.

But he had just signed Robinson, and other black players were about to be signed as well. Durocher was, as usual, getting feisty. Sam Breadon's Cardinals needed to be cut down to size. And even while he was unwell he had quietly hired black pitcher John Wright so Robinson might have a companion at the Royals' training camp in Sanford, Florida. Above all else, he wanted desperately to make Robinson's inaugural spring as easy as humanly possible.

To Bob Finch he wrote: "I think it might be well for you very quietly to find out about living accommodations. I don't believe I would take it up with white folks to begin with. No use to stir around them unnecessarily. It occurs to me that the first approach would be to some leading colored citizen who could be at least trusted with the inquiry ... if there would not be any real bad effects, then I would like to bring these boys on there. I think you see the point. So go to it." When the squad moved south, the two players were housed with a local black family since Rickey was unwilling to defy the state's racial codes.

A few days into the training season he watched as Robinson tagged Ed Stanky very hard in the testicles, a deliberate blow apparent to the entire club. He called for Robinson, raising his large, thick eyebrows quizzically.

"Mr. Rickey," said the aggressive Robinson, "if I was a white man you wouldn't have a second baseman."

"Control yourself, Jackie. You know what I told you."

Robinson looked squarely at him but softened his tone. "Don't worry, Mr. Rickey, I will."

Later in the week Cub pitcher Paul Erickson hit Robinson in the arm with a fastball. He was hurt, but he refused to rub himself or in anyway show his pain. In the stands, Rickey stared at his pioneer and, turning to a companion, said, nodding his head, "Courage."

He was trying to protect him as well. On the opening day of spring training he appeared before every Dodger and Royal player and employee and for thirty minutes lectured them on "fair play." After Robinson developed a sore arm, Rickey insisted Montreal manager Clay Hopper play him at first base, an unfamiliar position. "He got me a first baseman's mitt and spent more than an hour showing me how to play the bag, and just what to do under certain conditions," said Robinson. Three days later Robinson played his first game for the Royals against the Dodgers in Daytona before 3,000 spectators, including 1,000 blacks. He went 0 for 3, fouling out the first two times at bat and forcing a runner at second. Rickey sat in the stands with Jane at his side, talking quietly to her, but saying nothing to Shotton or the press.

For if Robinson was obliged to practice nonviolence on and off the field, Rickey had to withstand provocations himself. Among the most venal were the bigoted remarks emanating from the Durham, North Carolina, office of Judge W. G. Bramham, the minor leagues' counterpart to Landis. "A shrine to Rickey was being planned in Harlem by Nigras," Bramham reported. But more upsetting to Rickey were the remarks of his Montreal manager, the Mississippian Clay Hopper.

Rickey later recounted the incident: "This boy [Robinson] had made a great play in the fourth inning and I had remarked about it and the two of us—Clay Hopper, Jackie's first manager and I—were sitting there together in 1946 spring training. In the seventh inning Jackie made one of those tremendous and remarkable plays that very few people can make—went toward first base, made a slide, stabbed the ball, came up with it in his left hand glove, and turned with body control that's almost inconceivable and cut off the runner at second base on a force play. I took Clay and I put my hand on his shoulder and I said, 'Did you ever see a play to beat it?' Now this fellow comes from Greenwood, Mississippi. And he took me and shook me and his face that far from me and he said, 'Do you really think that a nigger is a human being, Mr. Rickey?' That's what he said. That's what that fellow said. I never answered him.

"And six months later he came into my office after the year in Montreal when he was this boy's manager. 'I want to take back what I said to you last spring,' he said. 'I'm ashamed of it. Now, you may have plans for him to be on your club but if you don't have plans to have him on the Brooklyn club, I would like to have him back at Montreal. He was,' said Hopper, 'not only a great ballplayer good enough for Brooklyn, but also a fine gentleman.'"

That first spring Rickey saw innumerable acts directed against Robinson. Once they left their training base, southern reception was almost universally hostile. The city of Jacksonville canceled its permit for a Jersey City–Montreal game. A day game with Indianapolis at Deland was delayed because perfectly adequate lights were declared to be broken. Local vigilante groups threatened reprisals against the Dodgers and Royals. Police with riot guns were called out in Macon. In Savannah and again in Richmond, as the Royals traveled north toward haven in Canada, Rickey was horrified and appalled at the games canceled but more so at the death threats and obscene calls directed at his two black athletes. Nor was he immune himself; the name of Branch Rickey was cursed and reviled everywhere by upholders of the racial status quo.

The hatred he witnessed was unlike any he had ever met and its passion staggered him. He had first encountered racism long ago in South Bend when Charles Thomas was denied a hotel room. But now he was stunned by its depth and strength. His assumptions of progress through gradualism and proximity were—at least for the time being—shaken. What Robinson and John Wright were passing through, he observed to his sympathetic family, staff, and a handful of reporters including Wendell Smith, was far worse than he had ever dreamed possible in the America he revered and loved.

"I could never realize the intensity of feeling and how bad it would be," he said to a friend.

Just the same, Rickey's pioneering move was stirring the conscience of a few courageous Southern sports writers, such as Hugh Germinio of the Durham *Sun,* who wrote, "If a colored player is good enough to make the major leagues, then I want to see him have that opportunity"; Smith Barrier of the Greensboro, N.C. *Daily News:* "I don't see anything wrong with the signing of Jackie Robinson"; and Frank Spencer of the Winston-Salem *Journal:* "If he is qualified, then give him the opportunity."

On the eighteenth of April Rickey was in his office when the phone rang. It was Frank Shaughnessy, the president of the International League, and he was very nervous. He had heard rumors of riots and bloodletting when the Royals reached Baltimore.

Shaughnessy expressed his fears if Robinson should dare perform in that city.

Rickey shook his head in disbelief.

Shaughnessy pressed on. "Don't let him go, Branch. People are up in arms." Threatening letters had been received, he reported.

A year earlier Rickey might have hesitated and perhaps postponed Robinson's debut in Baltimore, then still very much a predominantly Southern and racially restricted city. But too many things had happened by now and he was doubly certain about the rightness of his course. It was for him more than ever before a question of absolute right versus absolute wrong, of good versus evil.

As Harold Parrott stood alongside him, he explained to the distraught and overanxious Shaughnessy: "I don't think those awful things will happen, Frank. It's one more case of 'trouble ahead, trouble ahead'"—the commonplace expression he and Jane had used all their married life to dispel useless worries. Robinson, he insisted, would play for Montreal, and he would drive to Baltimore for the game.

Shaughnessy tried one more appeal, but Rickey refused to be swayed.

"I'm sorry, Frank, but I just don't foresee all the trouble you do. Anyhow, the time has come for us to give democracy a chance. We solve nothing by backing away. In fact, we'll encourage every troublemaker if we show fear."

On the four-hour auto trip south to Baltimore later that day he nonetheless expressed his concern to Bob Clements, a front office assistant who was driving, that Shaughnessy's worst fears could prove correct. As Clements turned toward Memorial Stadium, Rickey told him: "Bob, run down and tell Clay [Hopper] he doesn't have to play Robinson today unless he wants to." Clements raced down a long flight of stairs, jumped the railing onto the field, and ran toward the Royal clubhouse with the message. Hopper was unperturbed. "Hell, Bob, the boys have already voted and he's playing."

After the game, a surging crowd of blacks, overjoyed at the racial breakthrough, pushed their way onto the field and raised Robinson on their shoulders in triumph.

Returning to Brooklyn, Rickey shook his head and smiled broadly. "Bob, I'll tell you something. I'm an old man who spent a lot of his time worrying about things that never happened." Clements, a native southerner, was too overcome with emotion even to reply. He believed he had seen history being made.

A few days later, for the season's second game, the Dodger entourage drove to Jersey City's Roosevelt Stadium, where 25,000 fans witnessed Montreal's victory over the Giants. Robinson went on a rampage, collecting four hits including a home run, scoring four times, and driving Jersey City pitchers frantic as he pranced down the third base line time and again threatening to steal home.

After the game, Rachel was in tears outside the clubhouse. Inside, an army of writers spotted Rickey. "He'll make Montreal this year," he shouted above the din, "and is definitely a big league prospect."

The next day Joe Bostic, who one year earlier had accompanied two black players to Bear Mountain, assessed the event in his *Amsterdam News* column: "The most significant sports story of the century was written into the record books today as baseball took up the cudgel for democracy and an unassuming but superlative Negro boy ascended the height of excellence to prove the rightness of the experiment."

Back in his office the following day, Rickey turned to Durocher, coaches Red Corriden, Charlie Dressen, Mel Jones, a front office assistant, and Harold Parrott and said confidently: "I shall not be at all surprised if by the first of June the five men in this room will say we made a mistake by not putting colored men on the Brooklyn ball club. On the first day of August it would be my best guess that you will remove any man from Montreal easier than you will Robinson."

Montreal was the perfect place for the Robinsons. Its chic restaurants, shops, wine cellars, theaters, ballet, and symphony were far more hospitable to the beleaguered couple than any American city would have been. Not that Canada's record toward Negroes was that good, Rickey told a member of his staff after he had read some literature on the subject. No Negro sat in any Canadian legislature, federal or provincial. No Negro was permitted to be a dining or sleeping car porter on the Canadian National Railway. If their treatment compared favorably with that in the United States it may have been because other minorities, such as Indians and Eskimos and even the French in Quebec, bore the brunt of Canadian attention. "There's virtually nobody on our side," Rickey warned Robinson as he prepared to leave for Montreal. "No owners, no umpires, very few newspapermen."

Despite their apprehensions and Rickey's as well, Jackie and Rachel learned to love the city and many of its people. They found an apartment and Rachel awaited the birth of their first child. Sam Maltin, a sportswriter, befriended them and introduced them into his wide circle of sympathetic friends. On May 1, when Branch Jr. read him the proclamation of the Synod of the Anglican Diocese of Montreal praising the Dodger organization "for taking its stand in not concurring with racial discrimination," Rickey was beside himself with pride.

Opening Day: 15,745, the second largest crowd in shabby Dolorimer Downs' history, paid their way in to see Robinson. Manager Clay Hopper was still skeptical and told the press before the game that "Robinson would have to be Father Divine to get the shortstop job away from Stan Breard."

The Royals defeated the Jersey City Giants again, 12–9. Robinson went 1 for 4, played center field, and caught three flies. Next day the Montreal *Star* headlined: BUKER, HOWELL, BREARD SUPPLY ROYAL RELISH. ROBINSON ALL RIGHT, TOO.

As the season wore on, Robinson performed as the Dodger scouting reports had predicted he would. He was a solid, flashy performer, capable of playing many positions but best at second base and very quick, very smart. He ran, bunted, stole home faster and better than most major leaguers. Jersey City manager Bruno Betzel, a native southerner, said Robinson was the league's finest player.

After thirty-six games, Montreal was in first place and Robinson was batting .370, with 17 stolen bases and only two errors (he made only twelve all season long).

Montreal columnist Lloyd McGowan, who had been leery of the experiment, was by now a consistent booster. "Few baseball men thought Robinson would catch a place with the Royals," he wrote in the *Star.* "It wasn't thought that he would stay around very long. But he brought more crowd appeal than anybody else on the club."

Montreal won the pennant and in September traveled to Louisville for the Junior World Series (before television, an important event in much of America). Rickey was in St. Louis and phoned Ray Blades to meet him in Salem, Illinois, in order to drive together to the games. He picked up Blades and they arrived in Louisville late the night before. Blades was haggard and drooping, but Rickey, on the move since seven that morning, wasn't ready to quit yet. With the unfortunate Blades in tow, they set out to look for a farmer selling what Rickey called "turkins"— a new species of chicken bred for added breast meat. They drove beyond the city limits until 2 A.M., when Blades—who said that by now he could barely talk, walk, or drive—spied the farm. Rickey bounced out of the car and awoke the farmer. "The old colored gentlemen" he had been searching for strolled about with Rickey, extolling the birds' virtues, discussing prospective sales and profits, and examining them thoroughly. Rickey wouldn't leave until he was assured they would be shipped to his Chestertown farm directly. Four hours later, he was awake in his hotel, on the phone to Robinson to invite him to a breakfast of oatmeal and "some good talk."

The Louisville Colonels were a fine ball club and they won the first two games at Parkway Field. Far more bruising in the best four-of-six series was the roughhouse treatment given Robinson. He played poorly. Al Campanis, a Rickey protégé, watched the games but confided to Nemo Leibold, the Colonels' general manager: "Robinson hasn't played too well down here, but wait till you see him in Montreal where the fans are his friends."

On October 4, 1946, the Royals completed a remarkable come-from-behind, three-game sweep of the series, winning the title. Robinson's play was outstanding and when the last out was made the Royal fans started cheering, calling on Hopper, Curt Davis, and Robinson to return to the field for a salute. Hopper emerged first, then Davis, the grizzled and graying veteran forty-three-year-old sidearm pitcher who had just pitched and won a 2–0, nine-hit shutout (he had always been a special favorite of Rickey's, having worked seven years for him on the Cardinals and Dodgers), and both were lifted onto the shoulders of hundreds of laughing and applauding fans. Then came Robinson, who was also raised up. "Tears slid down Jackie's cheeks, so deeply moved by the tribute was he," reported McGowan.

In the Royal clubhouse, the players and visitors roared with laughter and joy. Branch Jr. put his arm around Robinson. Hopper, excited and ready to explode with joy, shook Robinson's hand. "I'll have you play for me anytime." Robinson beamed and embraced his Mississippi-born and -reared manager. Then he walked toward a player who called him the "real hero." Grinning, Robinson demurred. "Nah, nah, the real hero is this guy's father," gripping Branch Jr.'s hand and shaking it warmly. Jim Crow baseball was dead. Luck was indeed the residue of design.

All that remained was bringing Robinson to the Dodgers. Moving to another of the goals he set for himself, Rickey sought to obtain the support of the press. He hired Arthur Mann as his special assistant. Mann knew everyone there was to know in the New York press corps. He had been a reporter for the *World, Tribune, Mirror,* and *Graphic* and a successful freelance for major magazines. His first assignment was to deal with the men who were dead set against desegregating baseball. Before long, Rickey sensed that Mann was far more than a press agent. He was, instead, a very loyal retainer and friend. He wrote scores of articles, and in the mid–1950s, a biography of Rickey. He was also someone who understood every nuance of Rickey's thinking (Ken Smith, the *Mirror*'s man assigned to the Dodgers, said the two became so close a "mutter by Mr. Rickey behind a batting cage meant a sentence to Mann"), an intelligent and sensitive man capable of carrying out complex and delicate missions and posing sensible alternatives. He was, above all else, a strong proponent of bringing blacks into the game. In 1945, before he went to work for Rickey, he challenged him: "How can you call it an All-American sport if you exclude black Americans?"

For a time, Mann had served as the *World*'s second-string drama critic and he loved art and music and often free-lanced for radio shows as a writer. Rickey found his company soothing and comfortable, and at first in his Brooklyn apartment and later in his Forest Hills Gardens house they spent many evenings together singing the old church hymns they both loved, Rickey in his deep baritone and Mann playing the piano, harmonizing and singing.

But nowhere was Mann more appreciated by his fellow writers than when he wrote and acted in biting and satirical skits at the annual New York baseball writers' dinner. Once he poked irreverent fun at the venerable Connie Mack, who had peddled so many of his Athletic stars ("Nothing left to trade or sell/The whole damned club was shot to hell"). He composed a ditty about MacPhail ("I've Got a Pocketful of Schemes"). But his favorite topic was always the man he idolized but whom he loved to parody at each year's dinner. "That's nonsense," Rickey said in a huff to Ken Smith after hearing "Glory Massa Rickey," celebrating the signing of Robinson to a Brooklyn contract. In "Schnitzel bank" Mann had Rickey trying to explain his complex farm system to a group of small boys. It bothered some of Rickey's family and upset some of his staff, who resented Mann's closeness with Rickey, but as Jane told Marion Mann after Arthur died in 1961, "We often differed sharply but never with animosity." Rickey though was deeply grateful for Mann's support and companionship, and he happily encouraged what he knew to be Mann's greatest strength—the ability to carry out tough assignments.

During the summer of 1946 the two leagues established a steering committee "to consider and test all matters of major league interest." Robinson was starring in Montreal, the Pascual brothers' rival Mexican League was signing any major leaguers it could, a lawyer named Robert Murphy was trying to introduce player unions, and demands were heard for an end to the reserve clause and the institution of pensions for players. Confronted by this turbulence and instability, the owners chose to concentrate on race, or rather, ways of preventing Rickey from sullying the game.

The men who ran the game wanted above all else to keep the national game lily-white. Fifteen months earlier MacPhail had written a confidential letter to Chandler, taking the lead in urging the same course. "This problem is becoming increasingly serious and acute.... We can't stick our heads in the sand, like an ostrich and ignore the problem. If we do, we will have colored players in the Minor leagues in 1945 and in the Major leagues thereafter."

The lords of the game agreed wholeheartedly and in what was to be their last overt racist expression met in Chicago on July 8, 1946. Echoing

MacPhail, they stated, in secret: "One or two Negro players ought to be allowed in the major leagues" although nothing toward that end should be permitted in 1946. Besides, they went on, only "agitators—people [who] are not necessarily interested in baseball but are interested in other things" were behind the pressure to integrate.

Considering that Robinson was already on the Montreal roster, the tone was surprisingly antiblack. They then proceeded to reaffirm their stance formally. By a vote of 15–1 (with only Rickey dissenting) they voted against allowing blacks to play in the majors. Their report was issued *in camera* on August 27, 1946, and was signed by Ford Frick, Sam Breadon, Phil Wrigley, William Harridge, Larry MacPhail, and Tom Yawkey. Aware of its explosive potential, Frick polled each owner to make certain he understood fully what he was signing. He also asked that all copies be returned promptly to him personally, for destruction. All were returned and burned. Except one, which Chandler deposited in his files.

Under the heading of "Race Question" the secret report read:

REPORT

FOR SUBMISSION TO NATIONAL AND
AMERICAN LEAGUES ON 27 AUGUST, 1946

MAJOR LEAGUE COMMITTEE

| Ford C. Frick | William Harridge |
|---|---|
| Sam Breadon | L. S. MacPhail |
| Philip K. Wrigley | Thomas A. Yawkey |
| *National League* | *American League* |

RACE QUESTION

The appeal of Baseball is not limited to any racial group. The Negro takes great interest in baseball and is, and always has been, among the most loyal supporters of Professional Baseball.

The American people are primarily concerned with the excellence of performance in sport rather than the color, race or creed of the performer. The history of American sport has been enriched by the performance of great Negro athletes who have attained the mythical All-American team in football; who have won world championships in boxing; and who have helped carry America to track and field victory in the Olympic games. Fifty-four professional Negro baseball players served with the Armed Forces in this war—one player was killed and several wounded in combat.

Baseball will jeopardize its leadership in professional sport if it fails to give full appreciation to the fact that the Negro fan and the Negro player are part and parcel of the game. Certain groups in this country including political and social-minded drumbeaters, are conducting pressure campaigns in an attempt to force major league clubs to sign Negro players. Members of these groups are not primarily interested in Professional Baseball. They are not campaigning to provide a better opportunity for thousands of Negro boys who want to play baseball. They are not even particularly interested in improving the lot of Negro players who are already employed. They know little about baseball—and nothing about the business end of its operation. They single out Professional Baseball for attack because it offers a good publicity medium.

The thousands of Negro boys of ability who aspire to careers in professional baseball should have a better opportunity. Every American boy, without regard to his race or his color or his creed, should have a fair chance in Baseball. Jobs for half a dozen good Negro players now employed in the Negro leagues are relatively unimportant. Signing a few Negro players for the major leagues would be a gesture—but it would contribute little or nothing towards a solution of the real problem. Let's look at the facts:

A major league baseball player must have something besides great natural ability. He must possess the technique, the coordination, the competitive attitude, and the discipline, which is usually acquired only after years of training in the minor leagues. The minor league experience of players on the major league rosters, for instance, averages 7 years. The young Negro player never has had a good chance in baseball. Comparatively few good young Negro players are being developed. This is the reason there are not more players who meet major league standards in the big Negro leagues. Sam Lacey, Sports Editor of the Afro-American newspapers, says, "I am reluctant to say that we haven't a single man in the ranks of colored baseball who could step into the major league uniform and disport himself after the fashion of a big leaguer.... There are those among our league players who might possibly excel in the matter of hitting or fielding or baserunning. But for the most part, the fellows who could hold their own in more than one of these phases of the game, are few and far between—perhaps nil." Mr. Lacey's opinions are shared by almost everyone, Negro or White, competent to appraise the qualifications of Negro players.

These Negro leagues cannot exist without good players. If they cannot field good teams, they will not continue to attract the fans who click the turnstiles. Continued prosperity depends upon improving standards of play. If the major leagues and big minors of Professional Baseball raid these leagues and take their best players—the Negro leagues will eventually fold up—the investments of their club owners will be wiped out—and a lot of professional Negro players will lose their jobs. The Negroes who own and operate these clubs do not want to part with their outstanding players—no one accuses them of racial discrimination.

The Negro leagues rent their parks in many cities from clubs in Organized Baseball. Many major and minor league clubs derive substantial revenue from these rentals. (The Yankee Organization, for instance, nets nearly $100,000 a year from rentals and concessions in connection with Negro league games at Yankee Stadium in New York—and in Newark, Kansas City and Norfolk.) Club owners in the major leagues are reluctant to give up revenues amounting to hundreds of thousands of dollars every year. They naturally want the Negro leagues to continue. They do not sign, and cannot properly sign, players under contract to Negro clubs. This is not racial discrimination. It's simply respecting the contractual relationship between the Negro leagues and their players.

There are many factors in this problem and many difficulties which will have to be solved before any generally satisfactory solution can be worked out. The individual action of any one Club may exert tremendous pressures upon the whole structure of Professional Baseball, and could conceivably result in lessening the value of several major league franchises.

The vote infuriated Rickey. Now he began speaking as if Robinson would never be allowed into baseball. So agitated did he become that he returned from Chicago as if in a trance and his aides tiptoed around him. He had cast the only negative vote yet had remained silent. Moreover, he had absentmindedly left his copy with Frick, unaware of the plans to burn the evidence. He phoned Frick for another copy, only to be told they had all been destroyed.

He had Robinson, Roy Partlow, Newcombe, and Campanella under contract; pitcher Dan Bankhead and other blacks were at that very moment under consideration. The more he pondered the vote the more his mood swung from anger to depression and back to anger again. One afternoon he rose and fled his office, shouting at Mann that it was the most un–American declaration he had ever heard.

He flew to Kentucky to meet with Chandler. Arriving late in the day the two men walked about Chandler's property, discussing the problem from every angle. Behind the commissioner's main house stood the two-story, luxurious "cabin," and following dinner, they seated themselves in the walnut-paneled room on its main floor, Chandler behind his huge desk and Rickey in the black leather chair.

"I can't go ahead in the face of that vote," Chandler says Rickey told him. "I can't do it unless I'm assured of your complete support."

"Can this man play?" asked Chandler. "He could make the major leagues today."

"Then the only reason he's being kept out is because he's black," said Chandler. "Let's bring him in and treat him as just another player. I'll keep my eye on him."

"The fifth step toward bringing Robinson to the Dodgers was the Negro race itself," said Rickey.

He sensed a danger in "overadulation, mass attendance, dinners of one kind or another, of such a public nature that it would have a tendency to create a solidification of the antagonism and misunderstandings—of overdoing it." Or, as a later generation put it, what he feared most was an ugly white backlash.

## Branch Rickey

In January 1947, Herbert T. Miller, executive secretary of the Carleton Avenue branch of the Bedford-Stuyvesant YMCA in Brooklyn, asked Rickey to meet with a representative group of local blacks. Yes, answered Rickey, but only if he might speak freely. He had been conferring with a growing number of black people and he had much on his mind. In a letter to forty prominent blacks, Miller wrote: "He has a matter of importance which he wishes to discuss with a select group of persons ... in connection with the projection of what seems to be inevitable."

On a frigid February evening, accompanied by Mann, NYU Professor Dan Dodson, and Judge Edward Lazansky, he entered the main hall to a standing ovation from the middle-class blacks Miller had invited.

Chewing tensely at his unlit cigar, he approached the dais. He stuttered as he tried to decide which of the three approaches to the topic he had prepared would be most suitable. He discarded all three and started speaking extemporaneously, asking his listeners to say nothing to outsiders and then abruptly admitting he was hesitant to tell them what was on his mind.

He began by speaking of Robinson. "If Jackie Robinson *does* come up to the Dodgers as a major leaguer..."

He stopped and the audience was still.

"...the biggest threat to his success—the *one* enemy most likely to ruin that success—is the Negro people themselves."

Arthur Mann described the next moments: "The gasps of shock and amazement were audible as they cut through the ominous silence. Jaws dropped. Eyes blazed in indignation. It was a sharp slap against every Negro in the room." Rickey continued.

"I mean it and I'll repeat it. I say it as cruelly as I can to make you all realize and appreciate the weight of responsibility that is not only on me and my associates, but on Negroes everywhere.

"If Robinson enters the big leagues Negroes will celebrate Robinson Days and Nights. Negroes will fight among themselves, become drunk in ball parks, be arrested, spoil him on the banquet circuit and ruin his chances.

"For let me tell you this!" Rickey roared. "If anyone tried to use the Robinson affair as a symbol of social 'ism' or schism, a triumph of race over race, I will curse the day I ever signed him to a contract."

They stood and cheered, some in the audience unashamedly weeping. If the cause was only baseball, thought Mann, it was a major breakthrough for them. Rickey turned away from the men in front of him so overcome with emotion he could no longer speak.

"Speak, brother, speak," came cries from the seats.

When he had collected himself and the audience returned to their seats he outlined the way they could avoid "spoiling Jackie's chances." Essentially he asked them not to antagonize white fans too quickly. He asked them to help organize committees of prominent Negroes in every major league city and spread the word: "Don't Spoil Jackie's Chances."

One final step in bringing Robinson to the majors remained: winning over his white teammates.

In 1946, a New York City sports columnist, who allegedly opposed the desegregation of baseball from the very start, wrote that Rickey deliberately had the Dodgers lose the pennant race (the Cardinals won by a two-game margin) when he traded Billy Herman, a thirty-five-year-old second baseman, to the Braves, thus "postponing" the victory until the year Robinson's arrival would make it a "Negro triumph."

If Powers' columns had profoundly agitated Rickey, this hurt even more. He rarely entered player clubhouses, but this time he arrived unannounced, tears rolling down his cheeks, to damn the story as an unmitigated lie. Notwithstanding a writer's bigotry, he still had to deal with his players and the coming of blacks.

He shifted the Dodgers' spring training in 1947 from Florida and other southern towns to Havana. Just before camp formally opened he scheduled a series of exhibitions in Panama, where the Dodgers stayed at the United States Army Base in Cristobal while the Royals were housed across the isthmus in Panama City. Rickey approached his old friend and *Sun* writer, Frank Graham, and asked him to plumb player sentiment. Graham later reported to the "Squire"—a name he reserved for Rickey—that "Robinson will have to undo an undercurrent of resentment. Not all the Dodgers feel that way, but a great many do."

Not long after the Royals arrived in Cristobal for the games, Kirby Higbe, a garrulous, hard-drinking right-handed South Carolinian, went to Parrott and confessed that a plot was being hatched to kill Robinson's chances. Dixie Walker, Bobby Bragan, and Carl Furillo—an Alabaman, a Texan, and an Italian-American from Reading, Pennsylvania—were the supposed ringleaders of a petition attacking the signing of the black infielder. Also in the cabal, said Higbe, were Cookie Lavagetto and Hugh Casey. Peewee Reese was neutral, he reported, and Gil Hodges, Carl Erskine, and Rex Barney, among several others, openly sided with Robinson. (Barney, incidentally, would become the first Dodger publicly to shake Robinson's hand when he joined the team.)

Thoroughly alarmed, Parrott telephoned Rickey at the Tivoli Hotel in Cristobal. He also informed Durocher, who had been apprised of the rumors by another Dodger player. For some time Durocher had been testing the rumor with his men. What did they think about the Robinson thing, he would suddenly slip into a conversation. When Durocher believed the rumor was genuine, he moved into action.

"I made up my mind right there that there was going to be no petition. Not if I had anything to say about it."

He called a meeting in the middle of the night and went into a tirade directed against the petition. Scorning all subleties, he plunged ahead with a warning: "You know what you can do with that petition. You can wipe your ass with it. My. Rickey is on his way down here and all you have to do is tell him about it."

Warning the players that signers would be sent to other teams, he said, I'll play an elephant if he can do the job. This fellow is a real great ballplayer. He's going to win a pennant for us.... From everything I hear, he's only the first. *Only the first, boys!*"

Rickey started receiving the recalcitrants in his room that morning.

To each he delivered a sermon on Americanism. Some relented, either persuaded or intimidated or simply in fear of being traded or shipped to the minors. But one player, a substitute catcher, was not moved. He took the worst criticism of all.

"Do you want to play on the same team with Robinson?" asked Rickey.

"No, sir, I do not."

"Would you, then, like your contract transferred to another club?"

Standing next to Rickey, refusing to back down, Bobby Bragan answered that he would indeed but did not want to be the scapegoat.

"Then I may accommodate you, sir! Good night."

Rickey (said Mann, who was alongside) was "visibly moved by the emotional strain of the evening. His hands trembled and he couldn't light a cigar. His voice was hoarse."

The popular Alabama-reared outfielder Dixie Walker was also initially opposed to Robinson's presence:

"Dear Mr. Rickey," he wrote in March 26, 1947.

"Recently the thought occurred to me that a change of ball clubs would benefit both the Brooklyn baseball club and myself. Therefore I would like to be traded as soon as a deal can be arranged."

Rickey was surprisingly sympathetic to the dilemma of the white southerners, who, he explained, had a way of life to undo. Clay Hopper had changed and before too long Bragan would befriend Robinson and vindicate Rickey's faith in both of them. Walker, too, soon relented (although he wasn't traded until 1948, when he was two years shy of forty), saying, "It wasn't easy for me to accept Jackie when he came up. But he and I were shaking hands at the end."

Sitting with Mann one afternoon several weeks later, Rickey said:

"Alexander Pope covers it mighty well in his *Essay on Man*. Many people don't want Negroes in the major leagues but when it comes..."

Then he began reciting:

> Vice is a monster of so frightful mien,
> As to be hated, needs but to be seen;
> Yet seen too oft, familiar with her face,
> We first endure, then pity, then embrace."

He sat back in his chair, looked at the ceiling, and reached for the right words. "First they'll endure Robinson, then pity him, then embrace him."

On April 9, 1947—the day Chandler suspended Durocher—Rickey phoned Robinson, who was living at the McAlpin Hotel in mid–Manhattan. Would he come to Montague Street the next morning, he asked? The Dodgers were going to make it official. By now it was a poorly kept secret but such confidants as Arthur Daley of the *Times* were not able to publish it yet because Rickey had told him the news off the record earlier that spring in Havana. In spite of Durocher's pleas to "give the kid a break," Rickey refused to allow himself to be quoted on this story. "My boy," he explained patiently to Daley, the *Times's* sports columnist, "I'm afraid I'll have to hold you to your promise. This is the most important step I ever took in my life, and I can't risk a premature leak. It could destroy something I've dreamed of for years. When it comes, it has to be a fait accompli, too late for anything to stop it."

On April 10, while racial segregation was legal and discrimination a widespread practice, while blacks were barely visible in newspaper and magazine coverage and advertisements, Robinson signed his contract in Branch Jr.'s office. He was to receive $5,000 annually.

The announcement went out over Rickey's name. "The Brooklyn Dodgers today purchased the contract of Jackie Roosevelt Robinson from the Montreal Royals. He will report immediately."

A few weeks later the club drove to Philadelphia, where the pattern encountered in the southern states was repeated. Not only had Robinson been refused a room at the Benjamin Franklin Hotel, but Rickey had also been notified of further trouble even while the team was still on the highway motoring down.

To the problem of the reluctant hotel, Rickey's directive to Shotton was to move the team to the more hospitable Warwick. The other problem was stickier. "Trouble ahead, trouble ahead," he murmured after he hung up the phone in his office. The call had come from Bob Carpenter, the owner of the Phillies, and Herb Pennock, their general manager. Both men had asked him to keep Robinson out of Shibe Park. If not, they warned, the fans might riot.

"You just can't bring a nigger here with the rest of the team, Branch," said Pennock, who had spent twenty-two years as a pitcher in the majors. Harold Parrott was listening at Rickey's request on an extension phone and heard Pennock add: "We're just not ready for that sort of thing yet. We won't be able to take the field with your Brooklyn team if that boy Robinson is in uniform."

(The Phillie manager was Ben Chapman, a fifteen-year veteran outfielder with a lifetime average of .302 who had briefly pitched for the wartime Dodgers in 1944–45. He had already informed the local reporters of his plans for Robinson. "We'll ride him…. There is not a man who has come to the big leagues since baseball has been played who has not been ridden.")

When Pennock finished Rickey was agitated but remained cool. "Very well, Herbert. And if we must claim the game 9–0 [the score for any forfeit] we will do just that, I assure you."

The Phillies retreated and took the field, but Chapman's bench jockeys were especially brutal and vindictive; nearly all their remarks centered on Robinson's race and his wife.

Today, Chapman waves aside any intention of harming him. "Robinson was a great player. He took what we gave him, and I must say he was the best competitor I ever saw. Jackie never expected any special treatment. A few writers, knowing I was from Alabama, made a big issue of it. Had I been from New York, I doubt if anything would have been said."

But Eddie Stanky, who was aptly nicknamed "The Brat" and "Muggsy" by his teammates and about whom Rickey once said, "He can't hit, he can't run, he can't field and he can't throw but if there's a way to beat the other team, he'll find it," thought otherwise. That evening in Philadelphia, Stanky responded. Looking straight at Chapman the inquisitor and then at the raucous Phillie dugout, he screamed across the infield, "Why don't you guys go to work on somebody who can fight back? There isn't one of you has the guts of a louse."

Parrott, who had driven down after the Pennock-Carpenter phone call on Rickey's instructions, sat behind his dugout listening to the jockeying and Stanky's defense. He called Rickey and told him "at no time in my life have I heard venom and dugout filth to match the abuse that Ben sprayed on Robinson last night."

The news was disturbing to Rickey because Robinson was receiving identical treatment wherever the club went; no one, neither club owner nor manager nor player, had yet dared step forward to denounce the tactics. The next morning he phoned Chandler in Cincinnati to complain, but the commissioner was a step ahead of him. He had, he told Rickey, just hired Jack Demoise, a onetime University of Kentucky basketball player and American Association pitcher, to roam about the majors assessing reactions to Robinson. Demoise, a former FBI agent hired on J. Edgar Hoover's suggestion, was asked to identify the troublemakers. Chapman was one so identified by Demoise, and that afternoon Chandler phoned the Phillie manager and warned that his conduct would no longer be tolerated. He also called Pennock and bluntly informed him, "If you move in on Robinson, I'll move in on you."

In his office, the tension tentatively relieved, Rickey laughed at Parrott's frustration. "You see," he told him. "You and Mother [Jane] weren't very strong for this Robinson at the start. Now all of a sudden you're both fans of Jackie's and you're actually worrying about him. Fair men of quality will soon rebel against the treatment Robinson is getting, and they'll do something about it. There will be an incident, perhaps a small one, perhaps something big. But they'll be drawn closer to him and become a protective cordon around him. You'll see..."

Two weeks later, as the team was in St. Louis for the season's initial series with the Cardinals, Sam Breadon phoned Ford Frick with disquieting news about a possible Cardinal player strike. "I don't know how far they'll go," he told the league president, "but I've got to do something now." Word was out that the men would not play alongside a black, and although no vote had been taken, the consensus was clear. "They're talking on the bench and in the clubhouse," said Breadon, "and if it continues we might have some serious trouble. What do you think I should tell them?"

"Tell them," answered Frick, a former sports reporter and once Babe Ruth's ghostwriter, a man with a well-deserved reputation for timidity before the owners, "that this is America and baseball is America's game. Tell them that if they go on strike, for racial reasons, or refuse to play in a scheduled game, they will be barred from baseball even though it means the disruption of a club or a whole league." It was Frick's finest moment.

His warning might have gone unnoticed had the press not heard the same rumors. Rudd Renny was covering the Dodgers for the New York *Herald-Tribune* and during dinner with Dr. Robert Hyland, an eminent local physician and team doctor for both St. Louis clubs, noticed that he looked worried. Renny pressed him hard, and Hyland told him of the plot to prevent Robinson from playing. They were cursing Rickey for having conceived the whole idea. The more tolerant and liberal Musial, the team leader, might have been able to stop it but he was in a New York hotel room recovering from acute appendicitis. The Cardinals, Hyland warned, were on the verge of striking.

Renny rushed to a phone and called his editor, Stanley Woodward. Then the editor phoned Frick at his suburban Bronxville home.

"What are you going to do about it?" asked Frick.

Woodward told him that without his confirmation he hesitated running the story.

Frick paused, and then replied, "I won't deny it." The story ran, and the strike was aborted.

As the season ran its course Stanky became a prominent supporter of Robinson's right to play baseball. At Rickey's instructions, the black player was still silent, but men such as Stanky filled in for him. In one game Robinson was spiked by Enos Slaughter—who had been a leader of the abortive strike—in the eleventh inning, a game that the Dodgers finally lost. "I have always had the highest regard for Slaughter as a clean competitor," an angry Stanky told reporters afterward, as Rickey stood by. "But I've lost all my respect for him."

Even the hard-drinking Georgian pitcher Hugh Casey now defended Robinson, rushing onto the infield to threaten Slaughter.

"You'd hear a lot of insults from the opposing benches during games, guys calling him things like 'nigger' and 'watermelon eater,' trying to rile him," said Peewee Reese, the team captain and Louisville native. "But that was when Jackie Robinson started to turn the tables: You saw how he stood there at the plate and dared them to hit him with the ball, and you began to put yourself in his shoes. You'd think of yourself trying to break into the black leagues, maybe, and what it would be like—and I know that I couldn't have done it. In a word, he was winning respect."

For all the obvious heroics both Robinson and Rickey paid a price. According to Harold Parrott the infielder suffered a near nervous breakdown during the season. And Rachel said, "I tried again and again to get him to talk, but he didn't want to burden me. He never would talk about those things at home. But I knew they were eating at his mind, for he would jerk and twitch and even talk in his troubled sleep." Rickey was troubled more than ever by Ménière's disease, which caused him to pass through constant spells of dizziness and nausea.

The arrival of a subpoena to testify before the House Un-American Activities Committee created greater anxiety in Robinson. Called on daily by the international as well as American press for interviews, pressured by headline-seeking politicians and treated as a demigod by blacks

With his arm around Dodger team captain Peewee Reese, Rickey talks with the shortstop before the opening game of the 1949 World Series against the Yankees at Yankee Stadium. (AP/Wide World Photos)

and liberals, Robinson seemed bewildered by the furor. The subpoena demanded he testify on Paul Robeson's statement that American blacks would not fight against the Soviet Union. Far more politically liberal than Rickey, he and Rachel admired Robeson's talents and, even more, often lonely fight against racial bias, though not his pro–Soviet remarks.

They were two innocents caught up in a cruel political game. "We were not aware of the underlying intent of the committee and regret very much speaking against Robeson," says Rachel. But in 1947 she told Rickey that the pressure from Communists not to testify was enormous. Rickey heard them with interest and sympathy. He was in agreement with the committee's stated intent but he was unaware of its opportunism and its ugly vigilante spirit. Still, his primary interest was in helping the Robinsons and he turned to Lester Granger of the Urban League and Arthur Mann for assistance in drafting a statement for Robinson to approve and deliver.

"I don't pretend to be expert on communism or any other kind of 'ism,'" Robinson told packed congressional committee audience on July 17, 1947. He asked instead to be thought of as "an expert on being a colored American, with thirty years experience at it." He wasn't "fooled" because he had had opportunities denied to other blacks, he went on, to the discomfort of the committee's hard-liners who had expected a fiery anti–Communist speech. The fact that Communists preyed on injustice and brutality meted out historically to American blacks did not "change the truth of his [Robeson's] charges." And he went even further. "A lot of people try to pretend the whole issue is a creation of Communist imagination. Negroes were stirred up long before there was a Communist Party and they'll stay stirred up long after the party has disappeared—unless Jim Crow has disappeared by then as well.... And so, it isn't very pleasant for me to find myself in the middle of a public argument that has nothing to do with the standing of the Dodgers in the pennant race—or even the pay raise I am going to ask Mr. Branch Rickey for next year."

Gradually, Rickey's thesis won over the Dodgers, in a series of small and subtle ways. Carl Erskine and his wife befriended the Robinsons publicly. And one day Jackie Jr. was throwing a ball in the Ebbets Field clubhouse. "Throws like his daddy," someone said, and Robinson grinned. When the boy bobbled the ball, the Georgian relief ace Hugh Casey laughed loudly, adding, "He fields like his daddy, too." It was good-natured joshing and the men in the locker room joined in the laughter. He was getting teased because of his post–1947 theater and dinner tour. "Jack, have you got $20,000 with you I can borrow?" asked one Dodger. And when he missed a ball in fielding practice, Arky Vaughan shouted, all smiles, "When you were poor, you *made* those kind." During the off-season he formed an integrated barnstorming club with Rickey's encouragement and blessing, and Hodges and Branca joined North Carolinian Pep Young (a former Pirate, Red and Cardinal infielder) as the white contingent. Even the volume of anonymous hate mail was diminishing, Marion Mann reported (Rickey had asked her to help Robinson with his correspondence) to her husband, Arthur. Hearing of these promising developments, Frank Graham wrote his friend, the "Squire": "Everything is going well."

*We first endure, then pity, then embrace.*

Rickey kept hammering away at the theme, reminding the Robinsons of his optimistic views of better days ahead and making himself available to them at all times.

"We would go to his hotel or he'd come to us, in Florida, in New

York, anywhere," said Rachel Robinson. "We'd meet in hotel rooms, the three of us, and we'd look forward to being with him. Often he'd invite us to his home in Forest Hills, where we'd undergo counseling sessions and supportive backup. Always his wife was with us in their home, always feeling that Mr. Rickey was doing the moral thing. If he didn't call us or ask us out to the house, he'd accept our calls. We called him often, because we needed support in this. We knew that Mr. Rickey was always there, always responsive; there was a consistency in his support. He didn't back off when things got tough. In fact, Mr. Rickey became a kind of father-substitute for Jackie and kept urging Jackie to go back to U.C.L.A. and complete his bachelor's degree."

The Dodgers won the pennant that year; 1,807,576 attended games at Ebbets Field, a league record, and an even greater number saw Robinson on the road. Stanky, catcher Bruce Edwards, pitchers Joe Hatten and Hugh Casey had splendid seasons while Reese sparkled at shortstop. Ralph Branca won 21 games. Robinson batted .297, shone as a base runner, especially during the World Series against the Yankees, and captured rookie-of-the-year honors. "An adventurer," exclaimed Rickey with enormous pride. "A man after my own heart."

"Looking back," says Rachel Robinson today, "I can see how the conviction of Jackie and Mr. Rickey to bring a black into baseball was fortified by the fact that they were alike in so many ways. Jackie had had the good influence of older men in his life and he was deeply spiritual with a strong belief in God. Both were religious, and both always said I rather than 'we.'

"Nor were we ever distrustful of Mr. Rickey's motives. He was a man of integrity and we could trust him. Whatever his mixed motives may have been, he became a lifelong friend, someone we admired tremendously."

After the season Rickey criticized his beloved OWU upon learning its football team, scheduled to play Rollins College in Orlando, Florida, decided against taking Negro tackle Kenneth Woodward with them. Alumni, faculty, and students called on Rickey for help and he wired the president: "I think Ohio Wesleyan might make [a] great mistake relative [to] not playing a colored boy against Rollins with the resultant bad publicity based upon injustice to the player and an expression of intolerance that the university has never stood for."

Woodward went south with the team.

In 1948 the Dodgers trained in the Dominican Republic, Rickey believing the bigotry had now abated. Still, Robinson continued having a difficult time. One evening Parrott found him and Campanella slumped in an empty Greyhound bus after a hard game with the Yankees. The squad was inside an adjoining restaurant but Rickey had consented to the owners' wishes and asked the two blacks to remain outside. Said Parrott: "As I juggled the tray of plates onto the lonely bus in the dark, I found a Robinson who was politely grateful—but seething at the put-down. Campanella was pleading to avoid a scene. 'Let's not have any trouble, Jackie. This is the only thing we can do right now, unless we want to go back to them crummy Negro leagues.'" (Rickey had also appealed to Campanella to follow the passive public approach taken by Robinson. "Mr. Rickey once stuck his head out a window in Parrott's presence and said, 'Roy, please don't chop it off.'")

By then Robinson harshly viewed Campanella as just another Uncle Tom, an obsequious Negro happy for the white man's leavings. In time, he felt the same way about Don Newcombe. Both men had, he believed, traded on his sacrifices and his humiliation but were unwilling to do the same for those still on the outside, in baseball and elsewhere in America. It was simply untrue, but his growing bitterness was a measure of his pain and his passion.

"Robinson's eyes were aflame, and I knew what was racing through his mind," continued Parrott. "He had played a big part in winning fat World Series checks for all those guys inside the restaurant, even the third-string bullpen catcher and the humpties who hardly ever got into a game. And there they were, all of them, stuffing the food down and not seeming to care that he wasn't part of it, wasn't one of them."

Robinson had appealed to Rickey, but the older man had again counseled a bit more patience. They talked of Job's travails and Rickey ended up asking for Robinson's faith and trust, but only for a brief while longer. Soon, he told his combative infielder, "the wraps will be off and you can be yourself." Robinson agreed, reluctantly, because the man who had brought him so far had asked him to.

"Mr. Rickey had a personal commitment to seeing it through," says Rachel. "He anticipated a lot would happen to Jack and tried to cushion the blow. When we moved to Brooklyn, he contacted a lovely black family to help us. He made all sorts of efforts to involve us with friends and his family, to help us overcome the terrible stress. Jackie trusted him."

In 1948, Robinson batted .296 in 147 games, scored 108 runs, had 107 hits including 38 doubles, 8 triples, 12 homers (he had hit only 3 home runs in Montreal), 85 RBIs, 8 sacrifices, 22 steals, was hit by pitchers on seven occasions, and ended up with a slugging percentage of .453. The next year he hit .342 and won the league's batting championship and Most Valuable Player award.

Rickey then ended their pact of self-control and any separation from the rest of the team in housing and dining facilities. In Atlanta, Robinson and Campanella were scheduled to play on April 8–10, 1949, when Ku Klux Klan Grand Dragon Sam Green called for a state investigation of the "illegal exhibition series." Governor Herman Talmadge waffled, saying he "wasn't familiar with the laws governing such things and that any action would have to come from Fulton County [Atlanta] Solicitor General Paul Webb." Webb too demurred, adding he knew of no local laws that would prevent the games from being played. But State Attorney General Eugene Cook declared no such restrictive law existed. Stirred by the controversy, the Atlanta *Constitution* conducted a man-on-the-street poll and discovered that four of every five favored the games being played even if the two black players performed. The Associated Press also queried phone subscribers, with identical results. Typically, one white Atlantan's reaction was—as Frank Graham reported to Rickey soon after—"especially interesting": "Sure it's okay. In fact, I'll bet there will be less opposition to it in Atlanta than there was in Brooklyn the first time Robinson played there."

When he heard the news Rickey grinned, chewed on his cigar, and said to Graham, "Proximity, Frank, proximity."

The Robinson experiment transformed Rickey into an outspoken partisan of racial desegregation in the sport and throughout the nation. Mornings following night games at Ebbets Field, Rickey the ex-catcher would sit with Campanella talking about racial segregation, American and Christian ideals, catching. "Mr. Rickey kept telling me regularly about the importance of signals so that I could get the respect of the Dodger pitchers. Some of them were rednecks and he wanted them to respect me as a catcher and as a man."

In 1949, when Red Barber's assistant Ernie Harwell left for the Giants broadcasting team at the Polo Grounds, he and Mann talked about hiring a black announcer. "I know where there is a good Negro radio sports announcer," Mann wrote Rickey. "News of an interview with him would raise a few shingles, if not the whole roof." So intrigued with the idea was Rickey that he visited the Newell Emmett Advertising Agency, which handled announcing assignments for the Chesterfield cigarettes sponsor, only to learn they had already chosen Al Helfer.

His interest in furthering racial equality never flagged. When, for example, scout Toby Karam reported Bill Veeck in Cleveland was interested in Larry Doby, with whom the Dodgers had signed a binding agreement, Rickey told Mickey McConnell of the farm department, "As much as I would like to have Doby with us, I think it would be a healthy thing for the color line to be broken in the other league. If Cleveland will offer him a contract that will bring him as much or more income than our agreement, tell Doby we will tear up our agreement with him and let him go to Cleveland." Several weeks later he allowed Monte Irvin to go to the Giants for the same reason.

The warm friendship between the exemplary California black athlete and the elderly Ohio iconoclast continued for the remainder of their lives. When Rickey left Brooklyn after the 1950 season, Robinson wrote him:

"I have been intending to write for a month now and it seems that finding the right words comes hard so I will attempt at this time to put them down.

"It is certainly tough on everyone in Brooklyn to have you leave the organization but to me it's much worse and I don't mind saying we (my family) hate to see you go but realize baseball is like that and anything can happen. It has been the finest experience I have had being associated with you and I want to thank you very much for all you have meant not only to me and my family but to the entire country and particularly the members of our race. I am glad for your sake that I had a small part to do with the success of your efforts and I must admit it was your constant guidance that enabled me to do so. Regardless of what happens to me in the future it can all be placed on what you have done and believe me I appreciate it.... My wife joins me in saying thank you very much Mr. Rickey and we sincerely hope that we can always be regarded as your friends and when we need advice we can call on you as usual regardless of where we may be."

In 1959, Rickey expressed his own thoughts on the man. "Surely, God was with me when I picked Jackie. I don't think any other man in the Negro race or any race could have done what he did those first two or three years. Above all, he had what the boys call guts, real guts."

Each time Rickey visited New York City he phoned the Robinsons. In 1965 Robinson was involved with the Gibraltar Life Insurance Company and asked Rickey to join its board of directors.

"It would be a great honor for me if you would consider being a part of the company," he wrote. "Things have been very rewarding for me but had it not been for you nothing would be possible." Robinson added: "If you'd like a few shares [of Gibraltar] I'll see you get some on the ground floor," although he warned Rickey there were "no sure things." "Please don't feel you have to accept my offer, but I believe you would want to be a part of an interracial company."

Rickey quickly replied: "I am ready to go along with you in whatever capacity you wish."

The next month Robinson wrote again:
"Even though I haven't written very much you are always on our minds. We feel so very close to you and I am sure you know our love and admiration is sincere and dedicated. Please take care of yourself. We know where your heart is. We will take care of Selma, Alabama, and do a job."

In yet another of the many letters that passed between them, Rickey "had the temerity" to nominate the Urban League's Whitney M. Young ("a most complex mind, great courage") to the board of Gibraltar plus "two colored gentlemen" he had befriended, Archibald M. Carey, Jr., and Thurgood Marshall, "a very able interpreter of the Constitution, a stormy petrel as attorney for the NAACP, who gave no quarter and asked for none."

In the years following, Rickey's sympathies for and understanding of the suffering of minorities deepened. He recognized that bigotry, however cloaked in respectability, was a plague. For the remainder of his life his speeches were peppered with references to the Holocaust, in which six million Jews were murdered by the Nazis and their allies. "We shudder in amazement that a civilized nation, prominent for centuries in art and science and indeed in the practice of the Christian religion, of all things, could so deny the moral value of every individual human being that they could with clever and ingenious planning and systematized administration, sadistically destroy an average of one-half million men, women, boys and girls, and babies each year for twelve years. How could it be?"

He expressed chagrin that Japanese and other Asians weren't allowed to immigrate to the United States because of the exclusionary and racist McCarran-Walter Immigration Act. Scribbling on the subject on a yellow sheet of legal paper he added a note, as he had so often in his life, that Jesus' crucifixion and resurrection were His way of accepting moral responsibility.

Then too, he spoke frequently on the issue that became his central motif: "Why is there an epidemic of racism in the world today?" On a steaming summer's day in Buffalo, New York, in the late 1950s he spoke to a crying, laughing, stomping ovation at the New York State NAACP convention. In Pittsburgh, after Rutgers University philosophy professor Houston Peterson came to call, he called out, "Let's go to church." They drove to a black church and Peterson recalls that as the seventy-six-year-old Rickey entered, cane in hand, people began shouting out, "God bless you, Mr. Rickey," while the minister intoned, "Amen."

He helped establish the National Scholarship Service and Fund for

Negro Students. And during the 1960s he motored through the Deep South to study at first hand the impact of the momentous *Brown* v. *Topeka* desegregation ruling on its schools and black people. Looking, ever looking, he was overflowing with ardor and passion for this cause and this principle. For Branch Rickey, the simplest of truths was that God had indeed created all men and women equal.

He provocatively challenged six hundred white ministers in Lakeside, Ohio: "I am contemptuous of the church's role to date in integration. Ministers, on the whole, are like other people. They want to go slow on integration. They're moderates. In fact, I can think of no major white figure in America today who *isn't* a moderate.

"They call you an extremist if you want integration *now*—which is the only morally defensible position. To advise moderation is like going to a stickup man and saying to him: 'Don't use a gun. That's violent. Why not be a pickpocket instead?' *A moderate is a moral pickpocket.*"

When Jackie Robinson died in 1972 of diabetes and hypertension, some wrote that his coming was no big thing and would have happened sooner or later. Others, more cynical, described Rickey's driving force as greed. But the fact is that before Branch Rickey no one had done it or even seriously proposed doing it. And that is his legacy.

# Chapter Eleven

By 1947, RICKEY HAD FASHIONED once again an extraordinary organization and the nucleus of a remarkable cast of athletes. At the start of the year he told a third-string catcher, Gil Hodges, and a fledgling outfielder, Duke Snider, "You two will someday be preeminent power hitters." At Vero Beach he spent hours teaching Snider to hit to left and left center. Daily he stood with George Sisler behind the batting cage as scout John Cary threw Snider slow curves and had him hit to the left side of second base. "I think you're getting it," Rickey spoke up one morning after an hour of practice. "Without him," said Snider more than three decades later, "I would never have made it."

At the close of spring training he composed—as he so often did in his life—a memo to himself of "things to do and things I am thinking about." He wanted to hire Allen Roth, the first statistician ever in baseball. O'Malley objected, but Rickey pushed ahead. He dealt with preseason games at Yankee Stadium, baseball for youngsters in the New York region, a promising Yale University pitcher "of good family." He wanted information about Donald Newcombe, a black pitcher on the Nashua, New Hampshire roster. He shipped Roy Campanella, the black ex–Baltimore Elite Giant catcher, to St. Paul to integrate the American Association. He traded for Preacher Roe, Billy Cox, and little Al Gionfriddo in May. For the final Saturday of the season he took a large part in organizing "Jackie Robinson Day" at Ebbets Field, inviting dancer Bill Robinson to serve as emcee.

Again, they lost to the Yankees in the World Series, this time in seven games. After the final 5–2 Yank victory, Larry MacPhail tearfully announced his retirement from baseball. Then, departing the stadium, he accidentally ran into Rickey under the stands. Spontaneously, he put his arm around the older man's shoulders, but as if stung, Rickey fell back, his evangelical wrath kindled, his blood stirred. "Never speak to me again," he spat out. "Never."

Two months later, Chandler reinstated Durocher. In a personal note to Rickey he enclosed a copy of sportswriter Earl Ruby's Louisville *Courier-Journal* column praising Rickey's "extreme loyalty" to Durocher. Chandler added a postscript. "I admire the way you had fought for him all the way." And then still another postscript. "I was the main source of Ruby's column."

In 1948, Durocher was back at the helm, to the chagrin of O'Malley, who felt his presence might hurt gate receipts. Rickey warned him again to stay clear of gamblers and gambling.

Durocher seemed impervious to the warning and insensitive to the man who had sought vainly to protect him. In their new quarters at Ciudad Trujillo in the Dominican Republic, Jane was astounded to hear Durocher boasting of his winnings in cards. When she told her husband, he was incredulous. "He even had the effrontery to tell Mrs. Rickey that he had won $300," he told an aide. Rickey was also bothered by Durocher's open criticisms of his Dodgertown training base and his teaching techniques. Then too, other complaints began mounting up in his mind: "Outsiders," said the shocked Rickey, "were still sitting on the team bench during practice, a practice I had expressly forbidden so as to deter hustlers and touts from hanging about." Parrott reported Durocher refused to stay in the hotel rooms assigned him and chose, instead, a far more luxurious suite; daily, he fed reporters cynical criticisms of the Dominican campsite, Rickey was told. Then Durocher mocked Rickey's friend coach Ray Blades before the players, "the same Blades," complained Rickey, more annoyed than ever with his petulant and adolescent manager, "whom Manager Shotton handled in 1947 throughout the season with Blades as the third-base coach and won a pennant and at no time during that year was there player criticism against Blades." To top it off, another coach, Clyde Sukeforth, told Rickey he too was unhappy with Durocher.

There was little Rickey could do with Durocher but accept him as he was or fire him. When Horace Stoneham let Giant hero Mel Ott go and asked Rickey for permission to talk with Durocher, he had his solution. "Accepted," he said to the Giant owner. He was at last rid of a man he deeply admired as a manager but could neither control nor make behave more conventionally.

They met for the last time as employer-employee during the Stoneham-Durocher negotiations. Leo was hurt and puzzled, but his feelings of respect for Rickey were sincere. Accompanied by his wife, he walked into Rickey's office and asked about his status in Brooklyn if he didn't take the New York job. "Your future lies over the river, Leo," Rickey said in his gentle, fatherly way.

Almost as important for the future were the championships won by Montreal, St. Paul, and Hollywood. Rickey estimated that the club had sold $600,000 worth of excess players during the year.

The search never seemed to end. When Mickey McConnell heard Rickey complaining about Montreal's second-base problem he mentioned a young black "borderline prospect who might become a utility infielder on a major league team." He was talking about Jim "Junior" Gilliam of the Baltimore Elite Giants. "Try to acquire him for $4,000," Rickey advised him. The Elite Giants owner expressed an interest in the sale but sent McConnell back with a counterproposal: Baltimore had debts and needed a new bus; make it $5,000 and he would throw in a pitcher as well, a right-hander named Joe Black.

In December he quit smoking. He wagered his $500 against his daughter Sue's $100, payable to whoever stopped before Christmas Day. They both did, but their laughter was tempered by the fear he had developed a malignancy in his urinary tract. In the early part of the month he underwent a thirty-five-minute operation at the Mayo Clinic and learned the blockage was merely a benign growth.

During his hospitalization, Branch Jr. had replaced him, and Rickey took pride in his son's efficiency and sense of order. "I want to tell you"—he wrote all his children in a round-robin letter that December—"that Branch has been doing, and is doing, a good job of it. He can run this show pretty well and my indispensability, which has been less apparent to most people for some time, now impresses me less and less. I think I must now learn how to use leisure. Yet I have got to do something continuously even though I will be sixty-eight two weeks from today."

Branch Jr. was indeed capable of running any major league organization. But would the father allow the son he loved so dearly to apply for a job elsewhere? "Everyone in baseball regarded Branch Jr. as his father's son," observed Red Barber. "The result was a rebellion of despondency in the younger Rickey, a raging fury inside of him." The son was reluctant to hurt his father; the father was oblivious to the hurt he was unintentionally inflicting.

Superficially they were so much alike: Branch Jr. smoked occasionally, rarely drank or attended games on Sunday, preferring to teach Sunday school in a Freeport Methodist church. But in truth he was the very opposite of his colorful and extroverted father. He read extensively but was drawn to comparative religion, mysticism, philosophy, Shakespeare.

He enjoyed operatic and symphonic music. Only the men in the Dodger front office knew that more than anyone else he could argue with his father when he thought him wrong. When Rickey wanted to release Buzzie Bavasi and Fresco Thompson, two assistants in the Dodger organization, he persuaded him to retain them. When Jake Pitler's role was challenged, he took Pitler's side.

Pitler was business and field manager at Olean in the Class D Pony League. Branch Jr. had watched him closely and respected his abilities so much he suggested his father pay him a salary tantamount to a promotion to a job with a higher-classification farm club. Branch Jr. argued—backed by McConnell, his deputy in the farm system—that "Pitler's value lay in teaching and motivating beginners rather than polishing their skills further at a higher level." But Rickey stubbornly insisted he was correct. The salaries of Class D managers, he told them, had to be consistent. To pay one man more than other men would only stir dissension.

Branch Jr. disagreed. As farm director, he knew the best coaching was teaching. To his father he argued that nurturing raw talent and serving as instructor and counselor were far too vital to any organization as deeply committed to the farm system as they were.

Rickey won, but it was a Pyrrhic victory. Not long after he promoted Pitler to the Dodgers as a reward for past services, a recognition of the work he would perform with the younger Dodgers, and as an awareness of his son's understanding of what Jake Pitler meant to the organization.

"I observed Branch Jr. when he worked for MacPhail's Dodgers before his father arrived. He was never happier," says Bob Clements, contradicting what Branch Jr. had once confided in friends. "He was a much freer soul working independently than working for the father to whom he was so devoted." "Mr. Rickey had such a powerful personality he could veto an idea by Branch Jr. even when his idea had validity," added Mickey McConnell.

# Chapter Twelve

UNTIL 1948, WALTER O'MALLEY WAS AN OUTSIDER. He was, though, a superb behind-the-scenes operator, working hard at cultivating sportswriters and influential and powerful political associates. Tough, cool and a master of intrigue, a man who kept his own counsel, he recognized almost from the start of his association with the Dodgers that baseball was more than a game and that vast profits were to be made. If at the start he knew little about the sport's intricacies, he knew a lot about its economics. Watching Rickey operate, he developed an ambition to displace him in the president's chair.

From 1948 on, Rickey slowly grew uneasy as O'Malley lay in ambush, waiting for him to commit blunders. "It is a sad and costly mistake to underestimate O'Malley," he complained to St. Louis columnist Robert L. Burnes, "but most people do." To Dodger scout Rex Bowen, he cautioned: "We have a man trying to take over the organization." When O'Malley schemed to push Jim Mulvey off the Dodger board, Rickey sarcastically told Parrott at Vero Beach in early 1950: "The time has come, my boy, to consider whether it's wise to say 'good morning' to Jim Mulvey if O'Malley is listening." And to Red Barber he confided, "Walter O'Malley is the most devious man I have ever met."

Walter O'Malley first began attending board meetings as Dodger counsel in 1943 when he replaced former Republican presidential candidate Wendell Willkie. He was at the time a corporate lawyer residing in the small seaside village of Amityville on Long Island's south shore. The men he courted in his world of mergers and acquisitions thought him good-humored and generous, and his idea of a splendid weekend was to invite guests—Rickey, too, on two weekends early in their relationship—aboard his cabin cruiser to fish, drink, and swap stories. The son of a Catholic dry goods merchant turned Democratic Party politician, O'Malley was born on October 9, 1903, in New York City.

"Our family circumstances were above average," he recalled. "My father had been successful. I remember when I graduated from engineering school at the University of Pennsylvania, he gave me a boat that slept eight. But the stock market crash caught him, and financially he never recovered."

Transferring from engineering to law, the younger O'Malley graduated from Fordham University Law School in 1930. "A lot of people were selling apples on street corners at the time but I was fortunate in building up an active practice, handling mostly bankruptcies." He quickly sensed that the road to authority and comfort—as opposed to subordination and struggle—lay in knowing the right people in the right places.

Using his position as a springboard, he bought into a building materials firm and wrote and had published privately a register and manual for subcontractors. Afterward he annotated the city's antiquated building codes, acquired part ownership of the Long Island Railroad—then privately owned—the Brooklyn Borough Gas Company, the New York Subway Advertising Company, hotels, and a beer company. Before long, his clout in certain commercial circles and the powerful Catholic-run Brooklyn Democratic Party came to the attention of George V. McLaughlin, who initially asked him to handle the bank's affairs and, later, the Dodgers. In return, McLaughlin allowed him to buy 25 percent of the team.

As the years passed, O'Malley attacked any action by Rickey he deemed inappropriate. He courted John Smith assiduously and they became allies, freezing out Rickey. When the football Dodgers lost $750,000—which Rickey lamely tried to explain away as merely "regrettable," caused (said Rickey) by his premature interest in the economic possibilities of pro football—O'Malley blasted the move as an unmitigated miscalculation caused by bad judgment and consistent (said O'Malley) with the growing number of "questionable strategies" Rickey was pursuing.

When Rickey spontaneously ordered that every player and coach be given a new Studebaker after the 1946 season as an expression of the club's gratitude, O'Malley was able to have the order countermanded. Three years later he overruled Rickey again and told the pennant-winning 1949 players they could not receive new World Series rings unless they turned in their older, 1947 versions. They also clashed over whether a beer firm was a suitable sponsor for Dodger games. O'Malley won that one, too. But when O'Malley was called on to rescue Rickey and the club from a potentially disastrous law suit, he knew that Rickey was losing ground. During the challenge of the Mexican League to sign all the players it could from both leagues, Rickey uncharacteristically lost his public composure and condemned former Cardinal pitchers Fred Martin and Max Lanier (who had jumped to the Mexican League) and their Wall Street lawyer, John L. Flynn, for "avowed Communistic tendencies." Flynn threatened a massive suit and Rickey turned to O'Malley to salvage the situation. Publicly, O'Malley soothed Flynn's temper and stated that "Mr. Rickey neither stated nor inferred" any association with the Communists; privately, he attacked Rickey as a fool, calling his attack "libelous," and agreed with Flynn's characterization of Rickey's words as a "vicious slander ... maliciously intended."

Rickey was forced to thank O'Malley and that pleased the Dodger counsel immensely: "Rickey lost his cool and I showed how I could act in a bad situation," said O'Malley.

As the expiration of Rickey's five-year contract neared, O'Malley sensed that he could see to it that the contract was not renewed. Smith, the principal owner, died of cancer in July 1950. O'Malley's appeal was always businesslike; he argued persuasively that Rickey was spending money extravagantly on the Vero Beach complex, on his far-flung farm system, on his private plane, and on air travel for his team. "Rickey sold surplus players," said O'Malley, "but that is a dangerous way to operate a business."

Behind closed doors O'Malley was even more critical. Harold Parrott, who worked for both men, admiring Rickey and hating O'Malley, whom he dubbed the Big Oom, claims O'Malley and his friends called Rickey the "psalm-singing faker" and once spent an evening in their Hotel Bossert haunt playing pin-the-tail-on-the-donkey on a photograph of Rickey.

Beyond the issues of power and personality, the two men differed sharply about what lay ahead for baseball. O'Malley interpreted 1949's record total baseball attendance of 22 million as only a harbinger of greater profits. Television was in its infancy, and to O'Malley, it meant continued and limitless economic growth. More than any other baseball magnate at the time, he foresaw the implications of that boom. Geometric increases in revenues could be expected for years to come, he predicted.

Rickey, on the other hand, took a less commercial attitude toward television, much as he had in 1935 when he opposed night games because of the damage he thought it might inflict on family life. "Radio created a desire to see something. Television is giving it to them. Once a television set has broken them of the ball park habit, a great many fans will never reacquire it," he claimed. Moreover, he argued, TV would

Rickey, Durocher and Walter O'Malley in the Dodger offices on Montague Street in Brooklyn. Rickey and O'Malley battled for control of the team and O'Malley won. Eventually he transferred the Dodgers to Los Angeles, a traumatic development for Brooklyn and its incredibly loyal fans. (Courtesy of the Los Angeles Dodgers)

seriously harm the minors along with the "basic structure of professional baseball."

In the short run, it was an argument O'Malley had to win inasmuch as they were comparing Rickey's baseball—a nineteenth and early–twentieth-century slower, bucolic and pastoral sport, constant, tranquil, uninterrupted, a sentimental mirror of a world now gone—and O'Malley's vision of change and technology, of jet travel, of the surge in population and hedonism, of amoral shifts of franchises lured by more and more revenue, and of the voracious appetites of television advertising.

To Rickey, baseball remained a civil religion which acted out public functions organized religion was unable to perform; O'Malley's faith rested on balance sheets and dividends.

# Chapter Twelve

Professional football was an interlude, but one Rickey thought worth pursuing. He believed the game was on the threshold of enormous popularity and growth. When Bill Cox visited the Sugar Bowl in New Orleans, he sat next to Rickey, watching quarterback Bobby Lane lead Texas to a 27–7 win over Alabama and pleading with Rickey to take over his Brooklyn Football Dodgers of the All-America Conference. Cox, who had once owned the Phillies and been barred from the game by Landis for betting on their games, was losing considerable sums of money on football.

Cox handed his club to the Dodgers, and Rickey, deaf to O'Malley's objection that the football team was bankrupt, stressed his belief that "civic pride" would induce Brooklynites to support football much as they had baseball. "Brooklyn should be represented in professional football," he declared to a press conference in January 1948. "I already have scouts on the job and am studying the draft list." Would he consider coaching, a questioner asked? "I would do that only if requested by the players and my board of directors. However, the odds against either the players or the directors asking me to be coach are tremendously high."

Arthur Mann was appointed as chief assistant for football. He then asked Pepper Martin to be his place kicker. When Martin protested his ignorance of the skill, Rickey waved aside the objection. "Don't worry, John. I'll teach you."

The venture proved an athletic and financial calamity. Under Coach Cliff Battles, the ex–West Virginia Wesleyan and Washington Redskin star, the club finished next to last in the AAC's eastern division with a 3–10–1 record. After that, Rickey tried to bail out as painlessly as possible, offering to sell the franchise to any buyer for any "reasonable" offer—rent free, for one year."

But when Rickey and O'Malley fought over a beer-as-sponsor contract and Rickey lost, his youngest daughter, Elizabeth, concluded he had lost his whole struggle.

"I knew then that Dad was leaving Brooklyn. 'I'm doomed,' he told me. 'He'll force me out.'"

Fred Saigh, who had bought the Cardinals from the dying Sam Breadon in 1946, had suspected trouble when Rickey called him at his Hotel Pierre suite some months before in New York City. Rickey sounded worried, says Saigh, and he wanted to drop by for an early breakfast. When he confided that O'Malley was forcing him out, he asked if Saigh knew Joseph Kennedy, the Wall Street and Boston millionaire. "I do indeed," answered Saigh, an investor of considerable wealth himself. Then, Rickey continued, would you ask him if he would buy my quarter share in the Dodgers?

Saigh had liked Rickey in St. Louis (after Saigh was imprisoned for tax evasion and ostracized by baseball people, Rickey continued to send him warm letters and associate with him, says Saigh), and he wanted to help him out.

"Not Kennedy," he said, "but I do know someone who might. How much do you want?"

Rickey hedged, vaguely cited some figures, and said he really needed more time to come up with a definitive figure. Saigh nodded. "Okay," he said. "I'll try to find a buyer if you give me some detailed numbers." Rickey promised to do so and left. But Saigh never heard anything more from him about the offer.

Instead, Rickey seems to have deluded himself into believing he might overpower the formidable O'Malley. For a time he tried to strike the specter of O'Malley from his thoughts and turned to the business at hand and particularly the men he surrounded himself with and genuinely liked and felt most at ease with. Roettger, Finch, Parrott, Sisler, Sukeforth, Mann, Kenneth Blackburn, Mickey McConnell, Andy High, Rex Bowen, and of course, his son openly returned his affection. Now more frequently than ever he would call them into his office for coffee and dessert and speak of matters far removed from baseball. McConnell remembered times when Stalin's mass murders in the Soviet Union were much on his mind. On another occasion, he and his wife visited with Rickey at 1:30 A.M. talking about Plato's *Republic*. "I remember translating it from the Greek," he told the McConnells, who had read the book in a Great Books seminar. "But I would like to refresh my memory."

Even so, the final days were witness to a stormy fight between Rickey and O'Malley. Red Barber recalls the final day of the 1950 season in Ebbets Field. As the Phillies and Dodgers battled on the field below, O'Malley and Rickey sat in the press box, only a partition separating them from Barber's radio team, "screaming at each other all afternoon." It got so loud Barber had to turn his microphone around to avoid the din.

In December he was sixty-nine years old, on the edge of defeat. At his last Brooklyn spring training season, he had asked to meet with the minor leaguers. Rather than speak of baseball or their careers directly, he referred to their concerns as human beings and uncertain ballplayers and the role Jesus had played in his life.

"He left a life. He left a philosophy. He left a religion—so great, so marvelous, so wonderful; and yet to me the real revelation—even if we strip him of divinity, boys; just strip him of divinity—say there's no God in him—he's just a man like us. I don't think that. But let's say for the moment that he was. Just that. The explanation of a great life—of a marvelous life that can leave that kind of an impression on the world for two thousand years and now surely must enter into some of the great international problems if we're to solve them at all, and certainly ought to have full consideration in the personal life of everyone of you.

"Don't you shift too much responsibility for your success in this game to somebody else. You rely pretty much on yourself. Be anxious about it. Be persevering about it. Be firm about it. Have a high purpose. Pay the price; pay whatever it takes, and you'll probably come out about where merit takes you. I hope to see a lot of you next year and I hope that you are everyone in a higher classification than you are this minute. I hope that many of you go to the major leagues and you're in an organization that will send you there as fast as it can—either our club or some other.

"Fresco [Thompson], take care of these boys the next eight days. Lecture morning and night. You've got some wonderful fellows here—they'll enjoy it. See if you can't take care of all of them.

"Goodbye, gentlemen."

He turned to leave, his baggy pants and large, floppy hat dancing in the warm breeze. Behind him, the young players rose spontaneously and applauded.

That spring he wrote a friend, Howard Williams, "I really would like to return to the St. Louis area for the rest of my days and I want to live on a farm, and I mean live on it and run it. I am doing everything I can to sell my stock. It is pretty difficult to sell a one-quarter interest in a baseball club. In my entire life I have never had any money of my own. For the past fifty years I have never been out of debt—not one minute."

It was evident, especially to Jane, that even if he were allowed to stay with the club it would have to be as O'Malley's subordinate. She recognized the impossibility of such an arrangement. "No one could make friends easier than Branch. But he can't take a back seat." Neither for that matter could O'Malley, and the stage was set for their final, if anticlimactic, showdown.

By now, O'Malley reeked with confidence, telling writers that Rickey's contract was terribly unfair (he was earning $100,000 annually plus dividends plus a percentage of the profits on the sale of players) to the other stockholders. "We had to get him out of there if the club was ever going to make money," he repeated decades later to Roger Kahn.

When Rickey heard the criticisms he was furious but helpless. O'Malley, he suggested in a letter to the Dodger board, was a liar. His contract had been authorized by the board, a board that also included his critic.

As for charges that the club was losing money, "a recent auditor's report showed [in mid–1950] a capital surplus in excess of two and a half million dollars."

The argument, however, fell on deaf ears. O'Malley had the votes and the muscle to oust Rickey. Even more, O'Malley now believed himself to be Rickey's equal if not superior, a professional who had risen in the ranks, served his apprenticeship, and bested an aging reactionary twenty-two years his senior.

There was one remaining hurdle. A contractual clause between the two men stipulated that if either of them chose to sell his shares (and had a genuine offer), then the other had the option of buying the stock at the price offered.

Rickey demanded one million dollars. All he needed was a bona fide purchaser. Turning to his old friend John Galbreath, the Pirate owner, he asked for help. Like Rickey, Galbreath was the child of a poor Ohio farm family and a fraternity brother. He had amassed his fortune from real estate and, once informed of Rickey's plight, went to aid "the master salesman," as he fondly referred to him, "a man of great desire who accomplished whatever he set out to do."

Indeed, Rickey had been a supersalesman to the Pirates, having sold them $700,000 worth of surplus players since 1947, mainly the products of his fertile farm system. First baseman Ed Stevens, infielders Eddie Basinski, Monty Basgall, and Gene Mauch, pitcher Steve Nagy, along with over-the-hill Hugh Casey and Dixie Walker were among those sent westward. Bing Crosby, another Pirate owner, once paid a call on the team's offices and discovered Rickey trying to peddle Marvin Rackley, an outfielder. The crooner listened for one hour and then rose to leave. "Where are you going?" asked Rickey, looking up. Said Crosby: "I'm going to hire a three-piece ensemble to play soft music while you put on this sales talk." Outside the office he was spotted by some reporters. Rickey, he told them, ought to be in films. "I never saw his equal in Hollywood."

What was annoying to Crosby was most appealing to Galbreath, the club's principal owner. Not only did he continue to buy superfluous Dodgers but he also found a prospective buyer for Rickey—William Zeckendorf of the prestigious New York real estate firm of Webb and Knapp. When O'Malley heard that Zeckendorf was willing to put up $1,000,000, he paled, since he had hoped to pay a far smaller sum. But even more galling was Zeckendorf's additional insistence that, if O'Malley matched the offer, Zeckendorf get $50,000, for "tying up my capital." O'Malley had to reply within ninety days, else the Brooklyn realtor would become a partner, team up with Mulvey, rehire Rickey, and leave the club with a 50–50 standoff between the antagonists.

The final price was $1,025,000 ($50,000 still went to Zeckendorf). Rickey repaid $300,000 to the Brooklyn Trust Company, which he had pledged when he borrowed the money to buy into the Dodgers. To pay the capital gains tax, he borrowed a good deal of money so that the principal sum could go to his estate. Once done, he sat down and dictated a final letter to the board of directors summing up his years in Brooklyn.

"The past eight years of my association with you have been full of interest and challenge.... In 1943 the club organization numbered only five clubs. We had twenty-five in 1950. In 1943 we had approximately 250 players, almost 100 of whom were on inactive [military] lists. Our reserve lists for 1951 show 637 active players. In 1943 the Brooklyn Club did not own real estate in any major league city. Ebbets Field was heavily mortgaged. Today Brooklyn owns valuable properties other than Ebbets Field in Fort Worth, Montreal, and elsewhere. There is no indebtedness on Ebbets Field ... there is no indebtedness throughout the entire organization, except between our own clubs. The assets are estimated in high figures. The book value exceeds four million dollars.... The players, too, are known everywhere as gentlemen—with high standards of personal conduct. Our ... players are chosen with care and special attention to other than simply physical qualifications.... The past eight years, I believe, have been marked by an identification of the Brooklyn Club and its personnel with community service on a broad scale to an extent unparalleled in the history of baseball.... The Brooklyn Baseball Club has come to be recognized as a vital civic force ... I wish now to advise you that it is my definite intention not to continue in any capacity with the company."

Before concluding his final report, he nominated Jim Mulvey to succeed him, a futile gesture symbolizing his feelings about O'Malley. "It is really with very deep sorrow that I take my leave of you," he ended.

The press conference formally announcing O'Malley's triumphant succession to the presidency was held on October 26, 1950, at the Hotel Bossert in downtown Brooklyn. Tommy Holmes of the *Eagle,* watching the sixty-nine-year-old apparently accept his relegation to a more placid and retiring private life, described Rickey as "almost radiant."

When his time to speak arrived, Rickey stood, smiled benignly, and opened his remarks with one of his pet biblical quotations:

"Comest thou here to see the reed driven in the wind?" Then, swiftly, he declared his resignation and introduced O'Malley as "a man of youth, courage, enterprise, and desire." The words and his victory pleased

O'Malley for the time being, and he in turn praised his erstwhile opponent. "I have developed the warmest possible feelings of affection for Mr. Rickey as a person," he announced.

Months later O'Malley sat with Red Smith on the New York-to-Philadelphia train on their way to a game at Connie Mack Stadium. Something was bothering him, he said unexpectedly, and he wanted to set the record straight once and for all. About the introduction of Robinson into baseball, did Smith know it was really he, not Rickey, who had accomplished that historic act?

Galbreath found another way to rescue his friend. After the sale to O'Malley was consummated, he phoned Rickey in Brooklyn. Was he planning to retire or would he like to run the Pirates? Rickey was jubilant. His pain in losing the Dodgers was genuine, but the chance to take

charge of another club was one more challenge, as well as a way of building a ballclub from the ground up. The Pirates were in complete disarray. For five years not one of their farmhands had reached stardom, and they depended excessively on the glamour of home run hitters Hank Greenberg and Ralph Kiner to boost their attendance, if not their standings. They were losers, at the gate and in their league. By 1946, the widow of baseball pioneer Barney Dreyfuss had had enough and sold the club to a syndicate composed of Galbreath, Bing Crosby, Pittsburgh lawyer Thomas P. Johnson, and Indianapolis banker and owner of the local Clowns farm team, Frank McKinney.

McKinney was selected

**Branch Rickey announces his resignation at a press conference, October 26, 1950, marking the end of an era with the Brooklyn Dodgers. (AP/Wide World/Rooney)**

to administer the team's affairs but between his sorry trades and lack of foresight, plus his emotional attachment to the Indianapolis Clowns, the Pirates floundered badly. In 1946 they finished in sixth place, wasting hundreds of thousands of dollars on failed players. The next four years they ended eighth, fourth, sixth, and then last again.

The syndicate discarded McKinney as operating officer and in the autumn of 1950 signed a contract with Rickey. He was to receive $100,000 yearly for five years, with $50,000 a year for a second five years in any capacity he wished. Galbreath also provided him with a single-engine five-seat Cessna plane and a strapping 6' 6", 280-pound pilot nicknamed Moose ("He really is a moose," said the startled Rickey the first time he laid eyes on the huge pilot), with strict, no-nonsense instructions to avoid all night or mountain flying.

Most of Rickey's front office men followed him to Pittsburgh, where they reasoned that in spite of the prevailing mediocrity, Rickey's formula for success would in time bring victory to the city.

The crucial man in his organization was, however, uncertain about moving to Pittsburgh. Unknown to his father, Branch Jr. had been offered jobs with the Giants and the Tigers. Surprisingly, the pragmatic O'Malley asked him to remain with the Dodgers.

"Mary," he said one evening on the steps of their home in Freeport, "I've been offered a job."

"He had such great respect for his father," says his wife, "he was reluctant to even tell him about the offers. He knew such news would get him all excited."

But he did tell him and in the presence of Bob Clements, whom both men had known since 1937. Rickey listened to his son but was dead set against any of the opportunities offered him. "If you don't go to Pittsburgh with me," he told Branch Jr. matter-of-factly, "I'll quit baseball."

Branch Jr. never again left his father's side.

Moving to Pittsburgh, living at Fox Chapel, his small stab at independence blunted, he submitted passively to his role as second-in-command. Once done, he seemed to cease thinking of his father as an authority figure or competitor, and started to bring order to the Pirate farm system. George Sisler became director of scouting and Don Beach the auditor. Ken Blackburn, Harold Roettger, Milton Stock, Bob Clements, and Rex Bowen moved west too. Bob Cobb, who owned the Brown Derby restaurant in Hollywood together with the Pacific Coast League's Stars, broke his working agreement with the Dodgers and shifted his allegiance to the Pirates.

O'Malley asked scout Howie Haak to remain, but Haak refused. "I owe Mr. Rickey this," he told O'Malley. Rickey had hired him as team trainer for the Rochester Red Wings in 1939 following a career-ending injury to Haak's throwing arm. He sent him gifts of money while Haak was in the navy. Later he hired him as a scout for St. Louis and Brooklyn.

"But don't you think you've paid off your debt?" asked O'Malley.

"No," replied Haak, "not at all. I owe him everything." O'Malley also tried to persuade Rickey's son-in-law Bob Jones, who was running the Elmira Pioneers of the Eastern League, to stay on. He and his wife, Jane, asked Rickey for his opinion. "By all means, stay," he told them, realistically. Yet they harbored too many resentments against the man who had displaced Jane's father, and Jones quit.

Bavasi and Thompson and Al Campanis stayed with O'Malley. Dressen replaced Shotton as manager. Parrott also chose to remain behind, as did Red Barber, who soon departed for the Yankee broadcasting booth bitterly critical of O'Malley. Robinson, of course, continued performing for the team but soon developed his own major grievances against O'Malley and rebuffed every effort the new president made to befriend him.

Even so, O'Malley's generosity had its limits. According to Tommy Holmes, the mere mention of Branch Rickey's name in 215 Montague Street was forbidden and violators were "fined a dollar."

In November, Branch and Jane sold their Maryland farm and flew to Pittsburgh. There they roamed the area with real estate agents and finally settled on Fox Chapel, an exclusive bucolic area north of the city. They now had sixteen grandchildren, and with their presence very much in mind, they invested in 101 acres of softly undulating wooded hills and farmland with an eighteen-room white main house. Nearby, in a smaller home, Branch Jr., Mary and their children took up residence.

Beyond both houses was a stone springhouse to cool melons from Jane's prolific garden, a redwood barn with one horse and one cow, a lake they had blasted out, dammed, and stocked with trout. Rickey's comfortable office was filled with sixty years of framed cartoons and caricatures, photographs and plaques. Files, jammed with his correspondence and observations, lined the walls. Jane had the bathroom papered with copies of the *Sporting News*. And as always, there were pet dogs and cats underfoot everywhere, although Jane and Branch's favorite was a Chesapeake retriever named Dodger. "It was a magical place," granddaughter Elizabeth Adams Klinger recalls. "You never knew when you would find a new foal in the barn or a brand new litter of kittens in the kitchen."

John Galbreath (right), the principal owner of the Pittsburgh Pirates, hired his good friend Rickey to run the Pirates after Walter O'Malley forced Rickey out of the Brooklyn Dodgers. Here they are in 1952 at Forbes Field, home of the Pirates. (Courtesy Branch B. Rickey)

Soon after they arrived, Galbreath told Rickey about a small, two-acre island in Canada, not far from the Ontario town of Sudbury and near Galbreath's own private vacation isle. Rickey explained to a friend that the island was for the family so they would always have a place to come together on summer vacations. But when the sardonic Bob Cobb first set foot on the island he asked, "My God, Branch, what were you *doing* when you found this place?"

His hair was still dark brown but his bushy eyebrows were almost entirely white when he moved into his Forbes Field office across from lovely Schenley Park. On his walls hung the motto he had long ago had framed:

> He that will not reason is a bigot;
> he that cannot reason is a fool;
> and he that dares not reason is a slave

Pirate General Manager Branch Rickey joins a group of Pirate farmhands, all from the Pittsburgh area, for a bite to eat during spring training at Terry Park in Fort Myers, Florida. Left to right: Bruce Taylor, Bill Mazeroski, Rickey, Ken Barbao and Jackie Brown. (Pittsburgh Post-Gazette)

and photographs of exceptional athletes he admired most of all—Honus Wagner, Sisler, Hornsby, Charlie Barrett, Durocher, and Robinson. There were also photos of Lincoln and Churchill. His ever present globe was put down behind his huge leather swivel chair, and the frayed and well-thumbed dictionary and *Bartlett's Familiar Quotations* placed at his side.

He was home.

"We're pointing toward 1955," he announced at his first press conference in Pittsburgh. "That's when the bells will start ringing as the red wagon comes down the street. That's when Pittsburgh folks will shout, 'By George, this is it!'"

Within a year his euphoria was over. He knew now that the club had few good ballplayers and too many untried youngsters. "I found we had on our list only twenty-two new players. Brooklyn started the 1951 training season with about a hundred and twenty and the Cardinals with more than a hundred."

The Korean War draft took away many young men, while injuries ruined the careers of prospects such as pitcher Paul Pettit, who had received a large bonus for signing. He also concluded that home run hitter Ralph Kiner "would not throw or run and could not field and was a self-appraised star and could have no part ever in a pennant winning club. Kiner was a gentleman and a fine person but I cannot be any respecter of persons, nor character nor anything else when it comes to winning a pennant." Another local hero, Wally Westlake, was only "run of the mill." In the strictest of confidence he told an Associated Press reporter: "My disillusionment was complete when I realized that I had nothing at all, substantially, to hold onto."

"We had a lot of triple threat men—slip, fumble, and fall," added Joe Garagiola, who came from the Cardinals in 1952 and after his retirement was recommended by Rickey for a sports announcing job in St. Louis. "George Metkovich, our first baseman, who had been around the big leagues, would holler at the umpires, 'For Pete's sake, grab a glove and help me out.'"

Yet something even more fundamental had occurred, so subtle that even his keen staff and sharp-witted son had let it pass by unnoticed. The truth was that to a certain extent his old wizardry had become obsolete. His pioneering formula in St. Louis had been to sign energetic and enthusiastic players en masse; in Brooklyn he had instituted a massive wartime recruitment program and added his historic recruitment of black athletes. Rickey's scouts had always scoured the country signing youngsters who could throw and run and had good body control. He had held mass tryout camps before anyone else; he sought out talented convicts on prison teams; his scouts watched army and navy teams.

By 1951, his first year with Pittsburgh, all these standard Rickey innovations—fresh and original for thirty years—were commonplace throughout baseball. Now the Pirates had to compete on the open market with fifteen, mainly richer clubs, including the free-spending Yankees, Dodgers, and Red Sox. He could continue his customary twelve and fifteen hour workdays, spur his minor league scouts and farm teams on, bid for younger players, but dramatic breakthroughs were no longer possible.

In 1951 the Pirates finished in seventh place, the only time they escaped the cellar during his five-year reign. Young Danny Murtaugh was helpless at the plate, hitting only .199. Shortstop George Strickland batted .216. Of the regulars, only Kiner (who slammed 42 homers) and

Gus Bell displayed any talent. Pitchers Murry Dickson, Mel Queen, Bob Werle, Howie Pollett, Vernon Law, and Bob Friend compiled mediocre records. One prospect, Cliff Chambers, no-hit the Braves in May (Ralph Kiner described it years later as the "worst no-hitter I ever saw; they were hitting line-drives everywhere") but by mid-season Rickey dealt him to the Cardinals for desperately needed operating capital.

By the close of the year the club was losing so much money that Galbreath was compelled to contribute personally to reduce the deficit since Crosby and Johnson, the other co-owners, refused to invest any more cash. Thomas Johnson, especially, was by now thoroughly disenchanted with Rickey.

"He had given the Pirates crap in deals when he was with the Dodgers," he complained. "Now, when he came over he was supposed to take a portion of the money received from the Zeckendorf-O'Malley deal and acquire a stock interest in the Pirates." (Galbreath denies this flatly: "He was never given an opportunity to buy into the Pirates.") "He came here and immediately started to spend, spend, spend. He refused to pick up his financial obligation, constantly calling on Galbreath and me to fund the losses he was generating out of our pockets. I didn't like that and we went to the carpet. Once he said to me, 'You don't like me, do you?' I answered, 'That's not so. I'd be the first to vote you into the Hall of Fame. I just don't like the way you operate!'"

Nor did the farm system seem promising. A young Dick Stuart, playing for Modesto in a Class C league, hit .229; outfielder Bob Skinner batted .277 in a Class B league but led the league in errors.

By the autumn of 1951 the possibility of failure was real and Rickey was overcome with deeply pessimistic moods.

He wrote a long, depressed letter to Arthur Mann:

"I am not disorganized; I am unorganized, or does that make sense? Nobody ever got me ready to be organized. I do a lot of work in spurts but I do not think I spurt often enough.

"It has rained here solidly for four days. It rained all day yesterday and all last night and it is now noon and it is really pouring down....

"Job started with bunions. It was a mild start, but most ominous. He couldn't get around. His cattle got diseased, his asses strayed, and he got sore eyes. Then his numerous family got sick and began to die all around him, his house burned down, and he finally lost all his property and ended up with fistula. He steadfastly decided to proceed along this line if it took all summer and he told the Lord Jehovah that he would continue to trust him even though he forsook him. Then, just when he found himself in the last stages of in extremis, one of his fair-weather but long-standing friends came to him and said, 'Job, you're at the end of everything. There is no way to turn. I'll tell you what to do. You just curse God and die.' ... I do know that Job came through."

Sometimes the physical strain was too great and he asked Pirate physician Dr. Joseph Finegold for a frank assessment of his health. On five separate occasions between 1950 and 1952 he had been hospitalized for Ménière's disease, once in New Orleans while inspecting the Pelican operation, twice in California while visiting the Stars, and twice more in Pittsburgh. Finegold's judgment was that while his health was comparatively good for a man his age, his blood pressure was "gradually rising" and he counseled him "to reduce his activities to a minimum."

Despite his moods and health, he sought diversion among people he liked. Bob Cobb spent a few days at Fox Chapel and regaled the Rickey family with stories, true and imagined. Cobb loved to tell Rickey about his alcoholic father who drank himself to death. "Indeed," said Rickey, his eyebrows arched as he detected another argument for abstinence. "At what age did he die?" Cobb smiled. He had the old man now. "At ninety-four," he answered to howls of laughter. Cobb's uninhibited taste for liquor never offended Rickey, who took to him as a father to son. Once Cobb sent the Rickeys a set of drinking glasses with their names engraved on each. Another time he took daughter Elizabeth aside and asked for a glass of water, then poured some of it into a flask of whiskey he carried with him, swallowing it before her father. Rickey beamed, as if in approval of an erring yet loving child: "It's only Bob."

His second year, 1952, was even worse for the Pirates. Greater sums of money had somehow been located and spent on scouting. In many instances, the club—and Rickey—guessed wrong. He raved about a Class D farm pitcher, Ron Necciai. "Look," he said expansively one afternoon to a magazine writer seated in his office, "I've seen a lot of baseball in my time. There have only been two young pitchers I was certain were destined for greatness, simply because they had the meanest fastball a batter can face. One of those boys was Dizzy Dean. The other is Ron Necciai. And Necciai is harder to hit."

Necciai pitched one season for the Pirates, won one and lost six, and had an earned run average of 7.08 before leaving baseball.

The failure of such promising rookies, the lack of money to operate as he had in earlier years, the terrible Pirate teams he fielded, and the resulting unhappiness of fans and newspapermen contributed to the emotional pressure he was facing. In the spring of 1952 he dispatched a lengthy letter to Galbreath marked "confidential" detailing why Pirate hero and home run hitter Ralph Kiner could not help the team. In real-

Spring training with the Pittsburgh Pirates in Ft. Myers, Florida. It's 1952 or 1953 and Branch Rickey (center), his son and baseball associate Branch Jr. (right), and grandson Branch Barry Rickey observe practice. (Courtesy Branch B. Rickey)

**Billy Meyer, who managed the Pirates from 1947 to 1952, at spring training with General Manager Branch Rickey. (Courtesy of** *Pittsburgh Post-Gazette***)**

ity, Rickey was trying to talk himself into selling Kiner to raise money to buy new players.

Rickey objected to the "special privileges" managers Roy Hamey and Billy Meyer had "granted" Kiner: "Coming, going, reporting as he pleased." Rickey had lectured Kiner, using "Eisenhower's very pointed

remarks about morale being the single greatest factor in winning a war."
Kiner, he charged, was getting special attention and damaging team
morale. Why, added Rickey, he was also "extremely extravagant" because
he had demanded the clubhouse be air-conditioned. The very idea
shocked Rickey. "Now air conditioning in our clubhouse is, in the first
place, impractical, and secondly, very expensive, and thereby highly
objectionable to the health of the players." He also objected that Kiner's
wife had "special seating" and that Greenberg Gardens—the short left
field fence built especially for Hank Greenberg in 1946—was contractu-
ally retained. And yet another objection:

Kiner was the club's player representative. "That in itself is bad for
Pittsburgh," he said, recalling the vote for a player's union by the Pirates
in 1946.

Kiner became a scapegoat for his failure to improve the club.

Rickey compared him unfavorably to Ruth, ignoring the Babe's womanizing, heavy drinking habits, and inability to get along with many of
his teammates and managers. Nor did he choose to remember the many
special rights Yankee owner Jake Ruppert had accorded Ruth but which
were denied other Yankee players.

Instead, he composed a ditty for Galbreath:

Babe Ruth could run. Our man cannot.
Ruth could throw. Our man cannot.
Ruth could steal a base. Our man cannot.
Ruth was a good fielder. Our man is not.
Ruth could hit with power to all fields. Our man cannot.
Ruth never requested a diminutive field to fit him. Our man does.

It was all a sham. The truth was that Rickey, who admired Kiner as
a man and ballplayer, was trying to demean his skills in order to receive
permission to sell him and then use the money to develop the sort of
all-round athletes he preferred.

Meanwhile the club performed horribly. Even worse, gate receipts
fell off dramatically. By the close of his second year, half as many people paid their way into Forbes Field as had on the eve of his arrival in
1950. The corporate loss was $677,263 and the two-year deficit was more
than one million dollars. The situation was so desperate that he and his
front office loyalists agreed to a series of postponements of their salary
checks.

"The club was not as strong as my St. Louis club in 1919 when I had
[Bill] Doak, [Jack] Smith, [Walton] Cruise and Hornsby, had only a total
of twenty-three in the entire organization and it took seven years to bring

the club to a world championship. I had an ownership in Pittsburgh that urged me to produce a winner as quickly as possible and regardless of cost. This I proceeded to do. And, in my first year here, I spent $496,000 for free agents. A large amount of this money was not wisely spent, as history proves, but I worked fast and with my very best judgment—following the recommendation of the scouts whose opinions I had good reason to follow. Suddenly, in mid–1952, I found out that the financial situation of the Pittsburgh club did not permit further competition with other clubs in acquiring free agent material."

Daily the papers were filled with criticisms of his administration. While the personal attacks were hardly comparable to those he had experienced in Brooklyn, he was nonetheless as sensitive to their sting as he had always been. The respected *Post-Gazette* columnist Al Abrams wrote: "Rickey has done little in Pittsburgh but give us Class C and B baseball. The hammer blows will continue so long as he insists on using youngsters who don't belong in a major league lineup."

Things were taking a sour turn. "There is a very real concern on the part of all of us," Rickey wrote the Pirates' principal owner. "Our attendance is falling off very much ... we are in need of funds."

The problems continued to mount. Billy Meyer, his manager, phoned him unexpectedly before the 1953 season to say that he could not continue due to serious personal problems. Immediately, Rickey went looking for a successor. He swallowed his pride and, for the first time since he was driven out of Brooklyn, phoned Walter O'Malley in Los Angeles for permission to sign Walter Alston, then managing the Royals in Montreal. But his old rival refused. He then turned to one of his favorite people, Bobby Bragan, who had resigned from the Dodgers' Fort Worth club in the aftermath of Rickey's departure from Brooklyn. Rickey had promptly hired Bragan as manager of the Pirates' Hollywood club, hoping to move him to Pittsburgh. Meanwhile, he had to have a manager to fill Meyer's slot and at the winter baseball meeting in Phoenix signed Fred Haney, partly on the recommendation of scout Howie Haak. Earlier, Haney, a onetime Hollywood Star play-by-play announcer, had been let go by Bob Cobb at Hollywood for daring to ask for a $4,000 raise to $20,000. But Rickey had paid Meyer $30,000 to manage, and a delighted Haney was given the same salary.

At the age of seventy-two Rickey's strong assertion of ego, drive, and insatiability kept pushing him to develop a winning team in the face of insurmountable odds. In June he finally traded the club's only hero, Ralph Kiner, to the Chicago Cubs. When the news was flashed, a reporter wrote, "The old man has lost his touch." He was excoriated in letters to

newspapers and hung in effigy. Several leading citizens proposed a formal boycott of Pirate games until he left office.

The Kiner-less Pirates played as poorly as ever. Rickey tried to bring Peewee Reese to Pittsburgh, but O'Malley vetoed the idea. The Pirates, meanwhile, continued losing large amounts of money until Rickey was forced to invest $200,000 to shore up the cash reserve.

Handcuffed by the lack of money for player development, Galbreath resisted the demands of his co-owners that Rickey be dismissed. Silently and slowly, though, Rickey bought time with an enlarged Pirate farm system. The future was already present in the form of talented athletes performing on obscure farm clubs, he told his despairing staff time and again. Regularly he and his secretary, Kenneth Blackburn, a tall, thin, and shy former army captain, wandered across the country examining a player here, a franchise there.

As if in a frenzy, trades followed trades. Players arrived and departed, often without explanation. Danny O'Connell, a much-praised infielder who hit .294 in 1953, was shipped to Milwaukee for six players and $200,000. The workhorse of the pitching staff, Murry Dickson, was traded to the Phillies for two players and $72,500. The eight players he obtained in the two trades all failed, but Rickey now at last had ample money he believed necessary to build a winning team. Immediately he formed minor league camps in Huntsville, Alabama, and Brunswick, Georgia. His sprawling system was showing signs of improvement in talented youngsters—or so his staff and Branch Jr. believed. And quietly, but now without the intense emotionalism and fanfare of past years, he started signing black players. Curt Roberts became the first black Pirate and played second base for three years.

"Failure was a complete stranger to him and his anxiety to conquer his latest challenge was acute," says Blackburn. "There were even stretches when he worked without salary, so hard-pressed for cash were the Pirates [only the Browns were more impoverished in 1952, according to figures released during the Celler congressional committee hearings that year]. When it came to work he never spared himself, even at his advanced age."

During one frantic four-day period, with little or no sleep, Rickey and Blackburn flew in their Cessna to inspect farm teams in Hutchinson, Kansas; Waco, Texas; Lincoln, Nebraska; Billings, Montana. Traveling through the Middle West and big sky country, wandering with purpose but at times seemingly possessed, Blackburn recalls the peripatetic Rickey as "coldly calculating in all this but often there was an air of unreality about him too." Approaching an air field, he was informed

by their pilot that the field was closed by dense fog and they would have
to land elsewhere. "By Judas Priest," he exploded. "I must keep that
appointment." The pilot shrugged. He had his orders from the flight
tower. Rickey sulked for a moment and then brightened. "Moose," he
proposed, "try to land anyway. I'll take the responsibility." It might have
been very funny, thought Blackburn, except the man called the Mahatma
was deadly serious.

In all the coming and going of players there was for him one bright
note. Cal Abrams had come from the Reds in 1953 for Gus Bell, catcher
Joe Rossi, and utility player Gail Henley. It was hardly a brilliant exchange
since Bell went on to star for the Reds for nine years. But Rickey felt
strongly about the two principals involved, for, as he once said, he "loved"
Abrams, whom he first signed in 1942 for Jake Pitler's Olean club in the
Pony League. Just before the signing, Rickey had invited Abrams and his
father to Montague Street. When the elder Abrams asked how long
before his son might reach Ebbets Field, Rickey replied, "Five years."
"And," recollects Abrams in awe, "five years it took." Still, the young man
from Brooklyn would have been happy "to play for nothing." The
Dodgers offered him $75 a month and then Rickey sat back, the ever
present Antonio y Cleopatra cigar in his mouth, and tapping on his desk
for emphasis, leaned forward and whispered to the two Abramses: "I've
always been looking for a good Jewish player."

He saw Abrams as the prototype of an intelligent batter who was a
natural lead-off man because of his bunting and running skills. Rickey
once flew to Fort Worth to try to teach Abrams how to pull the ball to
right field. In his first year with the Pirates Abrams did indeed do well,
hitting 15 homers over the abbreviated *left field* Greenberg Gardens fence
and a respectable .286.

But skeptics weren't dissuaded. Who after all got the best part of
the deal when Gus Bell was sent in exchange to the Reds? Gabe Paul,
the Red general manager and onetime Rickey protégé, thought it the
best deal he had ever negotiated. "Know why Rickey didn't like Gus? He
said he was irresponsible, squandered all his money, and his wife was just
the same. 'Why,' he told me, 'she's always joining the club on the road
with that baby boy of theirs and she just throws away the child's diapers
because she won't do laundry.'

"I had a chance to talk with the Bells and asked her about it. She had
the baby with her. She explained that her father was a conductor on the
Louisville & Nashville and she could get passes on certain trains, and several times the ball club had been riding the same train. As for the laundry, she showed me a supply of disposable diapers, which were new then."

The next year, 1954, Rickey's revolving-door scheme continued as Abrams was shipped to Baltimore, where he hit .293. The men the Pirates received in return ended as failures.

By now, home attendance collapsed, as only 475,000 customers passed through the Forbes Field turnstiles. Again, they finished in last place. "It's the ninth year of a five-year plan," quipped the irrepressible Joe Garagiola.

As always, he continued to confide in Galbreath with complaints of not enough money, too few talented players, and the exhausting nature of ceaseless insistence on showing immediate improvement.

There was still another difficulty. Rickey decided Fred Haney was not as able as he had believed. Haney, in turn, lost respect for Rickey and thought him insensitive and unrealistic.

In spring training in 1954 Rickey began carping at Haney.

"Who has given Bill Bell [a rookie pitcher] personal instruction on his different pitches? Or examined him on control of the different pitches? Or has worked with him on improvement of this or that pitch? And I am pretty sure that the same thing can be said and I do say it about chaps like Dunn, or Face, or Hogue, or Pettit, or Macdonald. But why name all of them for it does include every single pitcher on the club? Not a man has received adequate work or instruction. Not one. Just what is it we are trying to do down here?"

He called scout Howie Haak and ordered him to report to camp. When Haak arrived, Rickey was untypically curt. "He isn't an instructor, is he?" he asked the man who had praised Haney as a minor league manager. "But Mr. Rickey," responded Haak, "you never asked that question of me. You just asked if he was a good manager."

When word leaked to Haney, the manager expressed his resentment to the reporters in camp. Both men remained silent for a while but two months later Rickey received a call from *Post-Gazette* sports editor Dan McGibbeny. He said he had a story from reporter Jack Hernon he wanted verified or corrected before publication. Was it true, he asked Rickey, that a serious rift was developing between the two men? Not so, Rickey said, just differences between two candid men. McGibbeny paused and then asked if he had any comment on Haney's public statement that trades were being made without his knowledge or consent. Haney had charged that pitcher Roger Bowman, just recalled from the Pacific League, was hardly major league caliber, while catcher Ed Fitzgerald, whom he wanted to remain with the Pirates, was shipped to the Washington Senators.

Rickey heatedly denied Haney's charges, claiming they had a "complete understanding that no player was removed or would ever be removed from the Pittsburgh club without the approval of the manager." All the same, he reserved the right to bring in players "about whom the manager might not be previously informed." More emphatically, he told McGibbeny that "players leaving the club were management's, not Haney's, concern."

Later that morning a player walked into the office demanding to see him. He was a young and unproven pitcher. Rickey was out of the office but he told Roettger that Rickey had deprecated his abilities. Why else would they be sending him back to Hollywood? Rickey, he went on, shouting, was mistreating him, even insulting him behind his back. Roettger asked him how he knew all that. "Why, Haney told all the reporters, that's why," he answered. "In all my forty years," Rickey sputtered with fury after Roettger related the incident to him, "this is the first time I have had a [press] story of this sort coming from the manager—major or minor."

His staff was outraged and urged him to fire Haney for insubordination and incompetence. Rickey was unwilling, since he probably was not eager for another battle of the headlines in the daily press. He also claimed to have a lingering feeling of affection for Haney, telling Branch Jr. that "Fred, regardless of all considerations of capacity, effort or circumstances, is kindly, thoughtful, and cooperative and anxious to do well and spares no personal effort. He does his level best."

He also knew that any managerial change would be cosmetic since he had hardly given Haney a roster of potential all-stars. As he saw it, Haney's difficulty was less in his public criticism than in his training of raw young men. Managing the hapless Pirates, he said, was "an organized Antioch College job which needed assignments in detail, individually and team, for specific kinds of work under skilled and experienced instruction"—precisely the system he had created at Dodgertown in Vero Beach. "I don't believe Fred or anyone his age is really physically able to meet the demands of our managerial job. It takes a younger man."

He and Haney declared a private truce, but when he read Red Smith's columns in the New York *Herald-Tribune* critical of his treatment of Haney, he wrote the columnist to deny he had been "inconsiderate or harsh in my dealings with Fred.

"Fred went to the World Series. He returned to Pittsburgh and came to see me in my office. We had what I thought was a very pleasant and friendly visit, ending up by Fred placing his arm about my shoulder and saying that when Mrs. Rickey and I came to Los Angeles he would like us to stay at his home. That surely indicates the cordiality that marked our last meeting."

The long and dreary season of 1955 dragged on for the Pirates until the autumn, when Rickey decided that for the moment he had had enough. When Rickey announced his retirement, his detractors chortled with glee. "Thank God," said Pirate part-owner Tom Johnson when he heard the news. Al Abrams expressed his "vague feeling of relief that at lengthy last the unsuccessful Rickey regime in Pittsburgh baseball finally was no more." Abrams also called Rickey "Mahatma," to which an infuriated fan took great offense. "Webster's Dictionary," the fan wrote, "states that a Mahatma is a wise and holy person, supposed to have unusual powers. Branch Rickey is nothing of the kind."

Abrams refused however to join in the bitter recriminations and commented that in spite of repeated failures, Rickey was "as wise a human being as I have ever met. He lived a clean Christian life which entitled him to holiness in the sense of the word and he was gifted with unusual powers in his chosen field of endeavor, baseball."

To which another exasperated fan wrote Abrams: "But the man didn't win a pennant for Pittsburgh!"

When Abrams showed the exchange to Rickey, Rickey shook his head and agreed with the fan. "Still, it's true, true. I did not bring Pittsburgh a winner. It was and still is the biggest disappointment in my baseball life."

To another visitor he repeated his earlier remark, "There can be no excuses or alibis for the lowly position of the Pittsburgh club. The Bell deal was a bad one, but I had no idea Bell would play as well as he has with the Reds. He had no adventure, he has none now." First base prospect Preston Ward did have "adventure," but when he was released from the army he was "unable to run" and lost "interest and agility" and became a "bust." As for the versatile Murry Dickson, whom he peddled to the Phillies: "I didn't need a twenty-seven-year-old pitcher like Dickson as much as I needed a twenty-year-old boy like Dangleis [who never reached the major leagues]. I needed numbers."

By resigning, he appeared to his critics to have acknowledged defeat, even though he had long intended to leave following the end of five years of active service. Time now seemed to have passed him by. His health was poor and his Ménière's disease condition deteriorating. The year before—within a span of five weeks—he had suffered three attacks. He had told his cousin, "I am actually afraid to appear in public." The slightest physical movement, even to his hand, caused a wave of dizziness and nausea. In September he collapsed again.

## Chapter Twelve

The ailment was generally unknown outside of his personal and official family. When, therefore, he announced on the last day of October he would remain as "adviser'" for $50,000 yearly he was accused of avarice and chicanery and of refusing to let go. A newspaper calculated the club had lost $1,850,000 since his arrival.

In truth, the seeds of Pirate respectability on the field and in their profit-and-loss statements were being assembled far from Forbes Field, on distant minor league farms, by the large scouting network he had assembled.

"Howie," he said in early 1955 to scout Haak, "one player on the Montreal Royals is outstanding and draftable. I'm not going to tell you his name. You go discover yourself."

Before departing for Canada, Haak learned the name of the prospect from Clyde Sukeforth: the Puerto Rican Roberto Clemente. Two days later he walked into the Royals' clubhouse and saw Glenn Mickens, a pitcher he had once signed. "Howie," said Mickens, who played one season with Brooklyn, "we've got the best damned player and they won't play him." (Clemente, of course, went on to become a marvelous performer for the Pirates until his tragic death in 1972.)

After Rickey's resignation he returned the next day to his office and dictated a letter to his children:

> I am not down and out—not at all. In fact, I think I am on the springboard of happier days—everything counted—more than I have ever been.
> Away back when, I told Mother I would regard myself as successful if the time ever came that I would be able to hire a stenographer....
> Then followed a substitute definition of my personal success when I said to Mother years later that I would regard myself as "successful" if I should be able to retire at forty-five years of age. "Well, forty-five years came along and I was very far from regarding myself as successful in any definition of that word. So, I had to shift my anticipated mastery of success. I changed it to something like "complete mastery of my time." My objective then, was to get to the place where I could do whatever I pleased—no clock punching, no doing anything that I didn't wish myself to do ... but this job of seeing to it that the Pittsburgh club comes to respectability at the earliest possible time has brought me to the place where I have to give up the idea that mastery of my time spells success. So you see, I am far from being successful.
> Doubtless you have been perplexed by no inside news of my so-called "retirement." If I shall be treated with kindly consideration by Joe Brown, then indeed I can be very happy in my new relationship. If not, I shall then do exactly what Judge Landis told the old reprobate when he sentenced him to Leavenworth Penitentiary for two years. Under repeated falsetto protests that "he couldn't stand it," the Judge told him,—"Well, sir, you do the very best you can."
> Meanwhile, look out for the Pirates. The team has turned the corner.

Writing on November 9th to his close friend Warren Giles, now president of the National League, he explained his plans for the years ahead. He had invested almost $250,000 in the Pirates and hoped to keep busy with "scouting" and "deals." He also thought the time had come to write a book, do a "weekly telecast" on baseball, and collaborate with Arthur Mann on an autobiography. He added a postscript to his letter telling Giles he had found a photograph of Giles's son in his files. Tell him, wrote Rickey, that if he ever needed "assistance or counsel I would give it to him with as much freedom and genuineness as if he were my own son. If something were to happen to you, Warren—may God forbid—I would be very happy if he were to feel I was indeed something more than his godfather."

"Now you can do nothing, Mr. Rickey," a reporter said to him as he sat cleaning out his Forbes Field desk drawers. He straightened up, indignant at the very idea.

"Do nothing, young man? You expect me to do nothing? Preposterous. I started out to do nothing for three days once. I never was so tired in all my life. Age in years, young man, is no criterion of a man's usefulness."

Just the same, fifty years of active duty had apparently come to an end. His sometime critics on the St. Louis *Post-Dispatch* saluted him editorially: "There are those—and they are not few—who would welcome Rickey back to St. Louis even if there are no baseball jobs open here." But Red Smith, who had been observing him closely for decades, said it better than anyone else, describing Branch Rickey as "a player, manager, executive, lawyer, preacher, horse-trader, spellbinder, innovator, husband and father and grandfather, farmer, logician, obscurantist, reformer, financier, sociologist, crusader, sharper, father confessor, checker shark, friend and fighter.

"Judas Priest!" the *Post-Dispatch* finished up. "What a character!"

# Chapter Thirteen

FOR THE FIRST TIME since 1912 he was on the sidelines. Not since his Cardinal years had he been subject to another man's directions, in this instance Joe L. Brown. The two had met during the summer of 1935 when film comedian Joe E. Brown brought his sixteen-year-old son Joe for treatment of a broken elbow by the eminent orthopedist and Brown and Cardinal physician, Dr. Robert Hyland. Rickey enjoyed the elder Brown, who was a fanatic ball fan, the star of Ring Lardner's *Alibi Ike,* and with Tris Speaker, owner of the Kansas City Blues of the American Association.

Young Brown spent the hot summer happily wandering among ballplayers, residing at exclusive Forest Park Hotel a few doors down from Patricia and Dizzy Dean, and dining on a number of occasions with the Rickeys at their Country Life home.

Years later, Joe Brown worked in the front offices of countless minor league clubs until Branch Jr. recommended to his father that he be hired to run their New Orleans Pelican ball club. Thus, when Rickey resigned, the Pirates decided to ignore the logical successor—Branch Jr.—and instead brought in Brown. Tom Johnson had no objection to his retaining Branch Jr. as farm director, but warned Brown that the elder Rickey was "a pompous windbag."

No sooner had Brown reached Pittsburgh than, realizing Rickey was not kindly thought of, he decided to ignore his advice.

"I'm sure Mr. Rickey was hurt but he was bigger than that," says Brown. "I found out quickly that the news media were disenchanted with him and that throughout Pittsburgh the Rickey name was anathema to the fans. I simply couldn't afford to be thought of as a stooge. I had never run a major league club before. Mr. Rickey was an overpowering man; we had no tension between us in that time, but I had to establish myself as the boss."

Brown believed that Fred Haney was "so overpowered, almost emas-
culated [and] Mr. Rickey was so strong that Haney wouldn't express his
convictions and consequently lost the respect of his players. Fred Haney
wasn't treated with dignity although Mr. Rickey wasn't really conscious
of the slights and hurts he caused Haney. It's just that he wanted a winner so badly in his last year. Thus, when I took over in 1956, I just couldn't
allow that to happen to me, no matter how much I respected the man."

Brown replaced George Sisler as scouting director and had him concentrate on teaching hitting. As for Rickey, he called on him only once,
asking him to scout two players in Hollywood: Cholly Naranjo was a
Cuban pitcher of limited talent and lasted but one season with the
Pirates; the other was the gifted second baseman Bill Mazeroski, whose
dramatic home run in the seventh game of the 1960 World Series against
the Yankees clinched the championship. Rickey raved about Mazeroski.

"Other than that," Brown says, "he never tried to interfere with my
trades."

Not quite. Rickey was at first frustrated and then turned petulant
and crotchety at his unexpected exclusion and isolation. For hadn't he
created the position of scouting and minor league director for Brown
in 1955 and given the job to him?

He complained steadily to Galbreath, obviously embarrassing his
old friend. Brown, he lamented in one of the many letters he wrote, had
hired a new assistant without asking his opinion; Sisler had been igno-
miniously demoted (Brown, privately, deprecated Sisler's administrative
skills); still other changes of the new regime were "completely unknown
to me." He wanted desperately to be consulted, needed, respected. After
all, he went on, *he* had given five years of his life to the Pirates, *he* had
found and nurtured Brown and brought him into the organization.
Wasn't it simple justice, then, that "some conversation about these various moves" involve him? It was painful for him to pull back, and Jane
fretted about the effect on his health as he retreated into self-pity, displaced by a younger man.

In April he wrote once more to Galbreath expressing his unhappiness with the new regime. Why wasn't he asked about trades? Why wasn't
he handling player negotiations as he expected to when he retired? "I
have spoken to Brown and I get the very strong impression that under
no circumstances was I to make any move whatsoever."

When he accidentally stumbled on the fact that Galbreath had been
asking about Jackie Robinson, Wid Matthews, and Gabe Paul without
telling him, he was beside himself with rage. "Insulted," he said. "The
thing to be ironed out is my relationship with this club and that ought

to be done immediately and firmly." Again and again, he phoned or wrote Galbreath about his discomfort at the unexpected turn of events, and time and again the owner put him off, refusing to tell him what was an obvious fact, namely that the second five years in his contract were intended as a gift to an old friend and not to be construed in any way as having a say in the way Brown ran the organization.

Nearly seventy-five, he finally conceded. "If that is the way ownership wants it to be, there is nothing, of course, I can do about it."

At home in Fox Chapel, he received a steady stream of visitors in his office. Each morning he dictated dozens of letters to correspondents around the country. He told Ken Blackburn of a trip south he had in mind to scout the younger crop of black ballplayers. Writers and reporters who remembered him fondly and still thought of him as great copy came regularly. Frank Graham spent a few days filling him in on the gossip and interviewing him for a magazine piece. Onetime Browns publicist Gerald Holland fashioned a superbly crafted article about Rickey in retirement for *Sports Illustrated*. Milt Stock—Stanky's father-in-law and ex–Dodger coach—called regularly to speak about the Mobile farm's problems. Jackie Robinson was in constant touch. Jake Pitler rang him in early October to wish him a belated happy New Year. "But it's only autumn, Jake," Rickey protested. "That's all right, Mr. Rickey," explained Pitler. "It's the *Jewish* New Year I'm talking about." Rutgers University philosophy professor Houston Peterson, who had written books about Havelock Ellis, Thomas Huxley, and Conrad Aiken, stayed with the Rickeys for several days, Peterson trying to talk baseball and Rickey interested only in philosophy. Invitations to speak or receive honorary degrees poured in, but when Morgan State College, a black school in Maryland, awarded him an honorary Doctor of Laws, he was inordinately proud of this recognition.

Rickey delighted in his grandchildren, especially young Branch Barrett, nicknamed Barry, and they often went skeet shooting together. His daughters flew in when they could. On holidays as many as sixteen grandchildren might be present, playing croquet, baseball, touch football (the game at times included Jane; Rickey wouldn't play but declared his wife had "the best looking legs I ever ran into").

And there were always the joyous Christmas holidays, family gatherings, when the Rickey clan would descend en masse on Fox Chapel. When the moment arrived for the distribution of gifts, the family gathered in a large room, the presents strewn about and the stockings hung on the mantelpiece. No one could open anything until Rickey entered

**Branch Rickey, stripped to the waist and holding a bat (the baseball is off to the right) executing a bunt at a family outing at their Chestertown, Maryland, home in 1947. His wife Jane (center) and their granddaughter Caroline (in white shorts) watch the 66-year-old display his skills. (Courtesy Branch B. Rickey)**

the room. One of his grandchildren, Christine Jones, remembers that "at last he appeared and sat down at the kitchen table, covered by a felt pad with sewn beads. The kids were all in a row, the youngest at the head of the line. Grandpa then rose, walked into the large room where we were all seated, and sitting in his favorite chair would dole out the gifts. Once done, he'd call us again, but this time passing out his favorite children's books—*The Swiss Family Robinson, Treasure Island,* and others. 'Who doesn't have *Little Women*' he'd call out to us, until the last books were distributed. At some time too, we all received Bibles."

Sundays were normally busy, with church services in the morning. Accompanied by Blackburn, he and Jane would set out in their four-door Ford Galaxie sedan or the powder blue Falcon Jane preferred, Archie their chauffeur behind the wheel as they bickered endlessly about the proper route. Sighing loudly, Archie invariably went his own way. One Sunday afternoon, Rickey had his companions dropped off at home and drove to the ultra-exclusive Duquesne Club after hearing a black guest had been barred. He brought Archie in as his guest, ordered a full-course dinner, and chatted amiably with him as the other diners stared uncomfortably at them.

Word arrived, too, of people he had known and worked with in the past. Harold Roettger drowned in a Miami Beach pool. Roettger, a diabetic, had been with Rickey since the old Cardinal days. "Harold," said Rickey upon hearing of his death, "was a man of first-class intellect and the utmost loyalty. I thought of him as a son and grieve deeply over his loss."

But when a former Dodger radio announcer appealed for money Rickey turned him down, offering an excuse about his own large debts. "It grieves me that I cannot find it advisable or possible to make the loan," he wrote him. He believed he was an alcoholic and would spend the money on liquor. To Red Barber, the announcer's onetime partner, he confided: "I am afraid that the placing of any cash in his hands might do more harm than good." Both notes were dictated to Blackburn, who became so distressed at the man's fall that unknown to Rickey he sent him $50.

Meanwhile, Rickey's dizziness and nausea continued to plague him. He also developed arthritis in his knee and ankle. On his poorer days Blackburn heard him say, "I am simply not equal to the jobs I have in front of me." Yet invariably he would snap back and schedule more activities and ever more speeches. That winter and spring he spoke at Wooster College and Ohio Wesleyan, in Chicago and Washington. By now he had perfected a theme he repeated over and again: "the perils of complacency." In one address he described the dangers of monolithic communism. In another, delivered in March 1956, he cited Indochina as a dangerous flashpoint ("We are really at war"), Formosa ("possibly tottering on the brink of invasion"), Germany ("the center of a hot 'Cold War'"), Alger Hiss ("the disgraceful presence of a traitor sitting with our president at Yalta"), and of "Communists" in Hollywood.

Histrionically, dramatically, sounding like the nineteenth-century evangelist he really was, he leaned forward at just the right moment, pounded the dais, his voice rising and falling, his deliberate pauses injecting expectation and tension, his tones exhilarating. Always he returned to the Gospels for his inspiration. He advanced the idea of "property of privacy" rather than "privacy of property" as the essential ingredient of freedom; "human rights, the right of ownership of one's own mind and soul" as the necessary components of dignity, integrity, and life itself.

"There is a radical individualism in the Gospels. Jesus took account of the number of hairs on the head. Two sparrows only worth a farthing—even these he made note of. The Samaritans on the roadside were enduringly important. The dissipated prodigal was beckoned to from afar. He rejoiced over one lost sheep that was found. He taught 'not to despise one of these little ones,' when a boy only twelve years of age. He so knew his direction and so firmly held His purpose in mind that he could say to his inquiring parents and, respectfully, too—'Wist ye not that I must be about my Father's business?' He founded a new religion when he actually advocated and practiced the love of his enemies. Strip him of any claim to divinity, and yet hear him pray for those who so spitefully used him.

> To go—to come
> To say—to speak
> To kneel—to pray
> To think—to believe

"These freedoms he died for, and it seems to me he must be saying to us apathetic children of a marvelous freedom, 'Forgive them, Father, for they know not what they do.' He left a life, a philosophy, indeed, a religion that could well enter as a solvent into the world's ills in this present hour."

In another speech that spring he elaborated on the theme:

"I don't like silent men when personal liberty is at stake, and I grow suspicious of them. This is not a time for silent men.

"In the midst of a hard winter at Valley Forge, George Washington wrote a letter to a member of the Continental Congress: In it he asked this question. 'Where is Jefferson?' Washington was in need of manpower and counsel and the whereabouts of the governor of Virginia were not known to him. But Jefferson was doing a great job at that moment. He was speaking to the undergraduates at Yale University. His theme was the hazardous service that was challenging these young men, to secure 'the blessings of Liberty.' Jefferson closed his address with six Latin words which Yale students at that time could translate without help, 'Malo periculosam libertatem quam quietam servitutem'—which he translated as 'I prefer a perilous freedom rather than a peaceful slavery.' I fervently hope for the early days when all of us everywhere will support the position of Mr. Jefferson by declaring that we, too, prefer a dangerous freedom rather than a peaceful slavery."

Above all, his essential theme remained the quest for social justice. After his resignation he started crisscrossing the eastern and middle western states to speak in colleges, churches, and conventions, whoever would have him probe their consciences and challenge them into action. A thousand people gathered to pay him honor in the Grand Ballroom of the Conrad Hilton Hotel in Chicago for his "opening of new vistas of opportunity to Negro-Americans" speech. When introduced, he strode into the huge room under a brilliant spotlight, escorted by the Reverend Archibald T. Carey, Jr., "as the orchestra struck up the Colonel Bogey march and there was a thunderous ovation."

By 1957, thirty-six blacks were in major league baseball and the last holdouts, Tom Yawkey's Red Sox, grudgingly capitulated two years later. Slowly, without class or character, baseball was granting black men the right to play alongside whites.

To ordinary blacks, the breakthrough was a major watershed, not only for baseball and sports, but for their vision of America itself. Shortly after the Chicago address, Rickey visited Prentice-Hall editor Stuart Daniels in his lower Fifth Avenue office in Manhattan. Daniels wanted Rickey to write a book. On their way down in the elevator for lunch, the black operator stopped the car between floors. He removed his cap, placed it over his heart, and bowing slightly, said, "Mr. Rickey, what an honor to have you in my elevator."

Still, speeches alone could not soothe his restlessness. He joined President Eisenhower's Committee on Government Employment Policy, the first executive agency designed to eliminate racial discrimination in federal employment. (Nixon drew his raves, while Lyndon Johnson, who joined the committee while vice president, was "a man of the lowest moral character he had ever met in his life, ruthless.") At home in Pittsburgh, he wrote the executive director of that city's Commission on Human Relations two years later, after experiencing a mild heart attack, "I wish I could do something really helpful in this whole field of human relations. If I am physically able to respond, I will do it."

People continued to call. Don McClanen, a young football coach from a small Oklahoma college, stopped by to ask for help in organizing Christian athletes into one organization, which he planned to call the Fellowship of Christian Athletes, and which he hoped would fortify the moral and religious beliefs of the country's athletes. "He was shielded by his son and a male secretary but I camped on his door and was finally given five minutes," recalled McClanen. "It turned into five hours. He advised me to build slowly and quietly. He said we needed $10,000 to start and he knew a man who had that money. Mr. Rickey stabilized me. I felt eerie. Some in sports said the idea was crazy. But Mr. Rickey had a solid commitment for FCA from the time he first heard the idea. He put the FCA on the road." He quickly offered his blessings and backing, seeing it as a way of working with young men. "Boys look up to men who have unusual physical prowess as their heroes," he told McClanen. Not only that, Jane interrupted, "did you know that Mr. Rickey's first hero was the champion bundle pitcher of the crew that came to thresh grain at Duck Run?" Grinning, Rickey shook his head in agreement.

"Tell you what, Don. I'll speak with Vernon Law, Robinson, and Erskine about this."

On September 24, 1957, as organist Gladys Gooding played "Auld Lang Syne," the Brooklyn Dodgers played their last game in venerable Ebbets Field. A few weeks before, while O'Malley's decision to move to the Pacific coast was not yet public knowledge, he commented on the issue. "Will the Brooklyn Dodgers move?" he asked rhetorically. "There is absolutely nothing wrong with Brooklyn, artistically or financially. The cry of 'bigger stadiums' and 'more parking space' is so much smoke screen. How can Brooklyn possibly get a new big stadium for private baseball ownership with the entire borough crying for new schools? And what would happen to the stadium, used only for seventy-five days, the rest of the year? Certainly not for fights. Not for football. For what, then?"

He also reflected on his years in Brooklyn. "My eight years in Brooklyn gave me a new vision of America, or rather America gave me a new vision of a part of itself, Brooklyn. They were wonderful years. A community of over three million people, proud, hurt, jealous, seeking geographical, social, emotional status

Branch Rickey hosting a television show on Pittsburgh's WQED, part of the "Heritage Series." Not shown in the photograph are his guests, Arthur Mann, freelance writer, early biographer of Rickey and close associate, and Ken Blackburn, his secretary and assistant. (Courtesy Branch B. Rickey)

as a city apart and alone and sufficient. One could not live for eight years in Brooklyn and not catch its spirit of devotion to its baseball club, such as no other city in America equaled. Call it loyalty and so it was. It would be a crime against a community of three million people to move the Dodgers. Not that the move was unlawful, since people have the right to do as they please with their property. But a baseball club in any city in America is a quasi-public institution, and in Brooklyn the Dodgers were public without the quasi."

He was talking about tradition and his deep-seated belief that baseball, that peculiarly indigenous sport, and the city-state loyalties it fostered, symbolized continuity in a world increasingly governed by particularism and disruption. For half our history as a nation, he told a visitor, we have seen and admired and played the game.

A few years later he was shown a photo of the destruction of Ebbets Field. He stared at the scene before him. A crane dominated the half-ruined rotunda where once crowds had lined up to buy box and reserve seat tickets. A fence was plastered with billboard ads for a dance, a bazaar, and a carnival.

"This dark, gloom-shrouded picture is a symbol of sadness for me and hundreds of thousands of people. Ebbets Field is a bleak and empty place here. All the joy and love and great devotion have left this diamond behind the torn and tattered posters. The grandstand is leveled, the voices are silent. By some strange coincidence the picture was taken on the day, almost the hour, that my son died. I lived in Brooklyn for eight years, but it doesn't take that long to fall in love with the place. I did. Branch Jr. did. Our whole family did. We were devoted to the people, the Dodgers, and the ballpark."

In March 1961 Branch Jr. was taken to Presbyterian Hospital in Pittsburgh to die. "The young roly-poly, quick-on-the-laugh Branch Jr."—as *Sporting News* editor J. G. Taylor Spink superficially described him twenty years before—was suffering from complications arising from acute diabetes, a disease first detected during his freshman year in law school and confirmed definitively in the summer of 1940. Four years later, still vivacious and powerfully built, he was warned even more forcefully by Dr. Elliot P. Joslin of Boston. The doctor clearly sensed the man's unsettled and struggling nature and candidly informed him that with self-discipline he might survive the ailment though "you are a problem unto yourself. I wish I could see your wife and talk with her because I am sure she could help you."

During his remaining years friends and acquaintances believed he was deliberately flirting with self-destruction, yet his personality was the same before and after the diagnosis. Still, people were horrified to watch as he casually injected insulin through his trouser legs or shirt sleeves or ate chocolate bars indiscriminately or ladled spoonfuls of sugar into his occasional cup of coffee. His son recalls a day at the ball park where his father ate countless hot dogs and drank cups of sugar-sweetened soda, cautioning the boy not to tell his mother, and then both of them roaming the darkened streets frantically searching for an insulin syringe to replace the one he had accidentally broken. Impulsive, ebullient, he loved to wrestle with players and coaches, a perpetual grin on his broad face, hiding his innermost feelings and deepest longings from almost everyone. Privately, away from the world he felt so much at ease with, his agony was growing. Jane had had a cataract operation in 1960 and his father had been felled by another heart attack in Sudbury the previous summer. His own health was deteriorating rapidly and he was forced to sleep upright because otherwise fluid filled his lungs. His eyes were failing and the painful cramps he suffered from were now interminable.

Pirate doctor Joseph Finegold warned him he could avoid premature death only if he cared for his body, but he laughed at the advice. And when Harold Parrott met him on the road and suggested he stay away from sugary junk foods he waved away the advice and swallowed twice the amount of forbidden food. There was, thought Parrott, an "impish immaturity" about Branch Jr. that was causing him to take such ominous risks.

A few months before, following the Pirates' clinching of the pennant in Milwaukee, he suffered a heart seizure on their flight homeward and was rushed home by Pirate official Joe O'Toole while thousands of joyous fans lined the Pittsburgh air terminal to greet their heroes.

On the eve of his final hospitalization, his farm system was flourishing. Columbus, Asheville, Grand Forks, and Burlington had all won their respective pennants. Future major leaguers Al McBean, Bob Veale, and Gene Alley were on the way to Pittsburgh; he was especially excited by the promise shown by a young Burlington outfielder named Willie Stargell.

Dying, he sent loving messages to his sisters through his wife, who came by daily. His daughter Nancy sat reading one of Shakespeare's comedies one afternoon as he dozed. Suddenly awaking, he asked what she was reading. "I know the act and scene" and recited it from memory. His parents came every day too, Rickey talking baseball while his mother attended to his needs.

Branch Jr. particularly looked forward to the visits of his friend and minister, the Reverend Dr. Frederick B. Speakman of the Third Presbyterian Church, an Oklahoma-born Harvard and Princeton Theological Seminary graduate and liberal churchman. The two had grown very close, Speakman committed to the church and Branch Jr., an indifferent churchgoer, almost a mystic in his deep sensitivity toward the eastern religions. Each was the other's intellectual equal and they had reached out to one another in love and respect. "Branch Jr. was a pilgrim, searching," says Speakman. "He was constantly questioning doctrines. He couldn't believe absolute religious 'truths' and was repelled by fanaticism.

"He was, though, without self-pity as he lay dying. I came by three days weekly, his brightest hours seemingly around eleven P.M. I was filming a series of television shows and would drop in at that late hour to sit with him. Except for his final week he never complained, although once he expressed his despair.

"During the last two weeks of his life, with blindness overtaking him, he considered suicide on several occasions. I would tell him to think of Mary and the kids but one night, near the end, he said, 'If I get home, I've got a gun.' He was exhausted, in a near-coma, and blind. On the last evening I saw him alive he awoke and asked me to move closer. Would I give Mary a message?—which of course I did. And then he asked, 'Fred, hold my arm and help me get across.'"

He died of hepatitis on April 11. An autopsy revealed the scars of twelve earlier heart attacks.

At the 21 Restaurant in Manhattan, Rickey was at a table with William Shea and Jack Kent Cooke when the call came. Returning to the two men, his face drawn and chalk white, he said softly, "God's will be done. My Branch will have to suffer no more." Briefly acknowledging their sympathies, he turned, saying, "I'd better go home to Mother."

"The fog softens the future," Jane wrote soon after his death.

"Each day brings a new world. [Yet] there is a time in everyone's life where the futility of living arises. What must we do to go on living with any content? One must contribute something to someone. But how? Can you put yourself in a state of contentment that an all wise Providence will show you the way, accepting each task that presents itself from hour to hour?"

When O'Malley decided to go west he never told his mentor and patron, George V. McLaughlin of the Brooklyn Trust Company. O'Malley had been planning the move for many months, but when the banker learned that his borough would lose its beloved Dodgers he was beside himself with anger and grief. Calling an emergency meeting to resolve the situation, he asked Mayor Robert Wagner what might be done.

Wagner glanced at attorney William Shea seated alongside him for suggestions. Shea was known in New York political circles as a "rainmaker," in political parlance a well-connected lawyer and power broker. He was also a passionate baseball fan and his judgment was the same as McLaughlin's: "Let's get another team here."

For several months, the group tried unsuccessfully to induce the Reds and later the Pirates to transfer to Brooklyn. When that maneuver failed, Wagner named Shea head of an official committee to develop a new baseball team.

"I thought it was a very easy job to be accomplished," says Shea, "that all I had to do was get some people with money together and go out on a white charger and pick up a franchise somewhere in the hinterlands.

"Well, I soon found out that wasn't going to be done. It was just impossible to accomplish, and we were getting nowhere with our franchise for New York."

The more Shea floundered, the more McLaughlin stewed. At last he called Shea impatiently. "Get Rickey," he advised. "Work with him. He knows everything."

Shea phoned Fox Chapel. Explaining his dilemma, he asked the seventy-six-year-old if he was interested. Squirming in his superfluous role with the Pirates, incomplete in his quasi-retirement, Rickey sprang at the chance. He had recently been hospitalized, "worn out and tired." But Shea's invitation was an opportunity to run at full speed again. Still, he had an important question to ask Shea: Did he and the committee simply want him to find a franchise for the city or might they be interested in an utterly unorthodox approach requiring risk and courage?

Virtually unknown to anyone but Blackburn, he had—at least since the end of the 1957 season, when the Dodgers and Giants departed—been thinking seriously about expanding the two leagues, either by founding new expansion clubs and having them absorbed, or failing that, by forming an entirely new third major league. Whatever the ultimate formula, he knew the notion of another league would be hardest to achieve. National League president Warren Giles was on record as asking "Who needs New York?" when the two teams left for the West Coast. American League president Joe Cronin and Commissioner Ford Frick were equally unenthusiastic about expansion. He knew too that O'Malley now dominated baseball's executive council and, as sportswriter Arthur Daley shrewdly observed, "What O'Malley wants, O'Malley gets."

Yet the more Rickey considered a new league the more he believed in its practicality. And the more he started preaching its necessity. Despite his past strong opposition to the rebels of the Federal and Mexican leagues, he was convinced baseball's monopolistic powers had drawbacks. He persuaded the tough-minded Shea that (as Shea asserted before a Senate committee afterward) the owners were "absolute dictators" who wanted "no part of ... free enterprise."

When word of Rickey's latest enthusiasm reached Tom Johnson's ears he was outraged. "Disloyal," he sputtered angrily, "that's what he [is] disloyal—to the league and us. Here he was working for me and out generating support for a competitor with Shea." Moving swiftly, he canceled Rickey's contract as consultant. Shea then negotiated a cash settlement on the balance of the five-year contract.

In 1959 Rickey returned to New York City as president of the newly formed Continental League, the first attempt to form a third league since the days of the Federal League. His office was on Fifth Avenue, and he and Shea threw themselves into the project.

"Twenty great cities cannot be ignored," he told everyone who would listen. Rounding up wealthy investors—Joan Payson Whitney, Jack Kent Cooke, Lamar Hunt, Craig Cullinan, Max Winter, Bob Howsam, and others—with the promise of tempting tax write-offs, shelters, and depreciation, he formed the new league with franchises in Atlanta, Buffalo, Dallas–Fort Worth, Denver, Houston, Minneapolis–St. Paul, New York, and Toronto. Eventually he planned to expand to Honolulu, Montreal, New Orleans, San Diego and Seattle.

Requests from ex–major leaguers poured into his office. Herman Franks, Mule Haas, George "Specs" Toporcer, Billy Southworth, Al Todd, Gil English, and many others wrote him. But as yet the league existed only in theory and the few jobs he filled were for the closest of aides. Ken Blackburn joined him, as did Arthur Mann. For the three of them it was as if the old and glorious days had been recreated and yet a new and uncharted adventure had begun again.

"He worked us all day, wearing us out. Then we'd go out to dinner and return to the office to work," says his secretary, Margaret Regetz.

Dashing across the country, generally accompanied by Shea, he conducted countless meetings and organized innumerable groups in support of the new league.

Alone in his Fifth Avenue office one afternoon, he decided to press the question directly to Commissioner Ford Frick. He walked several blocks to Frick's office in Rockefeller Plaza, where they sat chatting about the just concluded World Series, Frick denigrating the quality of play by the Los Angeles Dodgers and the Chicago White Sox. Then, after a moment of awkward silence, Rickey spoke. "Ford, I have believed for some time that you were definitely opposed to the organization of a third major league. I want to get at the nub of that thing right now by asking you a question."

"Amazingly," Rickey said later, "he did not interrupt when I said, 'I want to ask you a question and here it is.'"

"In here"—and Rickey pointed with his right forefinger to his heart— "in here" (he repeated) "are you opposed to the organization of the third major league?"

"I'm glad you asked that question," replied Frick. Then he proceeded into a lengthy explanation of how he had always favored the idea but could not support it because both leagues were opposed.

Rickey was unsatisfied.

"Ford, you have just made a statement you must never forget if you really believe the Continental League is now a definite project."

Rickey leaned forward. "Why, as commissioner of baseball, do you not embrace it and encourage it and lead it? We need your leadership as commissioner. You can take the place of Mr. William Shea and Mr. Branch Rickey and hasten and facilitate the proper organization of the league. Your people, and by that I mean the major leagues, cannot hurt you."

Frick was embarrassed. He couldn't do such a thing, he murmured. Besides, he never knew what the owners were thinking or what they were doing.

Rickey was ready to leave. Standing, he asked Frick to "listen to me and hear me through. I said to him, 'Ford, you must not miss your chance. Ol' man opportunity has long hair in front and he is bald behind. 'When he comes to you, you can snatch him and hold him tight, but when he is past, he could be gone forever.'"

Later, he spoke at a meeting in New York with league representatives and again Frick was present.

"We are prepared to start tomorrow, if necessary," Rickey began. "We are not looking for war. We much prefer to come in as friendly members of organized baseball. I think that every man in this room recognizes that expansion is necessary. All we request is that you gentlemen grant us major league membership as a third league. All we ask is that you gentlemen give us a chance.

Rickey sat down and Shea added his thoughts.

"Mr. Rickey has covered the situation well. One thing, however, I think should be understood. The Continental League is not a fly-by-night organization. The cities holding membership are pledged to mutual action. As individuals we cannot, any of us, go our own way or make our own decisions. As Mr. Rickey has said, we do not want a baseball war."

*Chapter Thirteen*

Was Shea really bluffing when he advanced the third league as a way of getting a New York club? He says he was in deadly earnest and while many people thought he had taken in the older man, Rickey believed him. Still, in a larger sense the league was a bluff, "a paper tiger which became a complete success," says Craig Cullinan, who joined the venture with Houston because he thought Rickey "an extraordinary man." He also believed the acumen of Rickey and political influence of Shea would force expansion.

At the end of July 1959, Rickey and Shea and others testified at hearings conducted by Senator Estes Kefauver's committee on a bill which would essentially have eliminated baseball's exemption from antitrust laws and weakened seriously their iron-clad control over player contracts and the allotment of franchises. "Baseball was scared," Frick admitted to the press as the hearings opened. "The nightmare of the Federal League war was common knowledge. Pressure was being applied by the press and public opinion."

Rickey and Shea had written a joint letter to the senatorial members of the committee: "The present major league franchise-owners apparently have a total lack of loyalty to the communities which support their enterprises. The major league owner today refers to the 'national pastime' with great reverence. And, when it suits him, he behaves as if he were operating a quasi-public trust. But let a better 'deal' be offered in another city and he reverts instantaneously to the hundred percent businessman whose only guide is the earnings statement. The men who would hold franchises in the Continental League are local, civic-minded, financially sound baseball fans of excellent reputation. They pray for legislation which will permit them to exercise their franchises."

Kefauver's bill was defeated in June 1960 but by only a handful of votes. Major league baseball had fought hard against the bill and the owners had been assured by their Washington-based lobbyist, lawyer Paul Porter, that the bill would receive only fifteen or twenty votes. Nevertheless, the strong backing given the bill by Senator Edwin Johnson of Colorado (who had once been president of the Western League and was the father-in-law of Bob Howsam) and Senate Majority Leader Lyndon Johnson almost pulled an upset.

Despite their defeat by a close vote, Rickey was pleased but still warned Cullinan that "something was going to happen." Within five weeks something did. The owners were so fearful of a second senatorial vote that their Executive Council met and voted expansion, thereby killing the Continental League. Promises had been made to both Rickey and Shea that any expansion would include Continental League franchises, but when the time to decide arrived on August 2, 1960, base-ball reneged on its word. They chose instead to expand to eight clubs each, the Nationals choosing New York and Houston while the Ameri-cans, in a complex move, allowed Washington to move to Minneapolis–St. Paul and Los Angeles to enter. They also decreed that within several years four additional clubs would be added. In return, the third league had to disband.

The news bitterly disappointed Rickey. In three typed pages he vented his rage. "Their action was not only unfair to the Continental League ... but it was unfair to the American public in defeating any proper concept of major league expansion into a number of great cities throughout our country.... It is difficult to understand how reputable gentlemen will explain this breach of good faith."

Even so, New York was to return to the National League. Jack Kent Cooke had bought a large minority share of the defunct Continental League club from Mrs. Isaac Killam, widow of a Canadian lumber king who was once part-owner of the *Brooklyn Eagle*. Cooke was fairly friendly with Rickey and doubtless Rickey was beginning to envision himself as chairman of the board of the New York Mets. He even had a candidate for its general manager, Eddie Leishman, then general manager of the San Diego club of the Pacific Coast League ("an old friend and one of the most capable general managers in baseball"). On February 15, 1961, M. Donald Grant, a Canadian-born stockbroker and minority share-holder but, more important, a close confidant of Mrs. Whitney's, offered Rickey a contract "to head up" the Mets. On the twenty-eighth Rickey responded that he was considering the offer but he was uncertain over assuming daily control; it may be too that he wanted Cooke to assume more control of the club.

Rickey tried to get along with Grant but his first loyalty was to Cooke. He had cautioned Lou Niss, an ex–*Brooklyn Eagle* sports editor and the Continental League publicist, that "when you have any ideas just pre-sent them. Then look at me and Grant. If I nod, then proceed but let Grant think he thought of them."

The resulting in-fighting for control was so intense that in the end, Cooke most likely sold out in disgust. With Cooke gone, Grant wrote Rickey in March telling him, "The proposal is withdrawn."

There was talk after that of naming the new stadium after Rickey—a stadium built with taxpayers' funds and presented as a virtual gift to one of America's wealthiest families. Instead, Rickey wrote the City Coun-cil and the mayor and asked them to honor Shea.

"The first one to agree with me about a third league was Shea. By

## Chapter Thirteen

George, he leaped into action. He was like a turkey in a tobacco patch, not caring if he knocked down the stalks to get the worm. That's when I got to know the man. The better I knew him the more I admired him and his effort. He's a marvelously unselfish person, asking and expecting no credit. By Judas Priest, he worked. He neglected his law practice for two years. He showed intelligence, resourcefulness, courage, indefatigability and tenacity. He brought back the National League to New York. The responsibility for the result is his and his alone."

Rickey returned home to Fox Chapel. He wanted to persuade Jackie Robinson to support Nixon, then campaigning against Pat Brown for the California gubernatorial seat. He also wanted the Republican Party to take a more active role in defense of civil rights, a step most national Republican politicians refused to take.

Rickey was determined to bring Nixon and Robinson together, telling the politician proudly that Robinson was "taking the stump as a Democrat for Nixon." Then he counseled Nixon to pursue black votes in 1964 with some "know-how and desire ... I could start it, but I am too old for it—in health, not in years—just past eighty, but I could be a fairly effective waterboy at the first meeting or two."

In 1963, a little more than twenty years after they left, Jane and Branch returned to St. Louis. He was eighty-two, "senior consultant" and elder statesman of the club he had first joined in 1917. Nearly everyone he once knew and worked with was gone. Augustus Busch, the multimillionaire beer baron, was his sole link to the present organization.

When Busch, on Bob Cobb's recommendation, asked him to rejoin the Cardinals, he and Jane agreed Fox Chapel's spacious acres and large house were too much for them.

Calling his daughters and Branch Jr.'s widow to his home to take whatever household articles they wanted, he was stunned when there were no bidders. "This is the saddest day of my life," he told them to waves of laughter. "I've lived eighty years and my children have all come in and instead of fighting over my possessions, not one of them wants a single thing I have."

But he was exhilarated with the offer though he sought to confront Busch with conditions.

"I'd make a lot of demands," he told Busch. "What kind of demands?" asked Busch.

"Well, I'd need a car and driver to get around, and I'd have to bring my secretary, Ken Blackburn."

Busch laughed. "Is *that* all?"

In spite of their wish to see him remain active, his family worried about the offer. "Life in Pittsburgh is an easy one for me with two people devoted to my comfort, all of which I accept and enjoy," complained Jane. "I am a bit old to take over the daily affairs, wandering around shops and cooking meals. It will take effort on my part to take up old ties. [But] Branch is so thoroughly engrossed in his new venture he has little time for anything else. I am not first nor second consideration, I am a sideline, a fill-in. He feels he has a new life at the age of eighty-two years."

On a less personal note, some of his children believed the role of undefined "adviser" would only repeat his unhappy experience with Joe L. Brown and the Pirates. Son-in-law John Eckler, a lawyer, suggested he reject Busch's invitation. Consultants, he argued, merely advised but had no authority. He was worried lest the arrangement bring the old man more unnecessary grief.

Jane's opposition continued to mount. Quoting Larry MacPhail's description of Rickey to him—"Rickey has a will that will go through a stone wall"—she excoriated his "discontent" at his stage of life, the exhausting journeys he expected to take for the Cardinals as their adviser, and his continuous neglect of a book for which he had signed a contract with Simon and Schuster. "Is there no limit to your ambitions? You have had a wonderful family life, the devotion and continuing love of children and grandchildren. Why not contentment of soul? Why not abiding feeling of joy and happiness in this faith? Why do you struggle and doubt? Why don't you trust life itself? Heap some of the rewards. Be thankful. Put trust in me."

He was stubborn and unyielding. Shortly before they left for St. Louis a reporter called and asked him for his greatest thrill in baseball. Snorting defiance, he shot back: "Son, it hasn't happened yet."

Archie drove them to 3 Warson Lane in suburban Ladue, adjoining St. Louis, where they had purchased a small house near their daughter Sue, her husband, Steve Adams, and their two youngsters. For the Rickeys, the children were a godsend, stopping by almost daily to or from school. Jane always had cookies on hand and when he was home, their grandfather would affectionately grab them, tickling and poking them with his cane and sometimes deliberately embracing them while his face was still covered with shaving lather.

Jane started sketching and drawing, decades after Ohio Wesleyan, and she enrolled in a neighborhood art school. Most of their friends were dead, but George and Katherine Sisler lived not far away and they spent many evenings playing bridge or chess. Ken Blackburn tried to make himself available whenever needed.

# Chapter Thirteen

*Globe-Democrat* sports editor Robert L. Burnes greeted Rickey's return to the city in his column:
"Less than two months away from his eighty-second birthday, Mr. Rickey is still a lion. The hair is still brown on top although the eyebrows are a startling white. The eyes are piercing. A cane with which he needs to move about is carefully hidden. The ever-present cigar is still there, and his mind leaps from subject to subject with lightning speed."

What, precisely, Busch had in mind for him was unclear from the start. All Busch knew was that their mutual friend Bob Cobb had told him, "The best brain in baseball is sitting in Pittsburgh doing nothing." Most probably, like Galbreath, Busch believed Rickey a wonder worker who would miraculously lift the Cardinals into contention. His team had fallen onto desperate days, ending up in fourth, then sixth, place the two previous seasons.

In many ways Augustus Busch, Jr., resembled a nineteenth-century plutocrat transferred into the technological world of the twentieth—hardly the sort who would consult subordinates about the advisability of hiring anyone he wanted to hire. His world, wrote a Busch watcher, was "all ball clubs, yachts, private railroad cars, land-cruising buses, blooded horses, a fabulous estate, and a hirefirehirefire sway over a far-flung and lucrative empire" born of the labors of three previous Busches and tens of billions of barrels of beer.

His fiefdom was run from his 281-acre estate, Grant's Farm, on the edge of the city where Ulysses S. Grant once resided before Lincoln chose him as his general. There Busch and his family lived in a thirty-four-room French Renaissance manor house set in a park stocked with exotic animals and through which the lord often passed on coach-and-fours, landaus, phaetons, or Russian sleighs. The question was: If Busch knew everything there was to know about the beer business, what in fact did he know about baseball?

Behind Busch there lay a trail of disaffected ex-associates. Some believed he loved the game and the idea of owning a ball club. It was only the details that bored him.

"When the Cardinals traded away Enos Slaughter [in 1953] Gussie had never heard of Slaughter," remarked Ed Vogel, who once worked at Anheuser-Busch. "Gussie couldn't figure out what all the yelling was about when Slaughter was traded.

"I was with Gussie at a game a few years after the brewery bought the club. The Cardinals are ahead 5–2 going into the ninth. The other team goes down one-two-three and I get up to leave. 'Where the hell do you think you're going,' Busch yells at me. 'We're not leaving till the last out.' Hell of a fan. He owns the team and he doesn't know that when you're ahead at home you don't bat in the last half of the ninth inning."

Whatever the local doubts, Rickey trusted Busch implicitly as he generally tended to trust successful men. It never dawned on him that other Cardinal employees might feel threatened by his presence. Two men were especially irreconcilable, Richard A. (Dick) Meyer and General Manager Bing Devine. Meyer had for years been the recipient of Busch's largesse, at the brewery where he served in an executive capacity and with the team. Harry Caray, a former Cardinal announcer, large stockholder in Anheuser Busch, and Busch's opponent, argued that Meyer's baseball background was minimal. "When Busch bought the Cardinals he asked his board if there was anyone who knew anything about baseball and Dick Meyer said he'd been a catcher for Concordia Seminary and Busch said, 'Well, then, you're running the team.'" True or not, Meyer worked in tandem with Devine, the other influential Rickey antagonist. Ironically, Devine was in baseball because of Rickey; years before Rickey had hired Devine as a young high school graduate and put him to work assisting a Cardinal publicist. But adolescent gratitude was one thing and adult insecurity quite another. The opposition to Rickey's second coming stemmed from their fear that their authority would be eroded by the strong-willed Rickey and the capricious Busch.

Unaware of such antagonism, Rickey unwittingly challenged them from the start. "The boys are building for 1963, because they believe they can *win* in 1963," he said soon after his arrival. "The boys" he referred to were Devine and Meyer and their associates in the front office, together with manager Johnny Keane. To their consternation, he suggested 1963 was premature and by no stretch of the imagination could they win the pennant that year.

When his old friend Frank Graham paid him a visit he told him, "But I must be honest, Frank, the Cardinals have neither the depth nor experience on their pitching staff."

When Graham departed he shook his head in concern. "Controversy is inevitable when an outsider is brought in to advise a proud young man [Devine]," he wrote ruefully a few days later, sensing that trouble was coming and Rickey, in the eye of the storm, was oblivious to it. "It is compounded when an outsider is Branch Rickey, who stirs strong passions."

At the close of the 1962 season Rickey suggested that the forty-two-year-old Stan Musial, who had just batted .330, was nearing the end of his illustrious career. Musial was "a fine hitter," wrote the man who had transformed the Donora, Pennsylvania, neophyte from a failing Class D pitcher into a superb outfielder two decades before, "but Stan doesn't have the arm [anymore]. He couldn't run the bases the way the others could." It was time, he proposed, that the city's hero and celebrity be asked to retire.

Devine sharply disagreed. And when the memorandum was shown to Musial, he termed it insulting, bringing him "embarrassment and unpleasantness." The press pounced on the incident, and once again, Rickey was embroiled in a public fight. Busch, who preferred to operate behind the scenes, was forced to take a position. "Since when do you ask a .330 hitter to retire'?" he asked, defending his front office.

Before long, Meyer and Devine sought allies elsewhere—in the newspapers, at the powerful private clubs, in downtown business circles. Unacknowledged off-the-record conversations brought tales of Rickey's alleged arrogance and aggrandizement: he was disruptive, went the charges, he didn't know when to quit; he was as cheap as ever; he had been unfair to Breadon; his Pirates had been a disaster; his Dodgers had won pennants but lost every World Series but one. *Post-Dispatch* sports columnist Bob Broeg reported, "He ordered Devine around."

In mid–September, as the 1963 season ground down to a bitter end—the Cardinals ended six games behind the Dodgers—Rickey was invited to lunch by someone with the improbable name of Fullerton Place. Place worked for Al Fleishman, a St. Louis political kingpin and a persuasive and shrewd public relations man whose major client was Busch and the brewery.

Rickey knew Place from his former Cardinal days and they chatted amiably for an hour. Yet Rickey kept wondering why he had been invited. Place had been talking about the team during dessert and suddenly lifted his eyes. Mr. Rickey, he said, why don't you retire at the close of the season? It would be the proper thing to do since an "unhappy atmosphere" had developed. Why end your illustrious career this way?

Rickey was startled. Busch, after all, had asked him to come to St. Louis; he had never sought the job. Innocently, he wondered whether Jane had something to do with the conversation, but he caught himself. She had never been duplicitous and "if so, it would be the first time in fifty-eight years that she would have proceeded in that fashion."

Then who wanted him out? And why?

Place was toying with a teaspoon, somewhat diffident about the errand he was performing. "It was very natural," Rickey thought, the truth finally evident to him, "that Mr. Devine and his associates would look with immediate and abiding disfavor upon my coming to the club, that it would be resented that I might be coming into some public attention and credit for the improved 1963 position of the Cardinal club in the pennant race; that he did not believe there was a chance for a change in that attitude on the part of Mr. Devine and his associates; that I was too old and dignified in position to endure it longer, etc. etc. But what would I say to the public and the press?"

Place smiled. Rickey was now on his turf. He had anticipated the question, he said. It would be appropriate simply to state he wanted at long last to leave the hurly-burly of daily activities and devote himself to his family and hobbies. Place's own firm would prepare the press release, he added.

"And my secretary, Kenneth? What will become of him?" Place had an answer for that one, too. "Any fine employee of yours for so long would be taken care of."

Rickey stared at Place and put down his coffee cup. Standing, he reached for his cane, his right hand trembling in fury.

"I don't believe you," he replied,

Vexed by the ugly edge the public argument was taking, Frank Graham called Rickey and tried to tell him that only he could be harmed by it. "But Frank, it's absurd to think that I'm after anybody's job," he insisted. "I'm too *old.*"

To others he appealed for understanding of his difficult situation.

"Mr. Busch invited me to come in as a consultant. This meant, as I understood it, that I was to help build a better Cardinal ball club. As a result I followed closely five minor league clubs and tried to become knowledgeable about their players. And what do I have to show for all this?" he asked in exasperation.

He also complained to Busch, as he had so often to Galbreath.

He outlined a litany of problems: he hadn't been consulted on player exchanges; developments among free agents were kept from him; a University of Wisconsin outfielder (who never made the majors) was scouted and signed by the club without his knowledge.

"I was completely surprised, in fact hurt, that I had never heard about the player and I did not know of our interest. Even after my inquiry I was never invited to see the player.... It would seem that courtesy for my age, if not for experience and ability, would have brought an early invitation to me to see the player."

In the winter of 1963-64 he was chagrined to hear that Devine had sharply restricted his role by ordering that any club expenditure greater than $15,000 had to have Devine's approval. "Apparently that final approval did not include myself at any point," said an offended Rickey to Busch.

Just the same, he embarked on a scouting tour assessing the players Busch hoped would bring them the flag in 1964. Dal Maxville, he reported, had a "quick and accurate arm and could be carried by any contending club—pennant bound"; new pitcher Ron Taylor was promising but needed a "third usable pitch"; Curt Flood, the Cardinal center fielder, was "perfection."

In June he was visited by Clyde King, the Cardinals' supervising pitching coach, who had played for Brooklyn and once been close to the Rickeys. He told an astounded but no longer surprised Rickey—his famous eyebrows arching as he listened to his onetime relief pitcher—he was in town for an important meeting on farm club prospects. "I was not invited nor do I know of the meeting," he complained to King. "It would seem that this sort of meeting would surely include me as a listener." Indignant and pained and wondering now what sort of Byzantine affair he had become embroiled in, he appealed again to Busch: "I have tried to make myself agreeable to everyone, happy to be in the organization, never seeking authority, and never interfering with the work of anyone, yet my opinions on players and deals have been disregarded."

In the midst of this gathering storm the book still remained to be written. Arthur Mann, who was to be his collaborator, had died, but still Simon and Schuster was pressing him to get on with the job, as did his own collaborator Robert Riger, a portraitist and photographer. "I know you are low on spirit and strength," wrote Riger, "but let us see if we can possibly put *one final effort into this book.*"

He was, however, reluctant to work "on my damn book" and he moaned, "I write and write. Then I read it over the next day and toss it in the wastebasket. I write copiously but not well."

Drafting a speech on the back of an envelope or a scrap of foolscap paper was one thing; writing, refining, and editing his thoughts into a book-length manuscript was quite another. Just the same, after innumerable calls, letters, visits, even Riger's threats to leave ("Unless I keep to this schedule or something close to it I must quit the project completely"), he finally relented and invited him to Ladue.

Riger's concept was a book about Rickey's decades in baseball—the people he knew so well, from the scared kids to the seasoned veterans, the teams he managed and administered, his general and specific feelings about the sport's meanings.

The first morning Rickey awakened later than usual and appeared at breakfast at 9:45 A.M. while Riger and Jane sat waiting for him.

"Good morning, Mother," he said, as he approached his wife,

dressed in his starched white shirt and tie and jacket. He bent to kiss her, with intensity, as if—Riger thought—they were newly married.

"And good morning to you Robert," he said, just before he uttered a brief grace. Their best china was set out and to Riger the two seemed quieter than ever, and very much alone.

After eating leisurely, they walked slowly to his basement office where Rickey took up an unlit cigar and sat in the large leather swivel chair he had carried with him from front office to front office. Then he began reading a draft of the manuscript Mann had researched for him but which he alone had written.

For the first seven decades of his life, he read, baseball had been a glorious fraternity. There were cruelties and racism and inequities but through it all he had found wondrous friendships and a degree of brotherhood unknown to most professions. When he mentioned Jackie Robinson's name he paused and smiled with sheer pleasure; for Judge Landis he now felt a measured gratitude for having upheld honesty in the game, although he never forgave him the Cedar Rapids ruling and his "despotic powers."

In his somber and resonant voice, clear and alive, he read aloud.

"I remember so well at the close of the college year in 1903 when I was leaving my old home in the hills of southern Ohio to report to the Dallas club in the Texas League as a player, that my mother, kneeling in prayer, asked God to give some kindly protection for her son. It was really stronger than that. She almost gave advice to her Heavenly Father. She felt that I was going into a very worldly association. And in 1903 she was right.

"I have a young seventeen-year-old grandson. He very recently pitched a no-hitter in his high school league and only yesterday, as I write this, struck out eighteen batsmen in an American Legion seven-inning game in California. It so happens that he is a straight-A student, especially strong in mathematics. He has entered as a freshman in an outstanding small college in California. If he shows sufficient ability, I shall do everything I can to have him go into professional baseball in America. There is no profession more worthy."

His large gnarled fingers turned the pages of his manuscript slowly, as he continued reading: "The Sisler family epitomized everything worthwhile about the best people in the game—they supported themselves through college, they married and loved, they were thoughtful and educated people. I always admired them greatly."

Writing painfully, laboriously, deliberately, altering words and phrases over and again, he wrote the entire book himself. He presented

Riger with dog-eared short pieces about the sixteen men he believed had contributed most to baseball. He wrote too of the years to come and the implications of expansion, the equalization of teams, and the deleterious impact excessive commercialization and television could have.

He was, Riger mused, like a great dramatist conducting a one-man show. Unpretentious now, with his audience of one, he still had an appreciation of the importance of the moment and the sport that sustained his life. Riger was ebullient at the progress he was making but kept asking him to rewrite drafts, to make the editorial changes requested by the editors, to clear his worldly concerns from his mind while writing.

As they approached the end, Riger revisited Ladue with the drawings and photographs to accompany the text. Seated in the living room, Jane and Branch looked at each of them over and again, portraits of people they had known so well and who were in most instances now dead. "Marvelous," he said over and over. "Just marvelous, Robert."

The book was finished in late 1964, but when Peter Schwed of Simon and Schuster delayed publication until the autumn of 1965 Rickey was vastly relieved. "It is a great relief to me," he wrote Jane then in Canada for the summer. "Poor Robert," one of his daughters sighed when she heard the news. "Poor Daddy." And then she laughed aloud.

The struggle with Devine and Meyer had grown more intense. Devine was so fearful for his job he visited Warson Lane twice—as did Johnny Keane—to ask Rickey's advice and help. "Mr. Rickey," complained Devine, "Mr. Busch wants to fire me."

After one visit, Rickey turned to his daughter. "Sue, I'm going to have a hard time convincing that man Devine that I'm his friend."

The difficulty lay in the fact that everyone's job depended entirely on Busch, who in turn watched the progress of the team closely. The Cardinals started the 1964 season in a horrid fashion and by midsummer were wallowing deep in the second division. Fans and writers demanded to know where the pennant was the management had all but pledged to win. Rickey's clubs had won nine flags between 1926 and 1946; now it was seventeen years with losers.

After Busch decided in July to make a change at the top and fire Devine, Rickey phoned and asked him to retain him until the end of the season. If he still wanted to dismiss him then, well and good. But why make a scapegoat of him now? Busch reluctantly agreed, but two weeks later, the team still losing, his patience snapped. Bing Devine was dismissed.

When Rickey learned the news he wrote Jane: "I had no idea that Busch was going to fire Bing. I would not have fired him at all." That day he was in Buffalo for the International League All-Star game. He was seated in his hotel room with Howie Haak when the phone rang. It was Busch. Haak recalled Rickey's conversation: "I'm eighty-three and there is no way I can be general manager. Bing Devine is a great general manager, Gussie. Keep him." There was a pause on Rickey's end and then he concluded, "No way. I'm too old."

Even so, he hoped the move would prove advantageous, and he promptly proposed Bob Howsam as Devine's successor. Meyer was furious at the firing but more so, perhaps, at the mere mention of Howsam, whom he considered Rickey's man. And to some extent, Howsam was just that. In mid–August then, while Rickey sat in an adjoining room at Grant's Farm, Busch signed Howsam to a contract as new general manager.

Howsam and Rickey had first met in 1946 at the annual minor league meeting in Columbus, Ohio. The next year they met again, in Pueblo, Colorado, where they chatted briefly about the Western League. Rickey was impressed with the young executive's acumen, and when Harold Roettger recommended that the Pirates and Denver sign a partial working agreement he quickly agreed. Soon after, three Howsams visited Rickey to sign the pact. In spite of their previous meetings, Howsam hardly knew the older and far more famous man but as he and his father and brother entered the Rickey suite, crowded with staff, scouts, and old baseball buddies, Howsam suddenly remembered a *Sporting News* piece. Rickey senior was "Branch" and his son, "Twig." "Hi, Branch, hi, Twig," he called out as they entered the room. Suddenly there was silence and everyone stopped to look at the brash newcomer. Branch Jr., who detested the name, was obviously annoyed, and Howsam felt like burying himself under a nearby bed. Rickey rose instead, smiling, shook hands and then, as if their conversation in Pueblo had been uninterrupted, plunged into an analysis of the Pirates and Bear players, asking Howsam for his judgment. It made an indelible impression on the younger man but never more so than later that year when Denver was driving for the pennant but found themselves short of relief pitchers. At 4 A.M. one late July morning Howsam's phone rang. "Bob," began Rickey with no apologies for the early hour, "I know we haven't done much for you but I haven't forgotten you and have been following your club all year. You seem to need a couple of pitchers. Right?" That day, two Pirate hurlers were assigned to Denver and they went on to win their first pennant in thirty-nine years.

By mid–August 1964, Howsam was running the Cardinals, then nine games out of first place. When the season ended, the Cardinals had come from behind in a tense race, beat out the Phillies and the Reds by one game, and gone on to master the Yankees in the World Series.

Despite the championship, which no one in St. Louis was willing to credit him with in any way, Howsam had entered a political ambush. Shortly after he assumed office Meyer told him candidly that he (Meyer) was a Devine man and moreover, he disliked Rickey. The highly regarded columnist Bob Broeg believed Howsam had offended everyone by "unfairly taking credit for the 1964 championship but also by his firing of lower echelon, longtime Cardinal employees."

At the World Series victory party at Stan and Biggie's Restaurant, Rickey arrived with Jane, Sue and Steve Adams, and Janet and Bob Howsam. He had been elated that morning when he received a congratulatory telegram from Terris McDuffie, the black former pitcher who had asked for a tryout in April 1945 in Bear Mountain. But once inside the restaurant he was shoved time and again by Cardinal employees and boorishly treated by people vaguely associated with the club. While his daughter bristled, he put his hand on hers and said evenly, "Sue, I understand their emotions."

Soon another bitter assault was launched, this time when Broeg revealed the contents of a leaked memorandum. Rickey had written it on August 10—three days before the firing of Devine and while the team were still relentless losers. The document, wrote Broeg, "would have run up the white flag of surrender in mid–August."

The memo had been given to Broeg by a secretary in the Cardinal office loyal to Devine and Meyer. Actually Broeg never saw the memo since it was read to him over the phone. According to Broeg, it called for "an early move with Bing," a recognition that 1964 was yet another wasted season and that planning for 1965 ought to begin immediately. Toward that end, Rickey suggested minor league pitchers Nelson Briles, Steve Carlton, and Dave Dowling be brought up to the parent club; an untried rookie replace veteran second baseman Julian Javier; and "to accommodate these new players on the Cardinal roster" Dal Maxville, Carl Warwick, and Charley James be sent elsewhere. "The Mahatma" continued Broeg, "proposed sending back Barney Schultz, just brought up, who would win one and save 11 games the last two months."

"The topper"—what he and others interpreted as Rickey's "Memo of Surrender"—was this paragraph:

"As an afterthought I would let [Mike] Shannon go back to Jacksonville for the balance of the season. I would even let Shannon go to the draft at Triple A if major league waivers could be secured. I don't believe we can win the pennant in 1965 with Shannon as a regular player on the Cardinal club, or Warwick, or James, or [Bob] Uecker or [Jerry] Buchek, for that matter."

Another stunning development exploded when Manager Johnny Keane resigned because he had been pained to read press reports of his impending replacement. Again, Rickey was blamed and accounts circulated of his efforts to bring in Leo Durocher as a replacement. Not one reporter, however, checked with Rickey, and deeply aggrieved, he drove to the *Globe-Democrat* and sought out reporter Rick Koster.

RICKEY SEES HIMSELF AS SCAPEGOAT ran the headlined story the next day. He denied heatedly he had urged Keane's firing (Keane had since joined the Yankees) and produced another memorandum dated February 1963 in which he concluded, "Given the material, Johnny Keane is a pennant-winning manager."

Koster, his reporter's instincts aroused, asked, "If not you, then who earmarked Keane for dismissal?"

"I'd have to say I don't know," answered Rickey. "Since that memo, everything Keane has done only substantiated my first impression. It certainly wasn't Bing Devine, he and I think alike on Keane."

Nor, he added, had he ever suggested that Durocher be hired.

"Even in my most incoherent dreams, I would never advocate that Durocher be hired as manager. Given twenty-five good players, Leo can produce a winner. At two o'clock in the afternoon, he's a great manager. But there's more to managing than just a ball game." (Unknown to Rickey, Busch had in fact approached Durocher after receiving permission from O'Malley to speak with his coach.)

Koster pressed him further. What about the August 10 "Surrender" memo, the one leaked to Broeg?

All his life, he explained, he had written memos to himself to clarify his thinking and simplify complicated problems. That memo was just another example of this practice.

"It was not from Branch Rickey to August Busch. It was from Branch Rickey to Branch Rickey. To my knowledge, Mr. Busch never saw it.

"At no time did I ever give up on the Cardinals. The memorandum, as it appeared, was an injustice. I can only question the motives of those who used it as they did."

He rose to leave but Koster had another question.

Could he have a copy of the memo?

"I have no copy of it. It has disappeared. I showed it to no one, but it is gone. Yes, I have an idea of what happened to it, but I'd rather not say."

Then Rickey was the scapegoat? Was that what he believed? "That, of course, is what I think. But it is not my place to say it," he replied as he left.

Archie was waiting in the car and he drove toward Ladue. Rickey was agitated, and once home, he hurried to his basement office and summoned Blackburn. Dictating rapidly, as his aide wrote in pen and ink in longhand, he directed a letter to Busch:

"It is a very old practice of mine to dictate memorandums on games, clubs, conferences and players that are never addressed to anybody and are very rarely ... available to or seen by anyone else."

He denied he had written off the Cardinals' chances or that he had denigrated the players. "I think that article is dishonest reporting."

He cooled down and the memo was never sent to Busch. But even so, his patience was at an end.

Actually, Busch was the principal cause of dissension in the front office since he had inexplicably invited Rickey, thus bringing unnecessary pressure on Devine and in the end blaming both of them for his own miscalculations. Swinging wildly, yet sincerely and desperately desiring a winning ball club, he ruled Rickey had to go.

He ordered Howsam to Grant's Farm and told him to fire the old man. Others wanted the task, but Howsam insisted he and he alone would do the telling for he owed too much to Rickey to allow anyone else to hurt him so. As he left the baronial estate Howsam had second thoughts. Perhaps, he remembers asking himself, he too ought to quit and let Busch do his own dirty work? Guilty and heartbroken, his hand shook as he reached for the phone to call Rickey in Hollywood, Florida.

Howsam could detect his mentor's agitation.

"But Robert, I had so looked forward to working together with you...," and his voice trailed off.

Howsam interrupted, as upset as Rickey.

"Mr. Rickey, I feel so bad about this that I want to hand in my resignation. I'd like to leave and..."

"Nonsense, Robert, if you did that it would accomplish nothing"— his voice stronger. "You just go ahead with your job and develop a winning team. I believe in you."

Years later Busch confessed the firing of Devine was a "mistake." (He fired him again in 1978.) Rickey though was quite another matter. A "baseball genius ... returning to the scene of his greatest glories, he forgot that he was just a 'senior consultant' and tried to run everything. I was sorry, but he had to go."

Howsam remained with the Cardinals for the 1965 (seventh-place finish) and 1966 (sixth-place) seasons. Devine's unrepentant backers and a few friends of veteran Cardinal players continued to harass Howsam, blaming him for their failures. His trades hardly endeared him to the old guard as he shipped off Ken Boyer, Bill White, and Dick Groat. In 1966, his final year, he executed two brilliant trades: Ray Sadecki for Orlando Cepeda and Charlie Smith for Roger Maris, which helped set the stage for the 1967 St. Louis World Champions. Then he left for Cincinnati. But why, a Cincinnati reporter asked him, would anyone in his right mind want to leave St. Louis for a club that finished seventh in 1966 and drew only 743,000 people at the gate? The new Red general manager paused, then answered, "Here, I have complete charge."

A few days after Rickey's dismissal, the first reviews of his book appeared. Entitled *The American Diamond,* the book got a mixed reception, summed up favorably by Ed Rumill in the *Christian Science Monitor* as "eloquent, dynamic and entertaining, with more depth of expression than ever before," and negatively by Roger Kahn in *Book Week,* as "trivial and pretentious."

Rickey now worked out of Warson Lane, as unquiet and tireless as ever, surprisingly nimble, hard at work on new projects.

Earlier, he had changed his mind about Lyndon Johnson and wrote him complimenting him on his approach to civil rights, and received a warm note in return. Archibald Carey, a Chicago black minister (and later a federal court judge) and onetime colleague on the President's Committee on Government Employment Policy, introduced him at a Boy Scout executive meeting in McCormick Place in Chicago in November. When he returned to St. Louis he called W. Arthur McCoy, Ross Clinchy, and Carey—all of them members of the federal antidiscrimination committee—to schedule a reunion the forthcoming summer on his Canadian island. His plans included inviting Eisenhower and Nixon as well.

Riger paid the Rickeys a social call. After leaving he decided Rickey was without bitterness at his final defeat. That he seemed to retain a degree of humility pleased Riger no end, but hardly more than the recognition that Rickey could not tolerate pretentiousness in people around him. When he could see properly, he was reading the books he loved while Jane painted and sketched. They still played a rubber of bridge almost every evening with Mabel and the Sislers. He limited his travel but found time to fly to Delaware for an OWU trustees meeting and then on to New York to meet old friends, as Jane wandered through the art galleries and museums and visited the theater. There he lunched with Riger at the Commodore Hotel, and then for the last time, Riger watched as the old man, cane in one hand, gingerly crossed East 42d Street, Blackburn's arm securely at his elbow.

## Chapter Thirteen

My God, thought Riger, watching him fade into the crowded street, his back is still straight and his hair dark brown. Only a few moments before, Rickey had asked after Riger's family and the artist-photographer knew then that the key to the old man's drive and unfettered creativity was his abiding and possessive love for his own large family.

His granddaughter Christine Jones announced her intention of marrying a New York Jewish businessman. She was aware her grandfather had been worshiped by his children and had often dominated their lives. When his daughter Alice became engaged to a Roman Catholic years earlier, Rickey had wanted to know and understand the man and his background. He did the same following Christine's engagement. The son of Ohio fundamentalists was struggling against what he deemed to be the religious disintegration of modernism and secularism and—to him—its unfortunate impact on family life. Never, though, did he rail against the precepts of either faith. Never did he permit himself a passing remark or witticism directed at Catholics or Jews. In fact, he told Alice she would be happier in her marriage if she embraced Catholicism.

Not long before he died granddaughter Christine visited him at the Commodore after he had a minor heart seizure. Her mother had warned her not to upset him but as she rode the elevator she knew this about her famous grandfather: one of the things that kept him vibrant and which made him so forceful and fascinating a companion was that people sought him out; whether they "upset" him was irrelevant inasmuch as it was their news and arguments that sustained and nourished him.

Seated at his bedside, he asked about her life. Some years before he had been bothered by the news that she wanted to live in Manhattan—"sin city," he now called it, at least for young, unmarried women—and that she had been introduced to famous celebrities whose feats were recorded in lurid headlines. Protectively, Rickey had offered her a job at twice what she earned as a model and aspiring actress if only she would leave the city.

Christine steered the talk away from her personal life and began speaking of religion.

"Religion is no answer for me," she said. "For you, yes, but not for me."

His eyes widened and he sat up.

"Not for you? Not for you?" He waved his finger at her. "If you were raised a Christian, Christine, at least explore it before you choose something else. Before you leave, find out about your original faith. If it doesn't work for you, then you are free to go."

He told her the story of Zacchaeus in Jericho, one of his favorite biblical tales. Jesus had gone into the home of the rich tax collector while the crowd railed at him, demanding to know why he was offering him help "joyously" and why he "was gone to be a guest with a man that is a sinner." And Rickey recited: "And Zacchaeus stood, and said unto the Lord; Behold, Lord, the half of my goods I give to the poor; and if I have taken anything from any man by false accusation, I restore him fourfold. And Jesus said unto him, this day is salvation. For the son of man is come to seek and to save that which was lost."

All the way back to her East Side apartment, Christine sobbed, knowing she had touched an extraordinary human being who just happened to be her mother's father. She knew then that he and her grandmother had succeeded in imprinting in her the belief that while people's support may be ephemeral, one could always rely on inner faith to weather life's crises. "The world doesn't mean this planet or this life," Rickey once said to some of his Brooklyn office staff shortly before leaving for Pittsburgh. "We can live right in this world and not be a part of it. Jesus said, 'I have overcome the world' while he was yet alive."

In early November in 1965 he returned to Pittsburgh.

"He was in my office for a meeting of the directors of the American Baseball Cap Company, which he had founded several years earlier," said Edward R. Lawrence, an attorney. "The meeting lasted for more than four hours, with no time for lunch. He had traveled to Pittsburgh from a World Series game in Minneapolis and his loud voice could be heard all over the floor. He suggested plans for A.B.C. far into the future. And then he told us a story, really a parable:

'My father was eighty-six when he died. As an old man, he was still planting peach and apple trees on our farm. When I asked who would take care of the fruit, he said, "That's not important. I just want to live every day as if I were going to live forever."'"

After that, he flew to Delaware for a fund-raising dinner and then decided to visit Cleveland, following a last-minute invitation to speak on racial integration.

Two weeks later he suffered his sixth heart attack and was taken to St. Luke's Hospital, not far from Warson Lane, where he soon seemed to be improving, although he complained to his daughter Elizabeth of abdominal pains. He picked up a pen and marked every ache on his stomach. "He looked like a zebra," she remembered thinking, thoroughly distressed.

Each day Jane and Sue came by and each time he nagged them to allow him to leave his bed and accept a speaking engagement at the Missouri Sports Hall of Fame dinner which followed the Missouri-Oklahoma football game in Columbia.

## Chapter Thirteen

On November 12, the day before the dinner, Archibald Carey was in Dallas. He had heard that Rickey was scheduled to be interviewed about *The American Diamond* on the "Today" television show, but when he turned his hotel set on was surprised to learn he had been hospitalized. He remembered Rickey with great fondness, recalling their first meeting at the Willard Hotel in Washington when they were present for a session of the committee to prevent bias in federal employment. A gruff voice had rung him very early one morning, asking: "Don't you want to have breakfast with me?" From then on they had become warm friends, traveling together throughout the nation on commission affairs, staying as guests at each other's homes. In 1964, Carey, a lifelong Republican, had convinced Rickey that presidential aspirant Barry Goldwater's commitment to civil rights was less than warm.

Carey flew to St. Louis and hailed a cab to the hospital. Entering St. Luke's, he carried as a gift a planter of Chinese evergreen and sanseviera the shape of a rainbow trout. When an attendant refused to let him pass, saying that only Rickey family were allowed in, Jane Rickey Jones walked by, put her arms about him, and told the guard, "He's family."

"Oh, Arch," Rickey said when he saw him. "I can't think of anybody I would rather see now than you."

They were alone, in a sick room high above the city Rickey had first seen in 1905 when he signed a contract with Robert Hedges' Browns.

"He grabbed a handful of his hair and with simulated petulance said, 'Arch, the trouble is these doctors want me to stay here so I can die in this hospital. I can die in Columbia as well as here. As long as the good Lord wants a man to get his breath, he'll get it.'"

Then they prayed silently and Rickey held Carey's wrist.

The next day, despite his doctor's refusal to sanction the trip, and against the wishes of his family, he stubbornly decided to leave for Columbia. He spent the morning giving Archie directions for driving and told him which luggage to take.

From his hospital bed, he was still in charge. It was all ego, a doctor said later to daughter Mary. But his eldest daughter knew her father far better than did the doctor. "He knew he hadn't far to go and he preferred to be among the living that night than lying dying in a hospital."

The Rickey entourage drove 125 miles on November 13 to Columbia, home of the University of Missouri. It was a particularly bleak and cold day and that afternoon on Faurot Field Missouri beat the Oklahoma Sooners 30–0 to clinch a Sugar Bowl invitation. In the stands, Rickey sat huddled under a blanket, uncomfortable and in apparent distress, his arms around his wife. Later, in his room at the Mark Twain Hotel, he continued to feel poorly and lay down to rest as the family tiptoed about.

In the evening, they drove to the Daniel Boone Hotel, and eventually as a scheduled speaker, he rose to speak, holding his cane for support.

His theme was courage. He began by telling the story of Sunny Jim Bottomley, one of the many brilliant young men on his Gashouse Gang, who once slid into third base on a grievously sore hip. Someone on the Cardinal bench, in admiration, shouted, "He paid the price." But, Rickey continued, there was a crucial distinction between physical courage and the far more difficult kind of moral and spiritual bravery. To illustrate, he turned again to the story of Zacchaeus, the unpopular publican who, having climbed a sycamore tree to escape a vengeful mob, welcomed Jesus into his home.

Rickey leaned forward at the dais. His voice soared.

"Now I'm going to tell you a story from the Bible about spiritual courage."

He suddenly faltered and staggered back into his seat and then slipped to the floor. "I don't believe I can continue," he said, the last words he ever uttered. Dr. Dominic M. Nigro rushed to his side, but Rickey never regained consciousness.

He was carried to the fire department across the street and later removed to Boone County Memorial Hospital's intensive care ward. Another granddaughter, Elizabeth Adams, who had grown close to him since their move to Ladue, watched as her mother rushed to her grandfather's side. Terrified, overwhelmed, the child thought, "It was almost like he betrayed me, I loved him so desperately. The speech robbed me of him." Jane meanwhile was offered sedatives by a Boone County physician but she refused, preferring to pass through the experience as controlled and as rational as possible, the better to help him if the need arose.

He lingered in a coma for twenty-six days and never regained consciousness. His brain was damaged when his breathing stopped momentarily, but his heart picked up its rhythm again. Even so, there was little anyone could do to save him. On Thanksgiving Day, the family gathered in grief, the first time in their lives the holiday had been celebrated without him. Their all-day vigils continued until at last, at 10 P.M. on December 9, 1965, Wesley Branch Rickey died, eleven days shy of his eighty-fifth year.

In New York City that evening, Phil Pepe of the *World-Telegram* phoned Stamford, Connecticut. It was just before midnight and he told Jackie Robinson the news.

For a long while there was silence while Pepe waited.

"Then I heard Jackie Robinson speak, but the voice was low and slightly muffled and I knew he was not speaking into the receiver.

"'Rae,' I heard him say, 'Mr. Rickey just died.'

"Again there was a long pause and then he spoke, clearly, softly.

"'It's hard to describe how I feel,' said the man whose life had changed dramatically nineteen years before. 'It's hard to say what is in my heart. We've always felt that Mr. Rickey was like a father to us. When I was in the hospital in 1963, he constantly called to check on my condition.

"'The thing about him was that he was always doing something for someone else. I know because he did so much for me. He got out of a sickbed to make a speech at a girls' college in St. Louis and he worked hard to hurry and finish his book. The doctors told him if he took it easy he would live three or four years longer, but he was not a man to take things easy. He had a commitment to finish the book and he endangered his life to fulfill the commitment. He was that kind of man.'"

Pepe, a sensitive and thoughtful writer, was moved. And the following day he wrote: "A man died in Columbia, Missouri, last night and in Stamford, Connecticut, a part of another man died, too."

Robinson flew to St. Louis for the funeral. In the Grace Methodist Church he spotted Arch Carey and without saying hello, walked up to him, dropped his eyes, and started shaking his head, "Aw, gee, Arch, how he loved you; he was always talking about you." Robinson sat next to Robert Riger and asked, rhetorically and plaintively, as his eyes swept the half-empty church, "Where are all the people?" Nearby Bobby Bragan whispered, "He made me a better man."

Ralph Sockman, a Methodist minister from Manhattan and an OWU alumnus, delivered the eulogy. He and Rickey had long before entered into a bargain that the survivor would conduct the funeral service for the other.

"We loved him as father and friend and companion of the long years. We knew him in a different way than the world knew him. We knew him in our homes and in church and among good friends. We knew something of his defeats as well as his victories. We have known more about some of his dreams and struggles than those who looked on from afar. We know him because we love him for all that he was and all that he will always be in our memories, a man of giant faith and dynamic action and dedicated purpose and selfless concern for others.... There are never very many who are truly great, but he was one of the few—a great mind, a big soul, a magnanimous spirit, a warm heart.

Branch Rickey was buried on a windy and steel-gray day near his parents, brothers, and son (and later, his wife, Jane) on a grassy knoll in Lucasville, Ohio, overlooking the Scioto Valley. (Courtesy of Stew Thornley)

'Like some vast mountain with its shoulders rounded,
And curved to splendid symmetry by Time,
With vision clear, and insight, wide, unbounded,
He stood among us, towering, sublime.'"

At the funeral home in Portsmouth, the Harlem Globetrotters, who
had come from playing a game in Kentucky, paid their respects. And then
on Tuesday, another windy and steel-gray day, he was buried near his parents, brothers, and son on a grassy knoll in Lucasville, Ohio, overlooking the Scioto Valley. Bob Clements, at graveside, thought to himself,
"This land was very close to his heart. I think he's at peace here."

# Epilogue

ALONE NOW BUT FOR MABEL, Jane had her bedroom moved to the den so she might be closer to her beloved garden and the sun's rays. Her radio was often turned on, the news of the world and daily ball games her main interest along with her family, music, and art. The Adams children continued to visit after school and she and the youngsters would sit and chat for hours. Jane and Elizabeth often watched the local educational television channel together and she delighted in the *National Geographic* and Jacques Cousteau programs. As they talked, and as Elizabeth began to mature, the child sensed the exhilarating life her grandparents had led, the people and places they had seen and visited together.

Jane was aware of her loneliness yet tried to steel those about her who tended to fall into fits of despondency. "Weep and you weep alone," she told a grieving friend.

To visitors, she retold stories of their life together.

She and Branch had been together in a boat during a savage storm, without food, radio, or life jackets. She was frightened and he was suffering from his endemic spells of dizziness. "Jane, if I go overboard," he instructed her, "here's what you have to do to survive." And she loved retelling the story about a drive they took one evening, on the way to dinner. She had a new hat on and Branch eyed it warily. "I don't like it," he finally blurted out. "I don't like it at all. In fact, I hate it." Jane raised her eyebrows, her eyes sparkling. "You don't like it? Well, then." And she rolled down the car window and threw it out. "We knew each other so well that whatever the other said was less out of pique and more out of love and concern." Branch, she said, had often described her as *mulier fortis*—by which he meant she was his strong, morally courageous, steadfast wife and friend.

Christine's fiancé, Arthur Rosenstein, sent her a plant. Jane was moved and wrote him:

My dear Arthur:

The only way I know you. I am Christine's grandmother. Christine spent her first days at our house, her father was at war.

I love her dearly and I understand you do too. Her grandfather adored her in a most protective way and constantly worked for her good. Her life in New York was a constant concern; knowing men of the world as he did, he felt she could lose her way and be hurt irretrievably. There are so many ways of hurting. If she now has found someone she loves and someone who loves her, who will put her first in all ways, the only true way of loving, I am so very happy.

We are a large family, a close family, each new member has become a link, and, there has never been a break. That is the caliber of the family. "One for all and all for one." We hope you will join our circle and contribute to its perfection.

Your gift to us when Dad left us was so very lovely indeed, and so completely thought out. I know you must know how to please. As the days go by I hope to make it into a terrarium, planting it artfully, care for it, watch it develop into something beautiful, symbolic of your devotion to Christine, and, watch it grow as I hope your love for each other will grow into something everyone will love to see.

I am lonely. If it were not for my devoted family I could be quite lost. Come to see me. I am eagerly looking forward to seeing you and Christine soon.

Christine and Arthur Rosenstein were married in February 1966, and Jane traveled to New York for the wedding. A few months later, with her daughters Mary and Alice, she flew to London for ten days of theater and museum visiting. But when Mabel died in 1969 she was even more alone. In her eighty-eighth year, on October 13, 1970, she phoned Christine. It was her granddaughter's twenty-seventh birthday. She wanted to say good-by. She had had a mastectomy and was suffering from cancer of the pancreas. "There are certain things I haven't told you," she began. "You've been under great pressure but I admire your innate dignity and strength, which I expect you will pass on to your son [Robert]. If you want a career in acting, go ahead. I've had my life, I've lived a long time. My friends, Branch Jr., and Branch have died. It was a most wondrous life and now I'm really ready to go."

Three days later she died of a heart seizure.

When Christine heard the news she was overcome by a wave of anger. Instead of tears, she thought, we ought to have a celebration of what had been two splendid lives. "My grandfather had his great years but it was my grandmother who gave him his energy, who was his dearest friend and most caring critic, and who in the end imparted the inner strength and joy in life which was passed on to me and which I hope to pass on to my son. I never felt she and Grandpa died. They live on in me and in all of us."

# A Bibliographic Note

THE BULK OF THIS BOOK GREW in large part from the Branch Rickey Papers, which are housed at the Library of Congress Manuscript Division and are presently closed to the public. [They have since been opened to the public.] In this regard, Rickey was a rarity among baseball personalities. Other than Kenesaw Mountain Landis— whose personal baseball papers still exist, particularly in scrapbooks and photographs, but whose working files of the Commissioner's office were apparently destroyed after his death in 1944—baseball executives and players do not generally maintain comprehensive archives. In addition, the Arthur Mann Papers, also on deposit at the Library of Congress, were a rich source of information. Particularly helpful was the material he collected for his biography of Rickey and which he did not include in his book. I also used the Albert (Happy) Chandler Papers, on file at the University of Kentucky Library, Special Collections and Archives, as well as portions of the Arthur M. Hyde, Jesse W. Barrett, Frank E. Attwood, and Robert E. Blake Papers, all housed at the Western Historical Manuscript Collection, State Historical Society, University of Missouri Library. In addition, I relied on the Chicago Historical Society for the Landis Papers; the Library of Congress for *Hearings Before the Subcommittee of the Committee on the Study of Monopoly Power,* House of Representatives, 82d Cong., 1st Sess., Part 6, Organized Baseball (1951); "Report of the Subcommittee on the Study of Monopoly Power" (May 27, 1952), and the "Senate Subcommittee Report on Antitrust and Monopoly" (1959), the latter dealing with the challenge by the Continental League against the established leagues. I also used the good offices of the Missouri Historical Society for Rickey's early years in St Louis; the Allegheny College Library for assistance in tracking his career as a coach and teacher at that school; the United Methodist Archives Center Beeghly Library, Ohio Wesleyan University, for information on his college years; and the New York Public Library, especially its Newspaper Division. The Charles Pfizer Chemical Corporation in New York City kindly granted me access to published and unpublished materials concerning John L. Smith. I also read the following newspapers: New York *Daily News, The New York Times,* Pittsburgh *Post-Gazette,* St. Louis *Post-Dispatch,* St. Louis *Globe-Democrat,* Montreal *Star,* Pittsburgh *Courier, Amsterdam News, Brooklyn Eagle, Sporting News,* portions of the *Zanesville* (Ohio) *Sunday Times-Signal, Baseball Digest,* and the *Saturday Evening Post.* In the Local History Division of the New York Public Library, I was guided to early histories of towns and cities where Rickey lived and worked before World War I.

# A Bibliographical Note

The Municipal Archives of New York City contained the records of the [Mayor Fiorello] LaGuardia Anti-Discrimination Committee; the Bentley Historical Library, Michigan Historical Collections, the University of Michigan, provided me with portions of the Fielding Yost papers; and the Great Neck (New York) Library was, as always, enormously helpful in obtaining books and articles.

A number of unpublished manuscripts were helpful:

Anderson, Donald Ray. "Branch Rickey and the St. Louis Farm System: The Growth of an Idea," The University of Wisconsin Ph.D. thesis, 1975. Ann Arbor, MI: University Microfilms.

Betts, John R. "Organized Sports in America," Columbia University Ph.D. thesis, 1951. Ann Arbor, MI: University Microfilms.

Craig, Peter. "Organized Baseball: An Industry Study of a $10 Million Spectator Sport," Oberlin College Library, 1950.

Fetzner, Arthur. "Once There Was a Farm: A Story of the Cardinal Farm System, Its Ups ... Its Downs ... Its First 44 Years," 1962, 59 pp.

Lowenfish, Lee. "A Tale of Two Titans: Branch Rickey and Walter O'Malley as Brooklyn Dodger Partners, 1944–1950," delivered at Long Island University–Brooklyn Campus conference on "Sports, Race and the American Dream: Jackie Robinson 50 Years Later," April 3, 1997.

Penisten, Edwin Harness. "Branch Rickey's Father," Ohio Valley Folklore Press, The Ross County Historical Society, Chillicothe, OH, 1958, 4pp.

Report. For Submission to National and American Leagues on 27 August 1946. Major League Committee, 20 pp.

Riess, Steven Allen. "Professional Baseball and American Culture in the Progressive Era: Myths and Realities," University of Chicago Photoduplication Department, 1947.

"Tentative Proposal for Report of the Mayor's Committee on Baseball," prepared by Dan W. Dodson, September 28, 1945, 6 pp.

Along with the Rickey, Mann and Chandler papers, I leaned extensively on the following interviewees, listed in alphabetical order:

Cal Abrams, Stephen Adams, Jr., Sue Rickey Adams, Fred Ankenman, Red Barber, Kenneth Blackburn, Ray Blades, Rex Bowen, John Bricker, Bob Broeg, Joe L. Brown, Roy Campanella, Al Campanis, Archibald J. Carey, Jr., Albert B. Chandler, W. Ben Chapman, Sr., Robert Clements, William D. Cox, Craig Cullinan, Jr., William DeWitt, John Eckler, Mary Rickey Eckler, Carl Erskine, Arthur Fetzner, Dr. Joseph Finegold, Arthur Flemming, John Galbreath, Warren Giles, Howard Haak, Roscoe Hillenkoetter, Bob Howsam, Bettina Hughes, Francis Hughes, Frederick A. Johnson, Thomas P. Johnson, Christine Jones, Jane Rickey Jones, Robert Jones, Nancy Rickey Keltner, Elizabeth Adams Klinger, Jim Kreuz, Edward Lawrence, Clay Littick, Lou Little, Marion Mann, Joe Mathes, Leslie Max, Mickey McConnell, Herbert G. McCracken, Charlie Muse, Lou Niss, Walter F. O'Malley, Joe O'Toole, C. Carroll Otto, Ethel Page, Harold Parrott, Norman Vincent Peale, Houston Peterson, George Pfister, Margaret Regetz, Branch B. Rickey, Mary Iams Rickey, Robert Riger, Rachel Robinson, Dr. Edward H. Rynearson, Fred Saigh, William Shea, Harry Simmons, George Silvey, Kathleen Sisler, Ken Smith, Red Smith, the Reverend Frederick B. Speakman, Gus Steiger, Pherbia Thornberg, Pinky Thornberg, Syd Thrift, John Titzel, Mrs. George Trautman, William G. Turner, Bill Veeck, and Elizabeth Rickey Wolfe.

I have also benefited from a number of books, most notably Arthur Mann's pioneering *Branch Rickey* (Boston: Houghton Mifflin, 1957). Moreover, I found the following most helpful:

Alexander, Charles C. *Rogers Hornsby: A Biography*. New York: Henry Holt, 1995.
Allen, Maury. *Jackie Robinson: A Life Remembered*. New York: Franklin Watts, 1987.
Barber, Red. *The Rhubarb Patch*. New York: Simon & Schuster, 1954.
_____. *1947: When All Hell Broke Loose in Baseball*. New York: Doubleday, 1982.
_____, with Robert Creamer. *Rhubarb in the Catbird Seat*. New York: Doubleday, 1968.
Barney, Rex, with Norman L. Macht. *Thank You for 50 Years of Baseball from Brooklyn to Baltimore*. Centerville, MD: Tidewater Publications, 1993.
Berkow, Ira. *Red: A Biography of Red Smith*. New York: Times Books, 1986.
Broeg, Bob. *Bob Broeg's Redbirds: A Century of Cardinal Baseball*. St. Louis: River City Publishers, 1981.
Cohen, Stanley. *Dodgers! The First 100 Years*. New York: Carol Publishing, 1990.
Dorinson, Joseph, and Joram Warmund, eds. *Jackie Robinson: Race, Sports and the American Dream*. Armonk, NY: M.E. Sharpe, 1998.
Durocher, Leo, and Ed Linn. *Nice Guys Finish Last*. New York: Pocket Books, 1976.
Edwards, Bob. *Fridays with Red: A Radio Friendship*. New York: Simon & Schuster, 1993.
Eskenazi, Gerald. *The Lip: A Biography of Leo Durocher*. New York: William Morrow, 1993.
Evans, Nelson W. *A History of Scioto County, Ohio, Together with a Record of Southern Ohio*. 2 vols. Portsmouth, Ohio, 1903, vol. 1.
Falkner, David. *Great Times Coming: The Life of Jackie Robinson, from Baseball to Birmingham*. New York: Simon & Schuster, 1995.
Frommer, Harvey. *Rickey and Robinson*. New York: Macmillan, 1982.
Goldstein, Richard. *Superstars and Screwballs: 100 Years of the Brooklyn Dodgers*. New York: Putnam's Sons, 1991.
Golenbock, Peter. *Bums: An Oral History of the Brooklyn Dodgers*. New York: G.P. Putnam's Sons, 1984.
_____. *The Spirit of St. Louis: A History of the St. Louis Cardinals and Browns*. New York: Spike, 2000.
Gough, David. *Burt Shotton, the Dodgers Manager: A Baseball Biography*. Jefferson, NC: McFarland, 1994.
Graham, Frank. *The Brooklyn Dodgers*. New York: G.P. Putnam's Sons, 1945.
Heidenry, John. *The Gashouse Gang*. New York: Public Affairs, 2007.
Holmes, Tommy. *Dodger Daze and Knights*. New York: David McKay, 1953.
Holway, John. *Voices from the Great Black Baseball League*. New York: Dodd, Mead, 1975.
Hood, Robert E. *The Gashouse Gang*. New York: Morrow, 1976.
Hornsby, Rogers, and Bill Surface. *My War with Baseball*. New York: Coward McCann, 1962.
Hubbart, Henry Clyde. *Ohio Wesleyan's First Hundred Years*. Delaware: Ohio Wesleyan University, 1943.

# A Bibliographical Note

Huhn, Rick. *The Sizzler: George Sisler, Baseball's Forgotten Great.* Columbia: University of Missouri Press, 2004.

Kahn, Roger. *The Boys of Summer.* New York: Harper & Row, 1971.

_____. *The Era 1947–1957. When the Yankees, Giants, and the Dodgers Ruled the World.* New York: Ticknor & Fields, 1993.

Lanctot, Nail. *Negro League Baseball: The Rise and Ruin of a Black Institution.* Philadelphia: University of Pennsylvania Press, 2004.

Lieb, Frederick G. *The St. Louis Cardinals.* New York: G.P. Putnam's Sons, 1947.

Lipman, David. *Mr. Baseball: The Story of Branch Rickey.* New York: G.P. Putnam's Sons, 1966.

Lowenfish, Lee. *Branch Rickey: Baseball's Ferocious Gentleman.* Lincoln: University of Nebraska Press, 2007.

Mann, Arthur. *Branch Rickey.* Boston: Houghton Mifflin, 1957.

_____. *The Jackie Robinson Story.* New York: Grosset & Dunlap, 1950.

Marshall, William. *Baseball's Pivotal Era 1945–1951.* Lexington: The University Press of Kentucky, 1999.

McGee, Bob. *The Greatest Ballpark Ever: Ebbets Field and the Story of the Brooklyn Dodgers.* New Brunswick, NJ: Rutgers University Pres, 2005.

Miller, James Edward. *The Baseball Business: Pursuing Pennants and Profits in Baltimore.* Chapel Hill: University of North Carolina Press, 1990.

Monteleone, John, ed. *Branch Rickey's Little Blue Book: Wit and Strategy from Baseball's Last Wise Man.* New York: Macmillan, 1995.

Mooney, Elizabeth. *In the Shadow of the White Plague: A Memoir.* New York: Thomas Y. Crowell, 1979.

O'Toole, Andrew. *Branch Rickey in Pittsburgh.* Jefferson, NC: McFarland, 2000.

Parrott, Harold. *The Lords of Baseball.* New York: Praeger, 1976.

Pietrusza, David. *Judge and Jury: The Life and Times of Judge Kenesaw Mountain Landis.* South Bend, IN: Diamond Communications, 1998.

Prince, Carl E. *The Bums, the Borough, and the Best of Baseball, 1947–1955.* New York: Oxford University Press, 1996.

Rampersad, Arnold. *Jackie Robinson: A Biography.* New York: Knopf, 1997.

Rickey, Branch, with Robert Riger. *The American Diamond: A Documentary of the Game of Baseball.* New York: Simon & Schuster, 1965.

Robinson, Jackie, edited by Charles Dexter. *Baseball Has Done It.* Philadelphia: Lippincott, 1964.

_____, as told to Alfred Duckett. *I Never Had It Made.* New York: G.P. Putnam's Sons, 1972.

Seymour, Harold. *Baseball: The Early Years.* New York: Oxford University Press, 1960.

_____. *Baseball: The Golden Age.* New York: Oxford University Press, 1971.

Simon, Scott. *Jackie Robinson and the Integration of Baseball.* New York: John Wiley, 2002.

Spink, J.G. Taylor. *Judge Landis and Twenty-Five Years of Baseball.* New York: Thomas Y. Crowell, 1947.

Sullivan, Neil J. *Dodgers Move West.* New York: Oxford University Press, 1987.

Tygiel, Jules. *Baseball's Great Experiment: Jackie Robinson and His Legacy.* New York: Oxford University Press, 1983.

Voigt, David Q. *American Baseball: From Gentlemen's Sports to the Commissioner System,* vol. 1. Norman: University of Oklahoma Press, 1968; *American Baseball:*

# A Bibliographical Note

*From Commissioners to Continental Expansion*, vol. 2. Norman: University of Oklahoma Press, 1970.
Warfield, Don. *The Roaring Redhead: Larry McPhail, Baseball's Great Innovator*. South Bend, IN: Diamond Communications, 1987.

Finally, of the hundreds of articles—perhaps thousands—written about Branch Rickey and his times, the following seem to me to be the most incisive and lasting in quality.

Barber, Red. "Game Today Would Make Rickey Ill." *Miami Herald*, February 15, 1970.
Behn, Robert D. "Branch Rickey as a Public Manager: Fulfilling the Eight Responsibilities of Public Management." *Journal of Public Administration Research and Theory*, January 1997, Vol. 7, No.1.
Berkow, Ira. "Where Did Happy Stand on Jackie? *New York Times*, June 29, 1991.
Bulger, Bozeman. "The Baseball Business from the Inside," by a Major League Owner as Told to Bozeman Bulger, *Collier's*, March 25, 1922, pp. 12–30.
Butterfield, Roger. "Brooklyn's Gentleman Bum" [Burt Shotten], *Saturday Evening Post*, August 20, 1949, pp. 28–29; 83–88.
Darst, Stephen. "The Very Last of the Marvelous Beer Barons," *St. Louisan*, January 1976, pp. 40–47.
Henry, Patrick. "Jackie Robinson: Athlete and American Par Excellence," *The Virginia Quarterly Review*, Vol. 73, No. 2, Spring 1997, pp.189–203.
Holland, Gerald. "Mr. Rickey and the Game," *Sports Illustrated*, Match 7, 1955, pp. 38–65.
Paxson, Frederick L. "The Rise of Sport," *Mississippi Valley Historical Review*, IV, September 1917, pp. 143–168.
Rice, Robert. "Profiles: Thoughts on Baseball [Branch Rickey], *New Yorker*, Part I: May 27, 1950, pp. 32–46; Part II: June 3, 1950, pp. 30–47.
Sailer, Steve. "How Jackie Robinson Desegregated America," *National Review*, April 8, 1996, pp. 38–41.
Taylor, Robert Lewis. "Profiles: Borough Defender" [Larry McPhail], *New Yorker*, Part I: July 12, 1941, pp. 20–28; Part II: July 19, 1941, pp. 20–30.
Wooley, E.M. "The Business of Baseball," *McClure's Magazine*, July 1912, pp. 241–256.

# Index

# Index

# Index

# Index

# Index

# Index

# Index

# Index